THE 120 DAYS OF SIMON

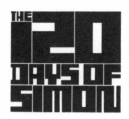

THE 120 DAYS OF SIMON © 2010 SIMON GÄRDENFORS.

PUBLISHED BY TOP SHELF PRODUCTIONS, PO BOX 1282, MARIETTA, GA 30061-1282, USA. PUBLISHERS: BRETT WARNOCK AND CHRIS STAROS.

TRANSLATED BY NAOMI NOWAK.
HAND LETTERING BY SIMON GÄRDENFORS.

ORIGINAL TITLE: SIMONS 120 DAGAR. ORIGINALLY PUBLISHED IN SWEDISH BY GALAGO (STOCKHOLM 2008).

VISIT OUR ONLINE CATALOG AT WWW.TOPSHELFCOMIX.COM

ISBN 978-1-60309-050-6

FIRST PRINTING, APRIL 2010. PRINTED IN CANADA.

THIS STORY TAKES PLACE IN SWEDEN.

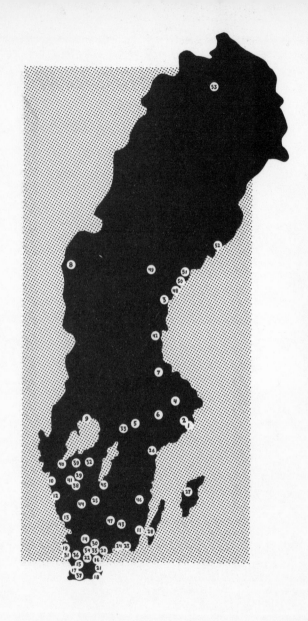

MY TRIP

THE PLACES I STAYED OVERNIGHT
(IN CHRONOLOGICAL ORDER)

STOCKHOLM (1), SOLNA (2),
STOCKHOLM, SUNDSVALL (3),
UPPSALA (4), FELLINGSBRO (5),
VÄSTERÅS (6), HOFORS (7),
ÅRE (8), KARLSTAD (9),
GÖTEBORG (10), KALMAR (11),
GÖTEBORG, KUNGSBACKA (12),
FALKENBERG (13), MARKARYD
(14), LUND (15), FORSAKAR (16),
MALMÖ (17), BORRBY (18),
HELSINGBORG (19), LUND,
MALMÖ, GÖTEBORG, NYMÖLLA
(20), MALMÖ, LUND, VITABY (21),
HÖRBY (22), KARLSKRONA (23),
RONNEBY (24), VÄRNAMO (25),
NORRKÖPING (26), STOCKHOLM,
VISBY (27), FÄRJESTADEN (28),
LJUNG (29), OSBY (30),
HELSINGBORG, RAMLÖSA (31),
HELSINGBORG, SKÖVDE (32),
ÖREBRO (33), FELLINGSBRO,
HÖÖR (34), HÄSSLEHOLM (35),
SVALÖV (36), SVEDALA (37),
BORÅS (38), VARA (39),
GÖTEBORG, TROLLHÄTTAN (40),
ALINGSÅS (41), STOCKHOLM,
UPPSALA, BOLLNÄS (42),
VÄSTERÅS, HOVMANTORP (43),
GISLAVED (44), JÖNKÖPING
(45), HULTSFRED (46),
JÖNKÖPING, VÄXJÖ (47),
HÄRNÖSAND (48), NÄSÅKER
(49), BJÄSTA (50),
ÖRNSKÖLDSVIK (51), UMEÅ (52),
KIRUNA (53), STOCKHOLM.

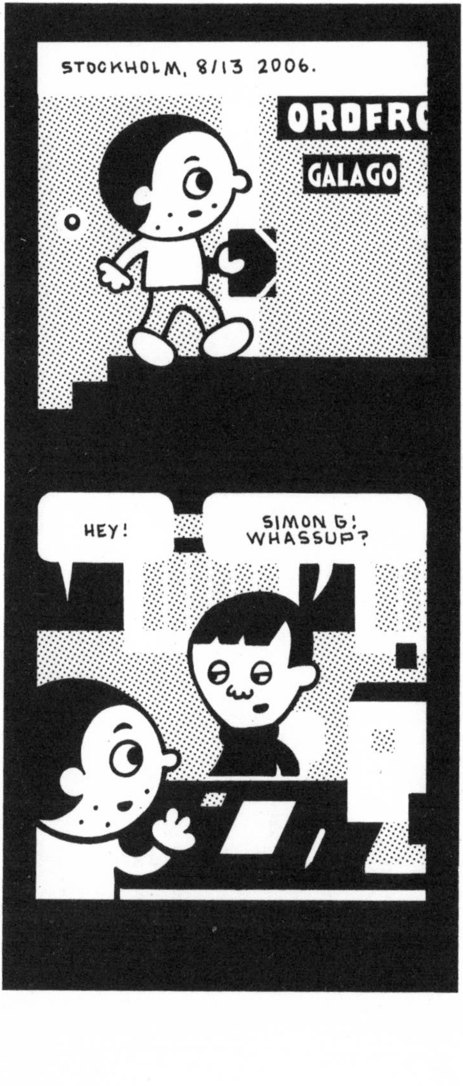
STOCKHOLM, 8/13 2006.
ORDFRO
GALAGO
HEY!
SIMON G! WHASSUP?

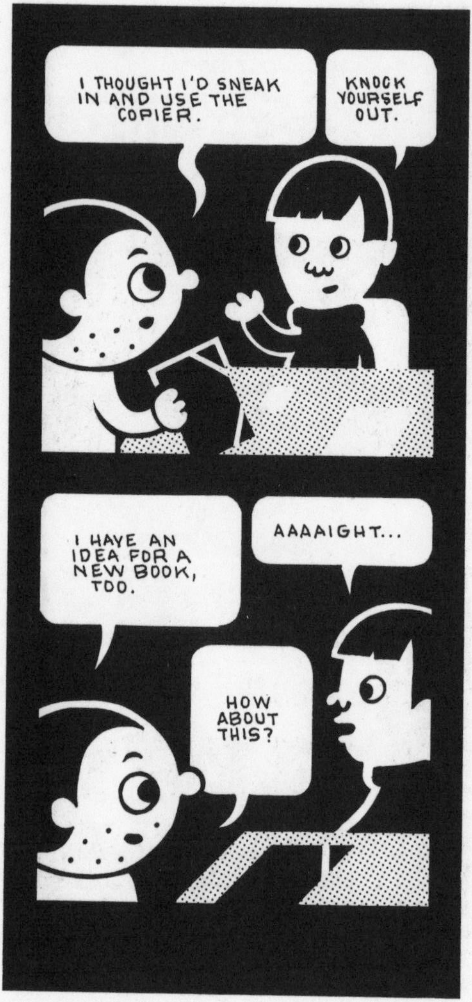
I THOUGHT I'D SNEAK IN AND USE THE COPIER.
KNOCK YOURSELF OUT.
I HAVE AN IDEA FOR A NEW BOOK, TOO.
AAAAIGHT...
HOW ABOUT THIS?

I'LL SUBLET MY APARTMENT AND MAKE A WEBSITE WHERE PEOPLE CAN SIGN UP TO OFFER ME FOOD AND SHELTER. THEN I'LL TRAVEL AROUND SWEDEN FOR FOUR MONTHS.
I'LL DRAW A COMIC ABOUT IT AND WE COULD CALL IT "THE 120 DAYS OF SIMON."
HEH HEH... SURE, AWESOME, WHATEVER.

THESE ARE THE BASIC RULES:
TWO NIGHTS IN ONE PLACE
TOPS... AND I CAN'T GO BACK
TO MY OWN APARTMENT FOR
120 DAYS.

HOW ARE YOU GONNA
SUPPORT YOURSELF?

I'LL ONLY HAVE TRAVEL
EXPENSES. WE'VE GOT
SOME GIGS BOOKED WITH
LAS PALMAS. I THINK THE
FEES WILL COVER IT.

"BLAH BLAH AN ODYSSEY THROUGH SWEDEN OF TODAY."
GIGGLE
SIMON SUBLETS HIS PLACE... TRAVELS AROUND AND STAYS WITH PEOPLE FOR 120 DAYS. TO GET SOME ASS.

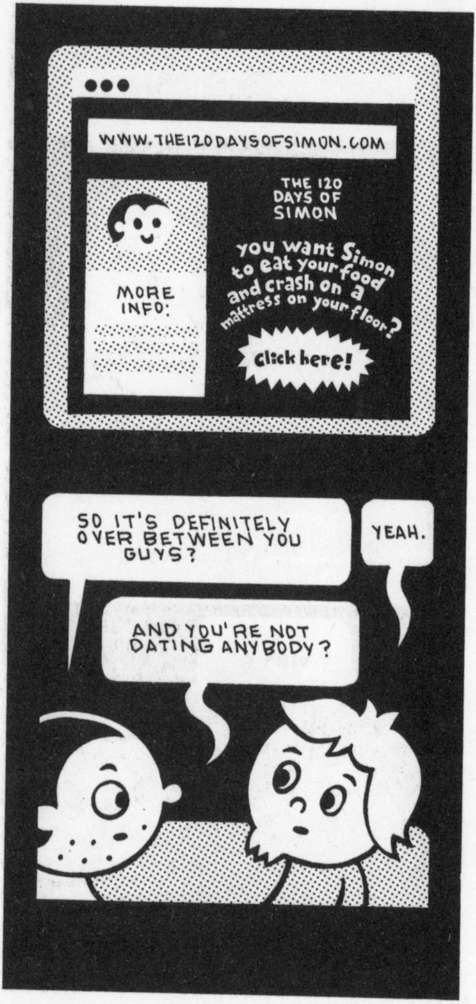
WWW.THE120DAYSOFSIMON.COM
THE 120 DAYS OF SIMON
you want Simon to eat your food and crash on a mattress on your floor?
Click here!
MORE INFO:
SO IT'S DEFINITELY OVER BETWEEN YOU GUYS?
YEAH.
AND YOU'RE NOT DATING ANYBODY?

NAW... I'M SO NOT READY FOR THAT.
YOU?
NO, LIKE, I HAVE TO ACTIVELY AVOID RELATIONSHIPS.
WHY?

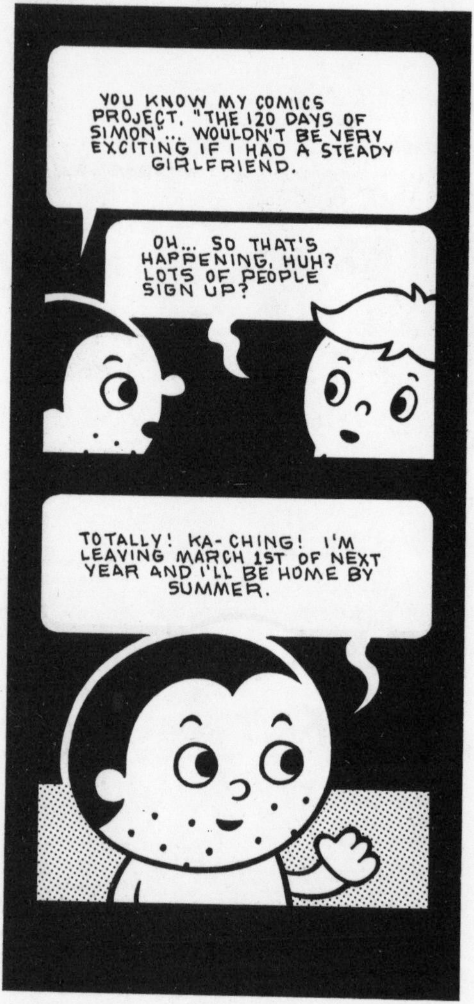
YOU KNOW MY COMICS PROJECT, "THE 120 DAYS OF SIMON"... WOULDN'T BE VERY EXCITING IF I HAD A STEADY GIRLFRIEND.
OH... SO THAT'S HAPPENING, HUH? LOTS OF PEOPLE SIGN UP?
TOTALLY! KA-CHING! I'M LEAVING MARCH 1ST OF NEXT YEAR AND I'LL BE HOME BY SUMMER.

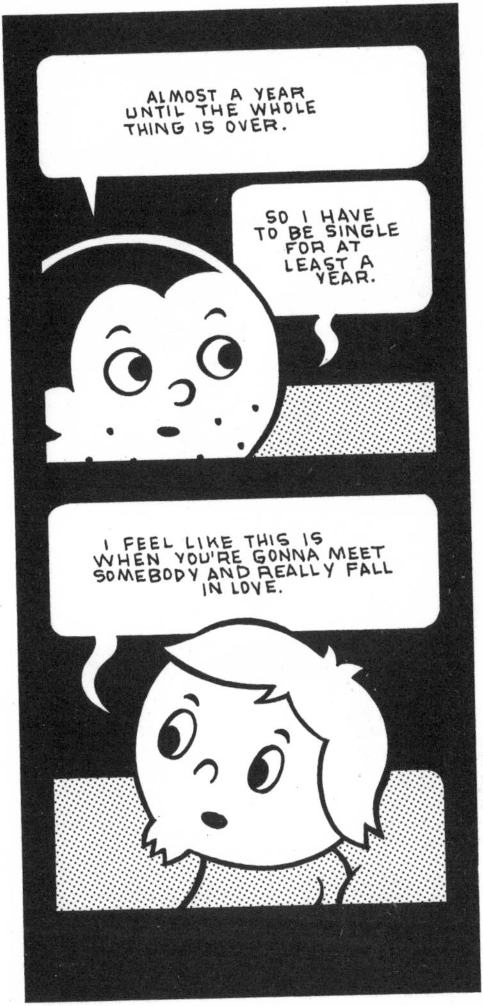
ALMOST A YEAR UNTIL THE WHOLE THING IS OVER.
SO I HAVE TO BE SINGLE FOR AT LEAST A YEAR.
I FEEL LIKE THIS IS WHEN YOU'RE GONNA MEET SOMEBODY AND REALLY FALL IN LOVE.

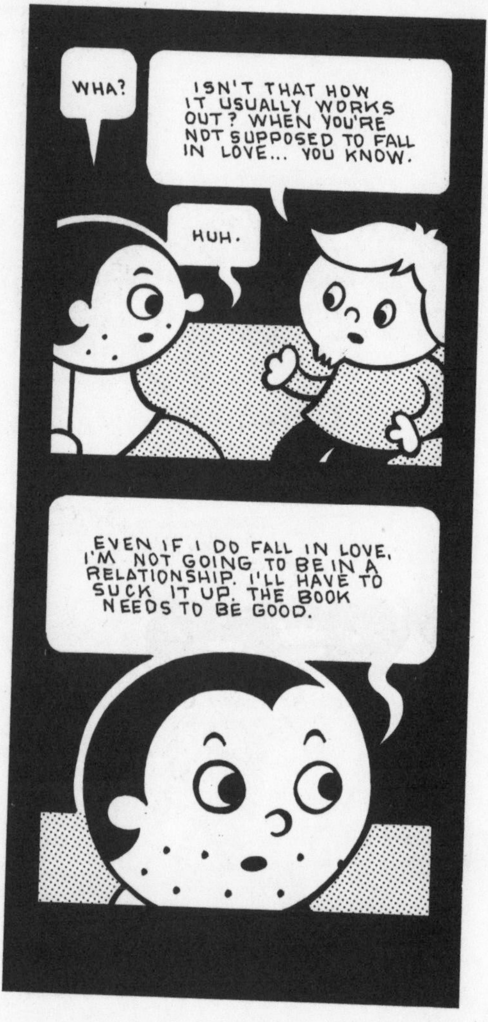
WHA?
ISN'T THAT HOW IT USUALLY WORKS OUT? WHEN YOU'RE NOT SUPPOSED TO FALL IN LOVE... YOU KNOW.
HUH.
EVEN IF I DO FALL IN LOVE, I'M NOT GOING TO BE IN A RELATIONSHIP. I'LL HAVE TO SUCK IT UP. THE BOOK NEEDS TO BE GOOD.

IT MIGHT SOUND SAD, BUT COMICS REALLY ARE THE MOST IMPORTANT THING IN MY LIFE.

DAMN IT, FINN... YOU WERE RIGHT. I THINK I'M FALLING FOR SOMEBODY.
WHAT? WHO?
.. JONNA BJÖRNSTJERNA. SHE DRAWS COMICS, TOO.
HOW'D THAT HAPPEN?

WE MADE OUT ONCE, A LONG TIME AGO WHEN WE WERE AT THE ARVIKA FESTIVAL WITH GALAGO. DIDN'T REALLY THINK ABOUT IT MUCH. IT WAS JUST LIKE, AWESOME, SHE ALWAYS TOPPED MY LIST OF HOT COMIC ARTISTS.

SHE LIVES IN NORRKÖPING, BUT WE'VE BEEN HANGING OUT WHEN SHE'S HAD MEETINGS WITH HER PUBLISHER HERE IN STOCKHOLM. SHE'S DOING A CHILDREN'S BOOK.

WE STARTED EMAILING EACH OTHER A LOT, AND THAT'S WHEN I CAUGHT ON TO HOW AWESOME SHE IS.

ONE TIME WHEN WE WERE BOTH WASTED SHE CALLED AND SUGGESTED THAT WE HAVE AN OPEN RELATIONSHIP. SHE WAS ONLY HALF KIDDING I GUESS.

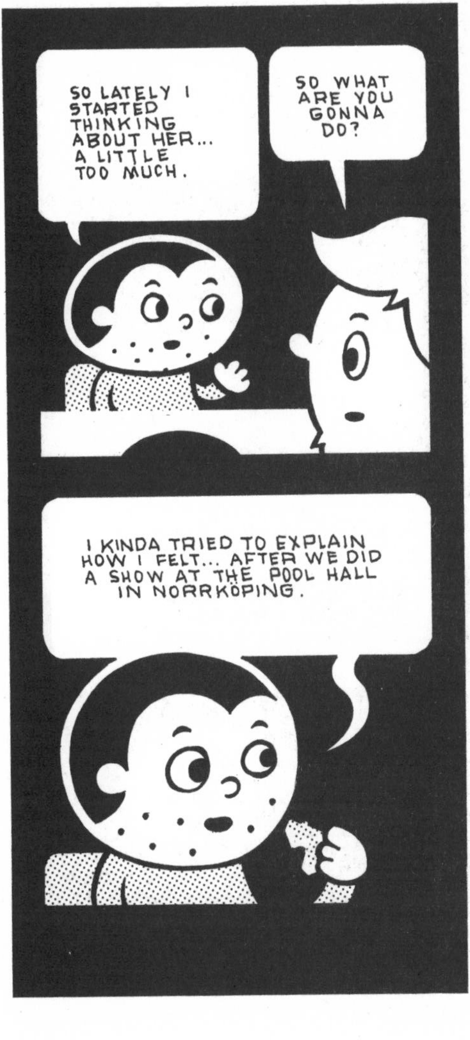
SO LATELY I STARTED THINKING ABOUT HER... A LITTLE TOO MUCH.
SO WHAT ARE YOU GONNA DO?
I KINDA TRIED TO EXPLAIN HOW I FELT... AFTER WE DID A SHOW AT THE POOL HALL IN NORRKÖPING.

JONNA, YOU'RE FUCKING AWESOME. WE SHOULD BE BOYFRIEND / GIRLFRIEND FOR REAL SOMETIME.
MMM... I'D LIKE THAT. WHEN DO YOU THINK IT COULD HAPPEN?

UH... I CAN'T MAKE ANY KIND OF COMMITMENT BEFORE MY 120 DAYS.
SHE SEEMED TO BE TAKING IT PRETTY WELL. BUT LAST TIME WE SAW EACH OTHER SHE SOUNDED ANGRY.
ACTUALLY I THINK IT'S FUCKING NASTY OF YOU TO SAY THINGS LIKE THAT.

SHOULD I SIT AROUND AND WAIT, LIKE AN IDIOT, WHILE YOU'RE OUT BEING A TOTAL PIG?
HELL NO... THE OPEN RELATIONSHIP THING WAS YOUR IDEA. IT'LL PRACTICALLY BE LIKE THAT.
AND THEN WE'LL SEE.

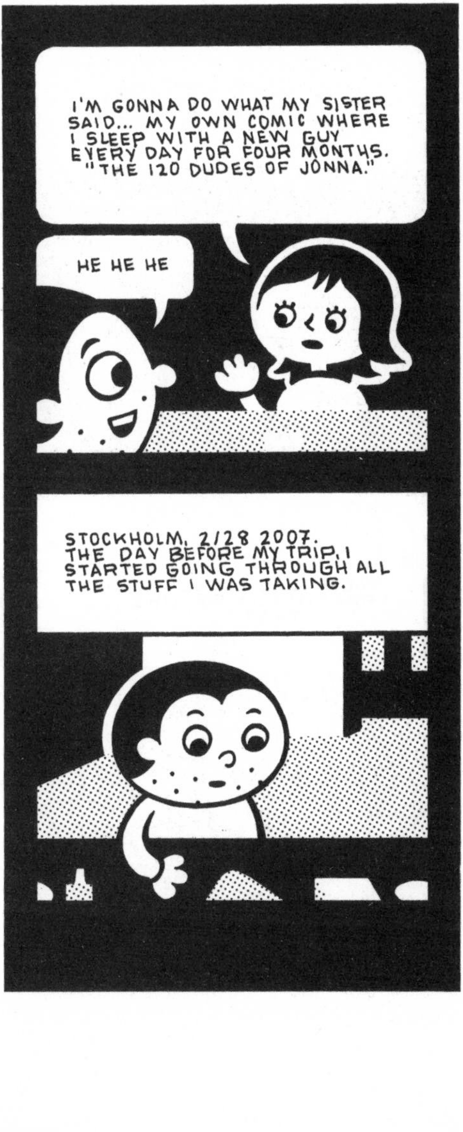
I'M GONNA DO WHAT MY SISTER SAID... MY OWN COMIC WHERE I SLEEP WITH A NEW GUY EVERY DAY FOR FOUR MONTHS. "THE 120 DUDES OF JONNA."
HE HE HE
STOCKHOLM, 2/28 2007. THE DAY BEFORE MY TRIP, I STARTED GOING THROUGH ALL THE STUFF I WAS TAKING.

TWO PAIRS OF SOCKS, A
BOTTLE OF WHITEOUT, A DIGITAL
CAMERA, A NOTEBOOK...

A POUCH OF TOILETRIES, A HAT,
THREE PAIRS OF UNDERWEAR,
A SHIRT, A PACK OF CONDOMS...

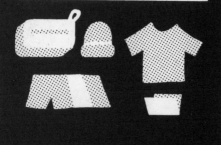

A USB MEMORY STICK, A PASSPORT (MY ONLY FORM OF I.D.), A BOX OF DRAWING SUPPLIES, A WALLET, A RULER...

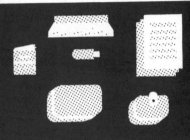

A CELL PHONE, KEYS, SIX CDS (LAS PALMAS INSTRUMENTALS AND SOME CD-RS), VARIOUS CARDS AND CHARGERS AND SEVEN WHITE, LETTER-SIZE PAPERS.

THE ONLY THINGS LEFT FOR ME TO DO: CLEAN UP A LITTLE AND GET A GOOD NIGHT'S SLEEP.

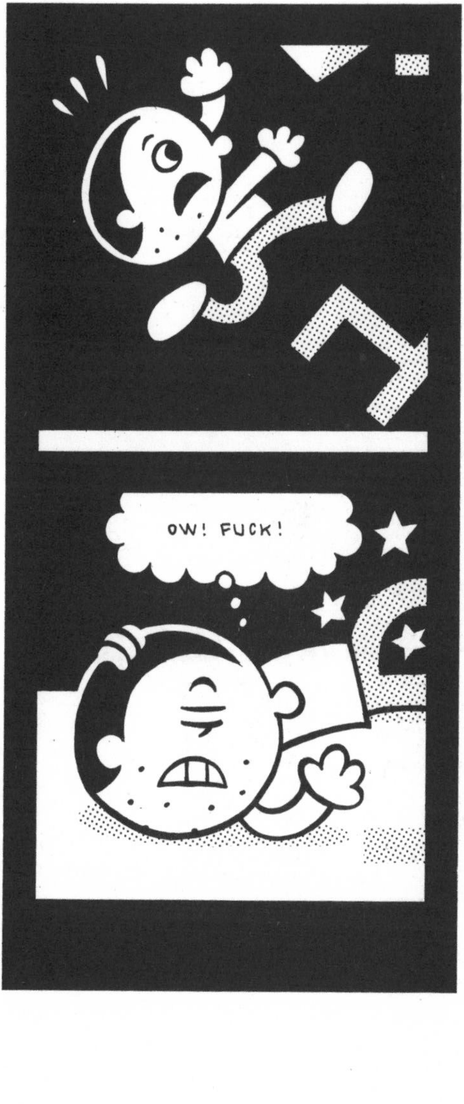
OW! FUCK!

IT TOOK A WHILE TO PINPOINT WHERE IT HURT THE MOST.
MY FOOT! THE FUCKING TOE IS AT A WEIRD ANGLE. SHIT... IT'S DISJOINTED!

OWOWOWOWOWOWOW...
I'LL HAVE TO TRY AND SNAP
IT BACK INTO PLACE.
OW!
SNAP

STOCKHOLM, 3/1 2007. HOST #1: JONAS "PIKE" DAHLSTRÖM
DAMN, SIMON G, YOU'RE LIMPING! WHAT HAPPENED?

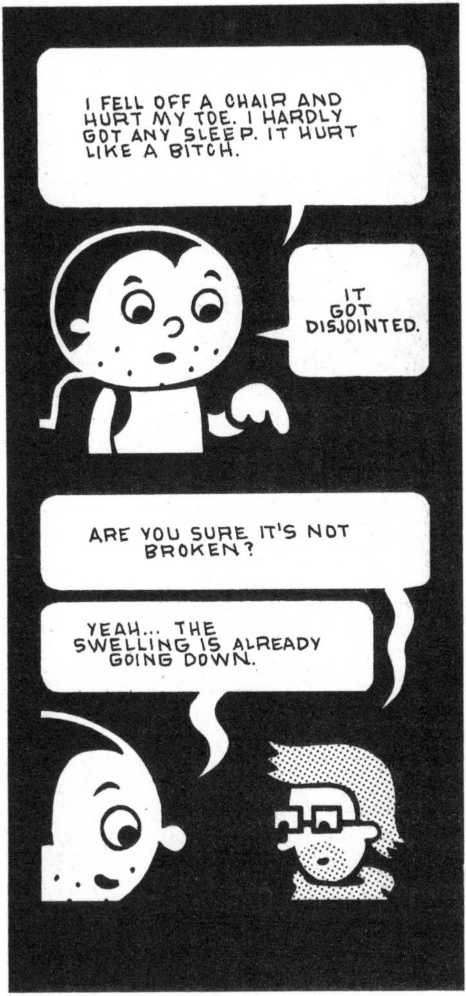
I FELL OFF A CHAIR AND HURT MY TOE. I HARDLY GOT ANY SLEEP. IT HURT LIKE A BITCH.
IT GOT DISJOINTED.
ARE YOU SURE IT'S NOT BROKEN?
YEAH... THE SWELLING IS ALREADY GOING DOWN.

RESTAURANT•BAR
NICE TO GET OFF TO A SLOW START WITH SOMEONE I ALREADY KNOW. I'M GOING TO SOLNA TOMORROW TO STAY WITH SOME CHICK I'VE NEVER MET BEFORE. I SHOULD GIVE HER A TEXT TO REMIND HER.

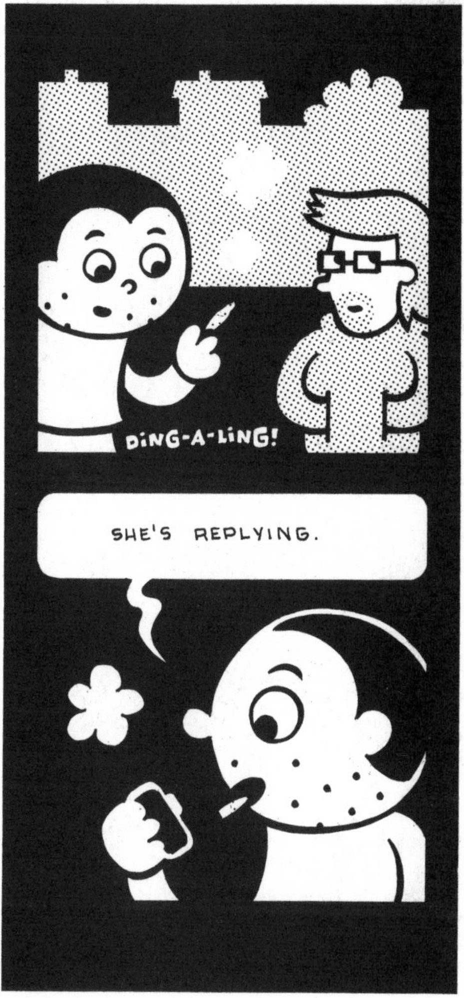
DING-A-LING!
SHE'S REPLYING.

"HEY! YOU'RE WELCOME OVER FOR DINNER TOMORROW, BUT I'M SORRY TO SAY I CAN'T OFFER YOU A PLACE TO SLEEP."
WHAT THE HELL? WHAT PART OF "FOOD AND SHELTER" DID SHE NOT UNDERSTAND?
SOMEONE FLAKING OUT ALREADY. THIS IS SO NOT A GOOD START.

SHE'S PROBABLY JUST NERVOUS. YOU CAN ALWAYS STAY WITH US ANOTHER NIGHT IF YOU WANT.
THANKS. THAT'LL BE MY BACK-UP PLAN. I'LL GO THERE AND EAT ANYWAY, SHE MIGHT CHANGE HER MIND ONCE SHE GETS TO MEET ME.

SOLNA, 3/2 2007. HOST #2: AMANDA NILSSON
DAMN... FEELING A LITTLE NERVOUS.
BZZT!
HELLO.
HEY THERE!

THESE ARE MY FRIENDS, JOHANNA AND FRIDA. HAVE A SEAT... I'M MAKING VEGETARIAN TACOS.

SO, LIKE, I THOUGHT MY MOM WOULD BE OUT OF TOWN FOR THE WEEKEND, BUT IT TURNS OUT THAT IT'S NEXT WEEKEND.
SO... IT WOULD'VE BEEN WEIRD FOR YOU TO SLEEP HERE. SHE'LL BE HOME IN A COUPLE OF HOURS, AND I DIDN'T REALLY TELL HER ABOUT THIS.

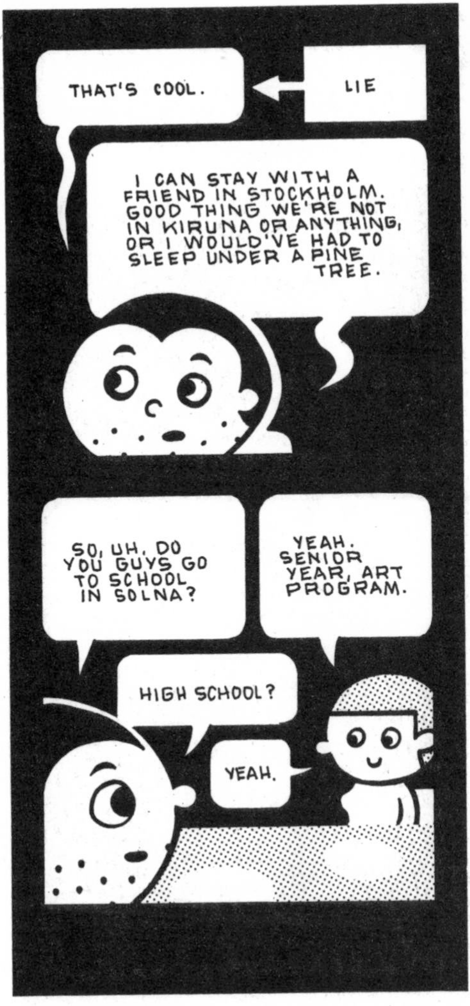
THAT'S COOL.
LIE
I CAN STAY WITH A FRIEND IN STOCKHOLM. GOOD THING WE'RE NOT IN KIRUNA OR ANYTHING, OR I WOULD'VE HAD TO SLEEP UNDER A PINE TREE.
SO, UH, DO YOU GUYS GO TO SCHOOL IN SOLNA?
YEAH. SENIOR YEAR, ART PROGRAM.
HIGH SCHOOL?
YEAH.

SO ARE YOU INTO COMICS? IS THAT HOW YOU FOUND "THE 120 DAYS OF SIMON?"

NAH... BUT WE LISTEN TO LAS PALMAS.

WHEN I WAS LITTLE I WAS REALLY INTO CARTOONS. I HAD A WHOLE BOX OF ALADDIN PARAPHERNALIA.

I STILL KNOW EVERYTHING ABOUT ALADDIN.

THESE DAYS I'M INTO OGGY AND THE COCKROACHES. I'M WITH THE ROACHES THOUGH, I LIKE TOTALLY HATE OGGY.
OKAY... LET'S GET DRUNK! WANNA GO DOWN TO DICK TURPIN?
YES.

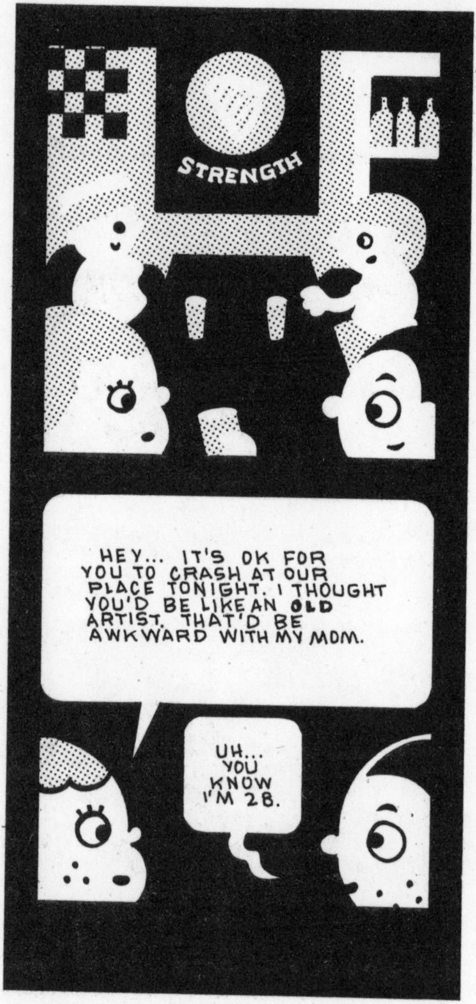
STRENGTH
HEY... IT'S OK FOR YOU TO CRASH AT OUR PLACE TONIGHT. I THOUGHT YOU'D BE LIKE AN OLD ARTIST. THAT'D BE AWKWARD WITH MY MOM.
UH... YOU KNOW I'M 28.

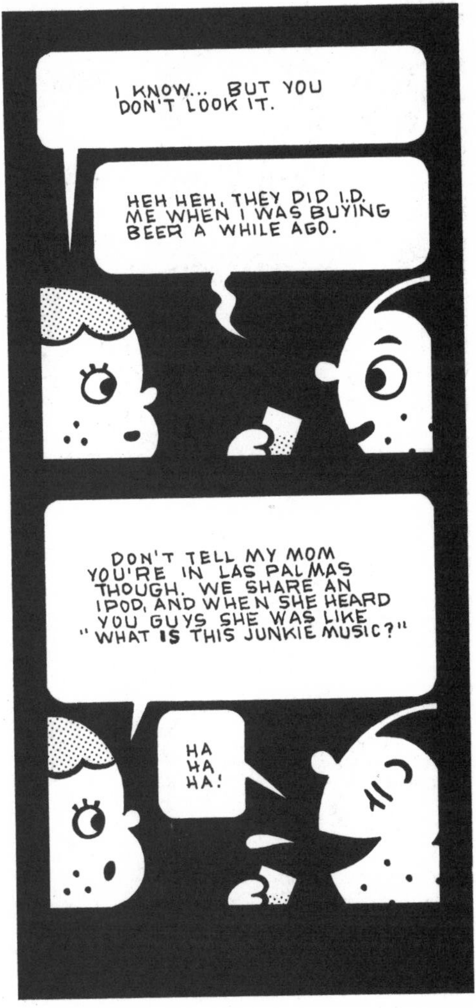
I KNOW... BUT YOU DON'T LOOK IT.
HEH HEH, THEY DID I.D. ME WHEN I WAS BUYING BEER A WHILE AGO.
DON'T TELL MY MOM YOU'RE IN LAS PALMAS THOUGH. WE SHARE AN IPOD, AND WHEN SHE HEARD YOU GUYS SHE WAS LIKE "WHAT **IS** THIS JUNKIE MUSIC?"
HA HA HA!

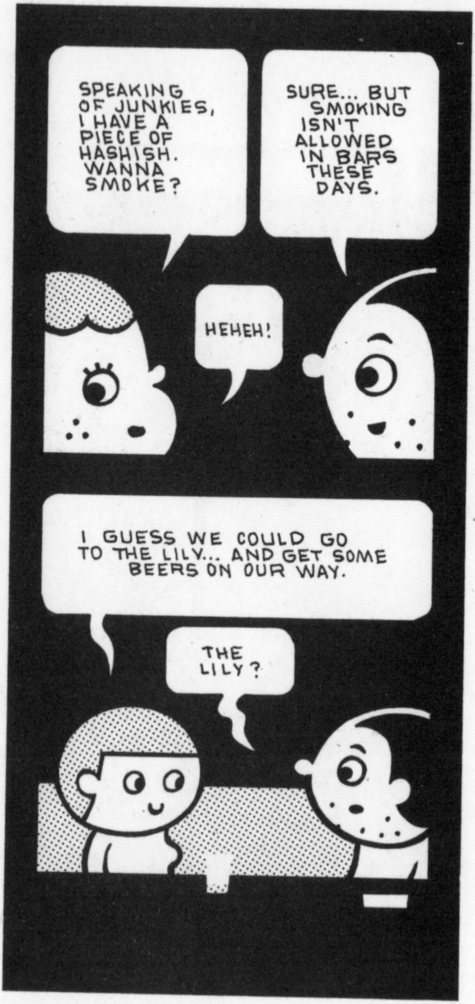
SPEAKING OF JUNKIES, I HAVE A PIECE OF HASHISH. WANNA SMOKE?
SURE... BUT SMOKING ISN'T ALLOWED IN BARS THESE DAYS.
HEHEH!
I GUESS WE COULD GO TO THE LILY... AND GET SOME BEERS ON OUR WAY.
THE LILY?

ME AND FRIDA HAVE A JOB CLEANING AT A DAYCARE CENTRE. IT'S PRETTY CLOSE BY AND WE HAVE KEYS.

WE'LL SMOKE OUT BY THE SWINGS OR SOMETHING... DON'T WANT THE PLACE TO SMELL.

HA HA! LOOK AT ALL THIS TINY FURNITURE!

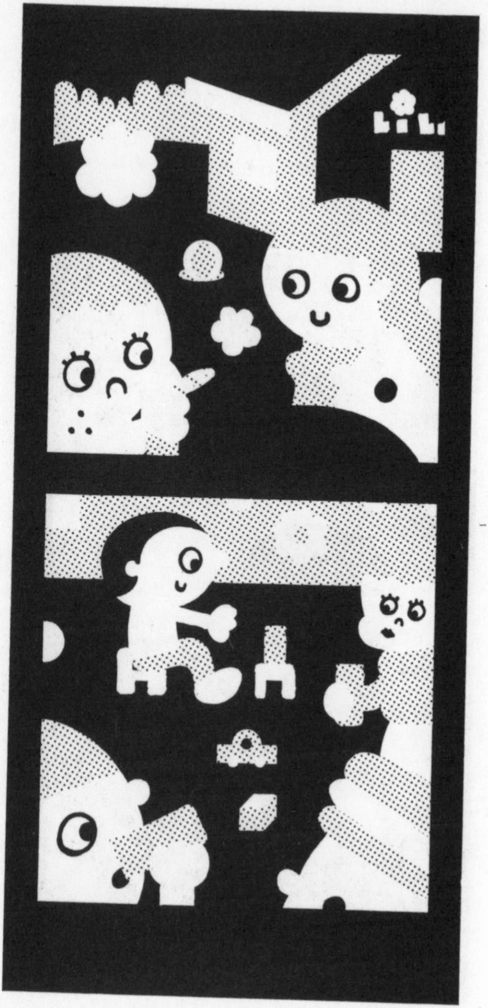

LOOK! THEY HAVE PILLOWS SHAPED LIKE LIQUORICE ALLSORTS. SWEET!

UH... WE'RE LEAVING.
PLEASE DON'T PUT THIS IN YOUR COMIC OR ANYTHING.
SURE.

IF I CHANGE YOUR NAME AND APPEARANCE, CAN I?
MM... ALRIGHT.

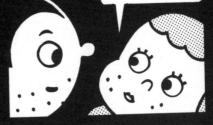

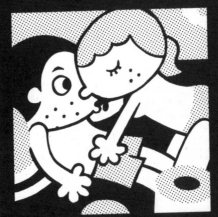

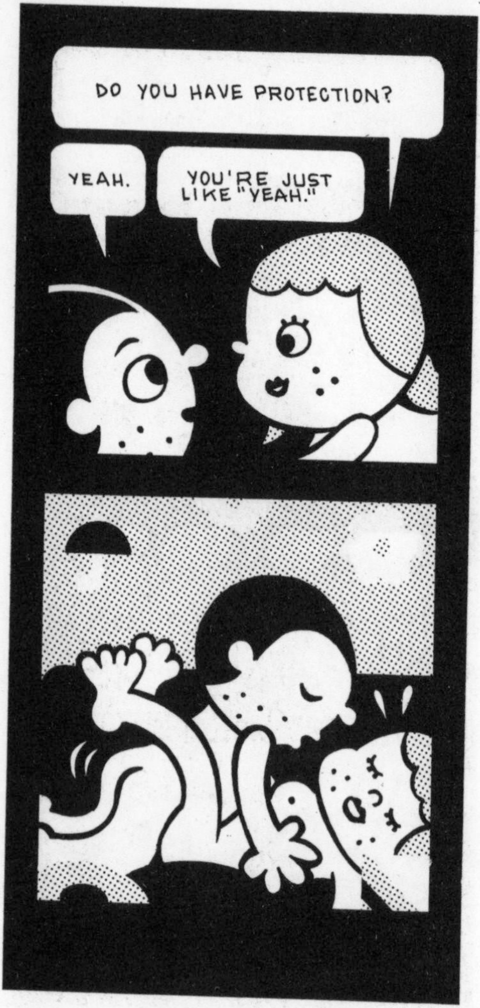
DO YOU HAVE PROTECTION?
YEAH.
YOU'RE JUST LIKE "YEAH."

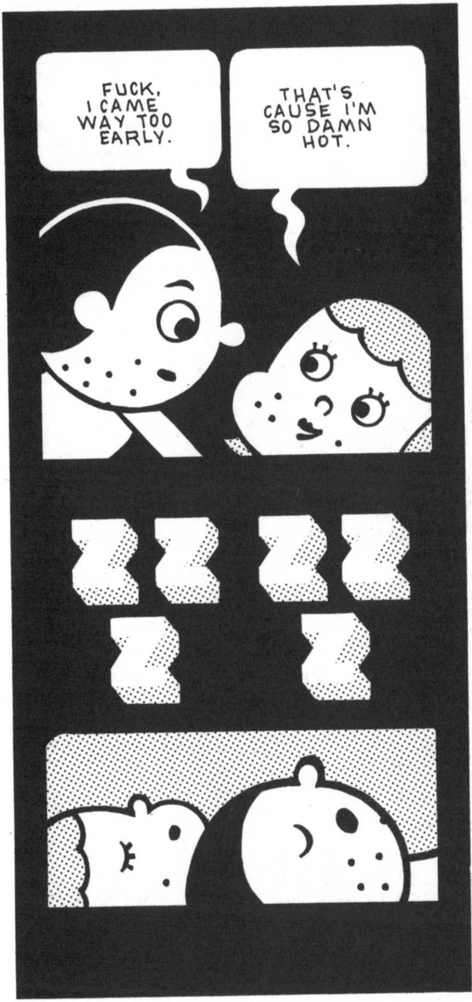
FUCK, I CAME WAY TOO EARLY.
THAT'S CAUSE I'M SO DAMN HOT.

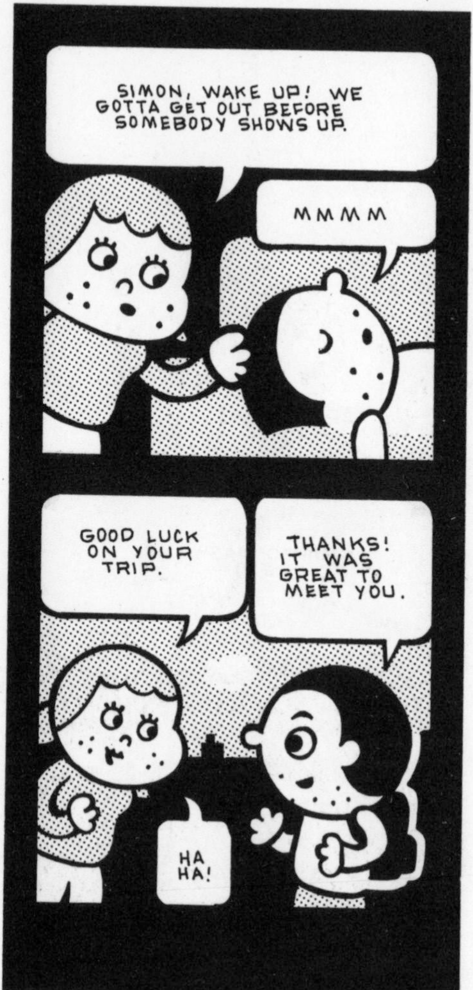
SIMON, WAKE UP! WE GOTTA GET OUT BEFORE SOMEBODY SHOWS UP.
MMMM
GOOD LUCK ON YOUR TRIP.
THANKS! IT WAS GREAT TO MEET YOU.
HA HA!

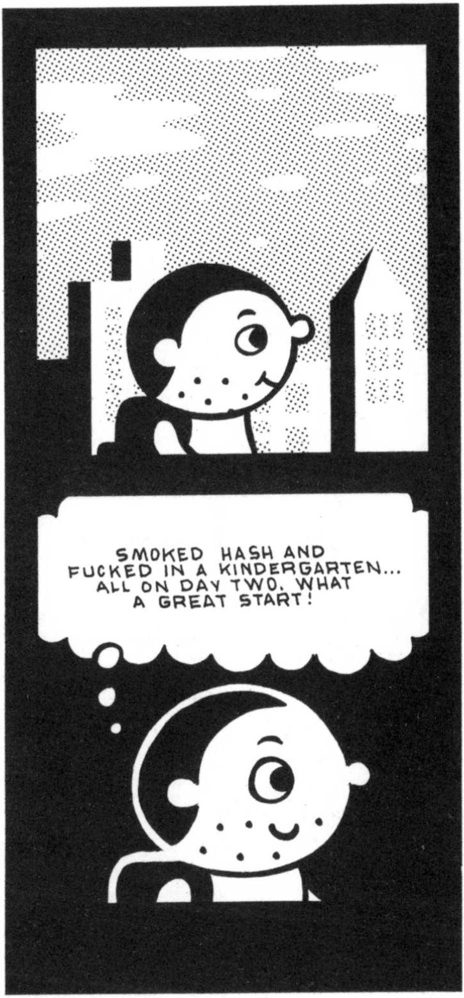
SMOKED HASH AND FUCKED IN A KINDERGARTEN... ALL ON DAY TWO. WHAT A GREAT START!

STOCKHOLM, 3/3 2007. HOST #3:
JOHANNES KLENELL

HEY KLENELL! CAN I COME
OVER? ARE YOU AT ORDFRONT?

IT'S SATURDAY, SIMON. I'M
AT CAFÉ EDENBORG. COME
HERE.

SO
HOW
WAS
LAST
NIGHT?

WELL, I'M NOT THE ONE TO KISS AND TELL OR ANYTHING... BUT SINCE YOU'RE ONE OF MY PUBLISHERS YOU HAVE A RIGHT TO KNOW. IT WAS AS GOOD AS IT GETS.
MADE LOVE, EH?

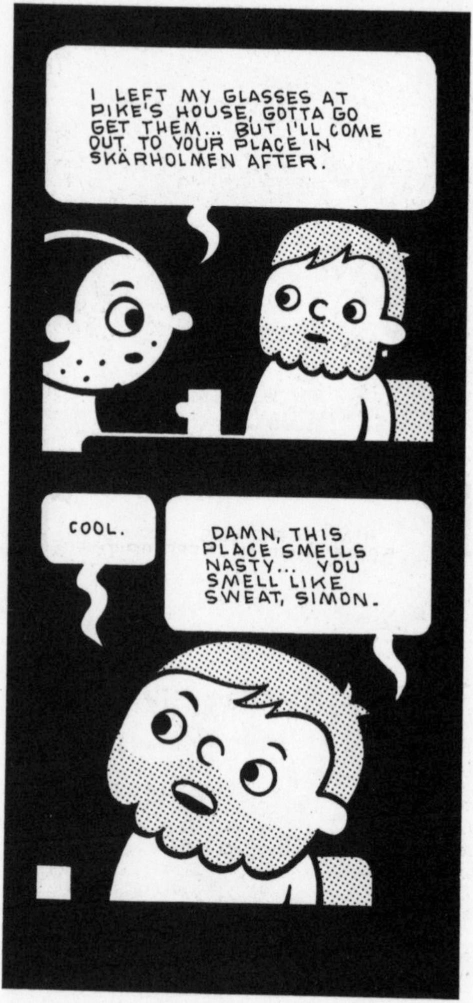
I LEFT MY GLASSES AT PIKE'S HOUSE, GOTTA GO GET THEM... BUT I'LL COME OUT TO YOUR PLACE IN SKARHOLMEN AFTER.
COOL.
DAMN, THIS PLACE SMELLS NASTY... YOU SMELL LIKE SWEAT, SIMON.

MOTHERFUCKER! I DON'T SMELL LIKE SWEAT AT ALL.
I'M SURE IT'S SOME KIND OF INFERIORITY COMPLEX, BUT WHAT THE HELL... HE DOES THOSE COMMENTS A LOT... TO MESS WITH MY SELF-ESTEEM.
"YOUR BOOK ISN'T SELLING FOR SHIT."

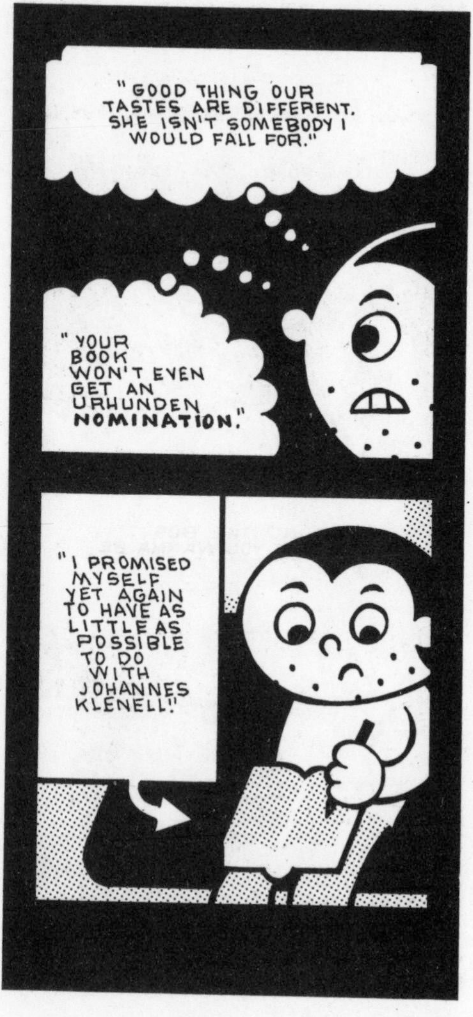
"GOOD THING OUR TASTES ARE DIFFERENT. SHE ISN'T SOMEBODY I WOULD FALL FOR."
"YOUR BOOK WON'T EVEN GET AN URHUNDEN NOMINATION."
"I PROMISED MYSELF YET AGAIN TO HAVE AS LITTLE AS POSSIBLE TO DO WITH JOHANNES KLENELL!"

LATER, IN SKÄRHOLMEN.

CAN I GO ONLINE FOR A SEC? I HAVE TO CHECK THE BUS SCHEDULES.

YEAH, USE THE COMPUTER IN THE OTHER ROOM.

I FOUND THE BUS THING. IF YOU WANNA BE SAFE THERE'S ONE AT 2:45 PM.

OH... I GUESS I SHOULD GET GOING PRETTY SOON. CAN I GRAB A SANDWICH OR TWO?
SURE, THAT'S PART OF THE DEAL. TAKE WHAT YOU WANT FROM THE KITCHEN.

SO YOU WANT AS LITTLE AS POSSIBLE TO DO WITH ME FROM NOW ON, HUH?
HA HA HA HA!
DAMN IT DAMN IT DAMN IT

YOU'VE BEEN READING MY DIARY?
WHAT THE HELL... IT LAY OPEN RIGHT BY THE COMPUTER AND I SAW MY NAME.
I DIDN'T GET IT WAS SECRET... BUT I'M NOT HURT OR ANYTHING. I'VE HAD WORSE THOUGHTS ABOUT YOU.

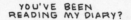

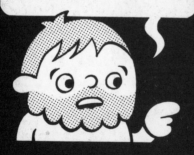

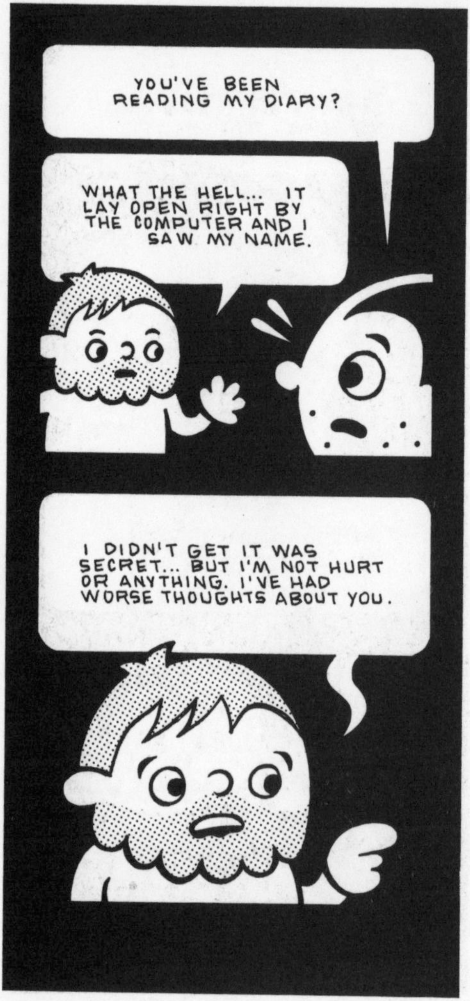

WHAT HAVE I DONE? HE LOOKS REALLY SAD.
LIKE... I DIDN'T MEAN IT LIKE THAT. I WROTE IT WHEN I WAS ANGRY.
IT WAS RIGHT AFTER YOU SAID I SMELL BAD.

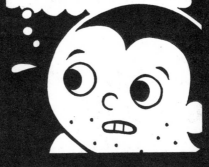

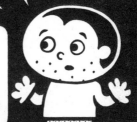

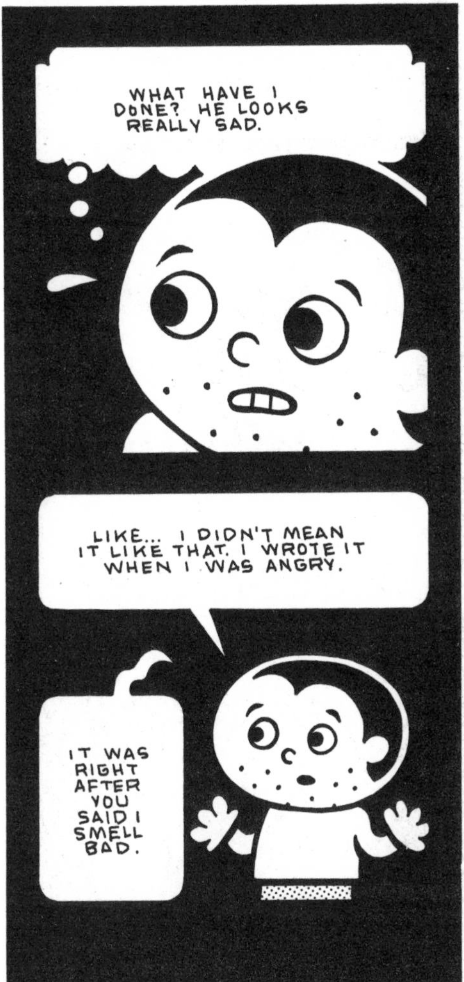

WHAT THE HELL! WHO DOESN'T SMELL BAD AFTER SMOKING UP AND FUCKING ALL NIGHT?!
IT'S NOT JUST THAT. YOU DO THOSE LITTLE INSULTS A LOT.
IT'S 'CAUSE I LIKE BEING HONEST WITH PEOPLE I KNOW WELL.

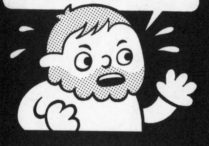

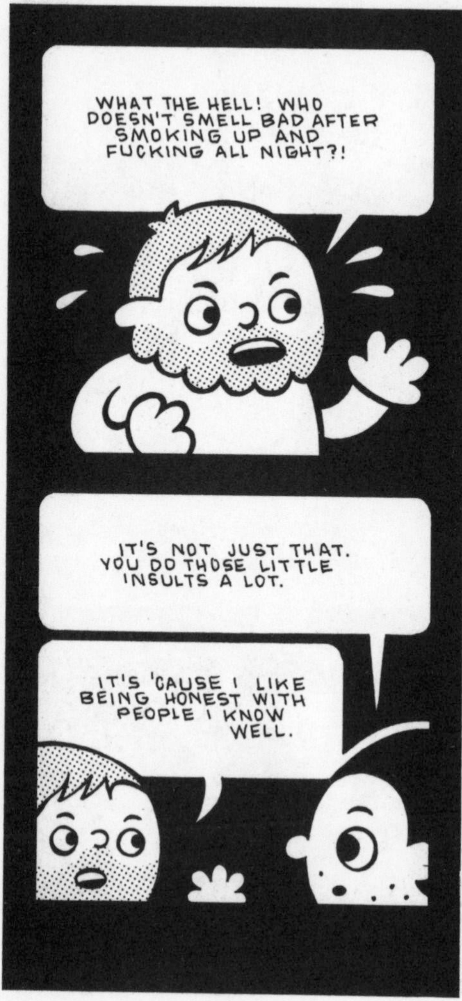

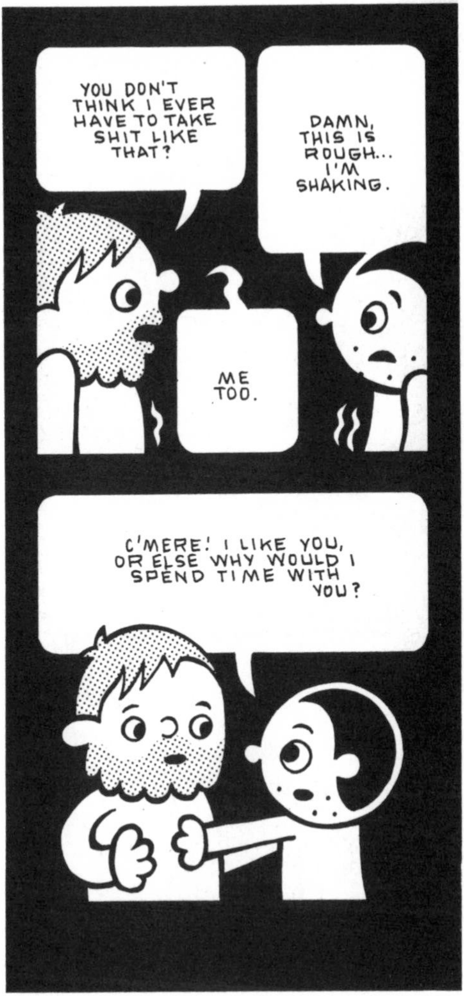
YOU DON'T THINK I EVER HAVE TO TAKE SHIT LIKE THAT?
DAMN, THIS IS ROUGH... I'M SHAKING.
ME TOO.
C'MERE! I LIKE YOU, OR ELSE WHY WOULD I SPEND TIME WITH YOU?

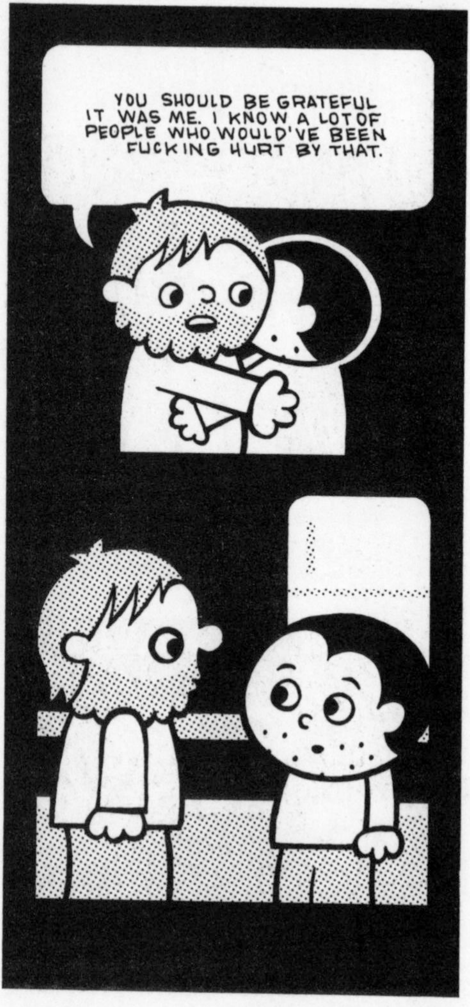
YOU SHOULD BE GRATEFUL IT WAS ME. I KNOW A LOT OF PEOPLE WHO WOULD'VE BEEN FUCKING HURT BY THAT.

CAN I STILL GRAB THE SANDWICHES?
SUNDSVALL, 3/4 2007. HOST #4: SOFIA JONASSON AND CARIN LINDEFELT

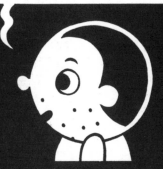

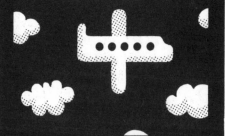

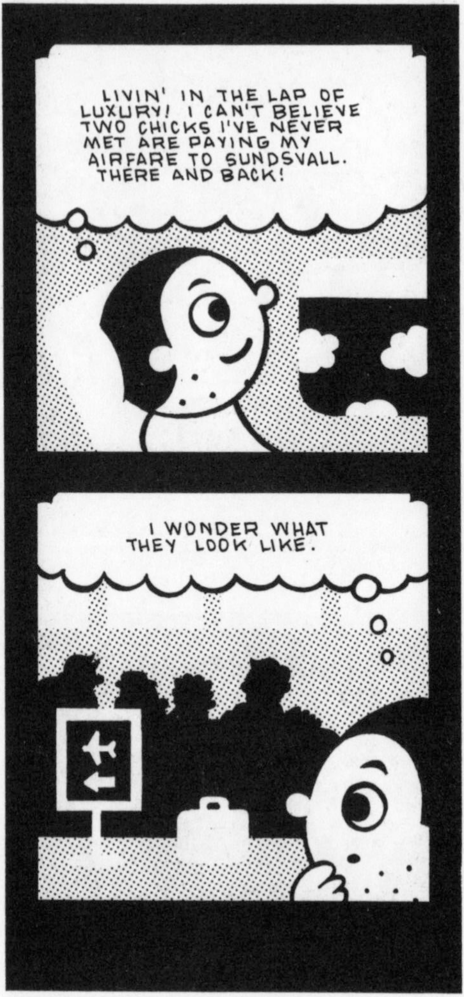
LIVIN' IN THE LAP OF LUXURY! I CAN'T BELIEVE TWO CHICKS I'VE NEVER MET ARE PAYING MY AIRFARE TO SUNDSVALL. THERE AND BACK!
I WONDER WHAT THEY LOOK LIKE.

SINGHA
OOOHMYGAWD. SOMBREROS AND BEER. SOME PEOPLE REALLY TRY HARD TO MAKE IT INTO THE BOOK.

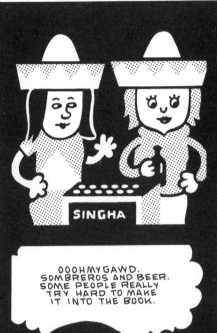

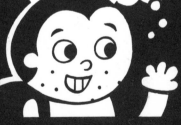

LATER THAT NIGHT.

WHICH ONE OF YOU THREW UP ON MY TOILETRIES?

ÅRE, 3/16 2007. HOST #11: BENJAMIN COVE

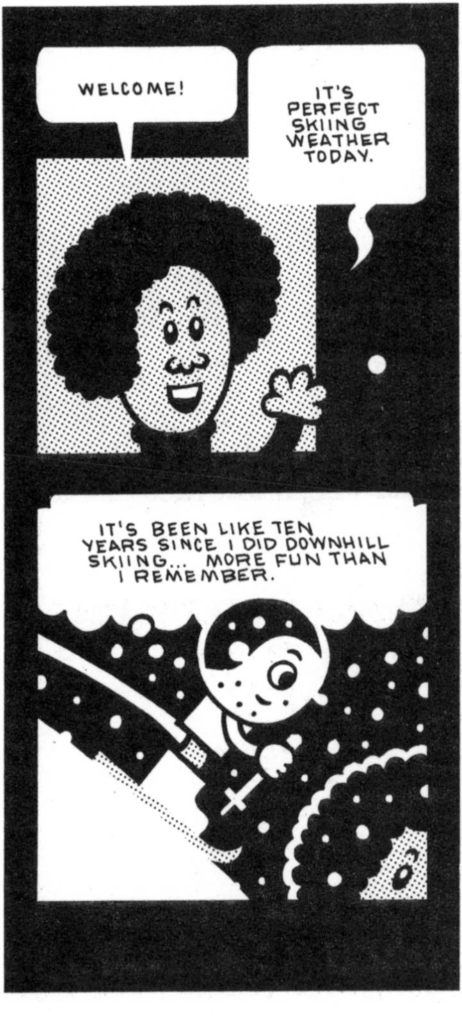
WELCOME!
IT'S PERFECT SKIING WEATHER TODAY.
IT'S BEEN LIKE TEN YEARS SINCE I DID DOWNHILL SKIING... MORE FUN THAN I REMEMBER.

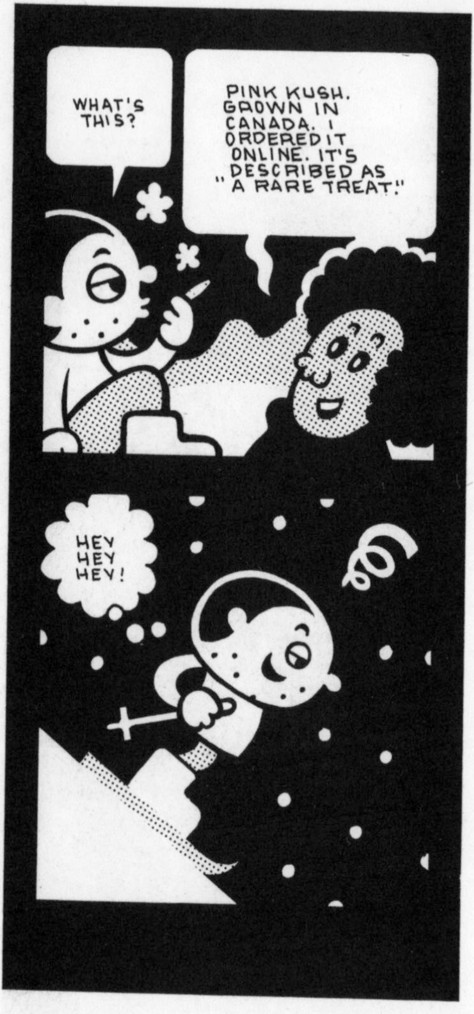
WHAT'S THIS?
PINK KUSH. GROWN IN CANADA. I ORDERED IT ONLINE. IT'S DESCRIBED AS "A RARE TREAT!"
HEY HEY HEY!

TOO BAD I CAN ONLY STAY ONE MORE DAY.

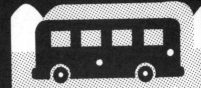

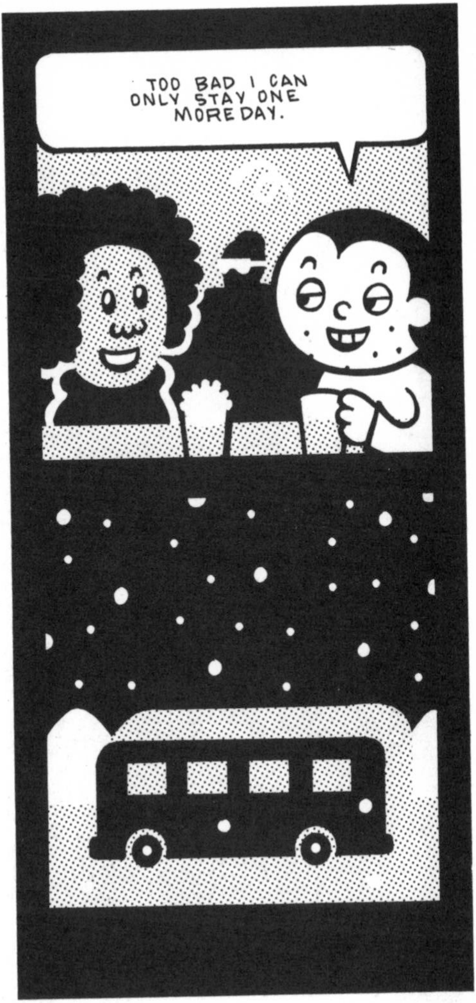

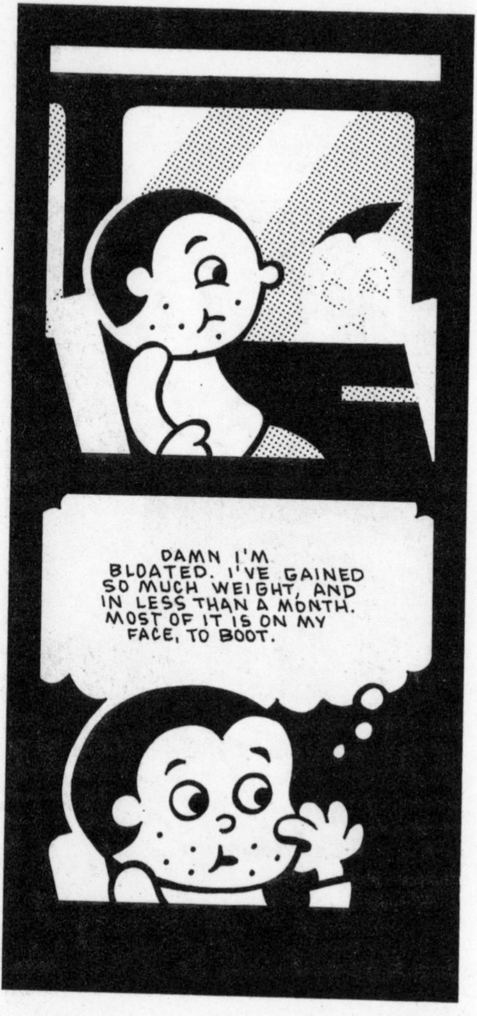
DAMN I'M BLOATED. I'VE GAINED SO MUCH WEIGHT, AND IN LESS THAN A MONTH. MOST OF IT IS ON MY FACE, TO BOOT.

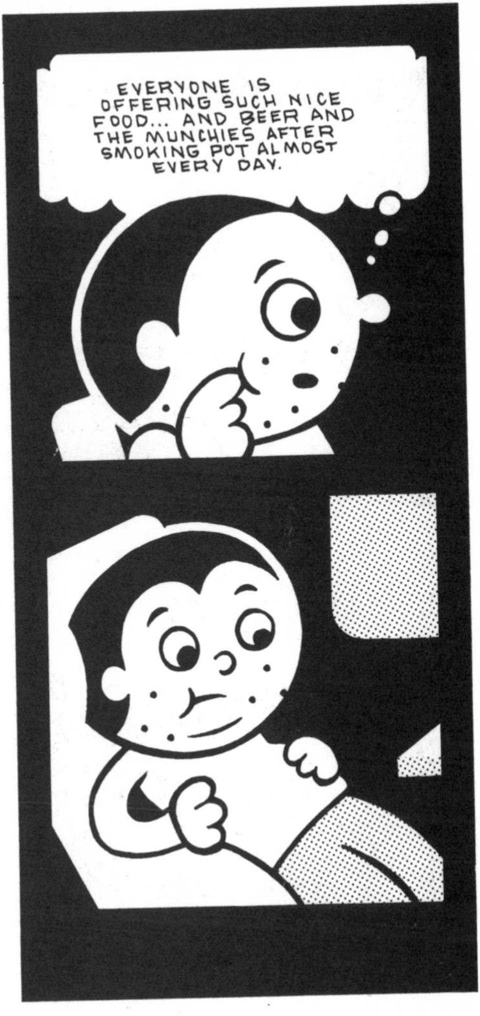
EVERYONE IS OFFERING SUCH NICE FOOD... AND BEER AND THE MUNCHIES AFTER SMOKING POT ALMOST EVERY DAY.

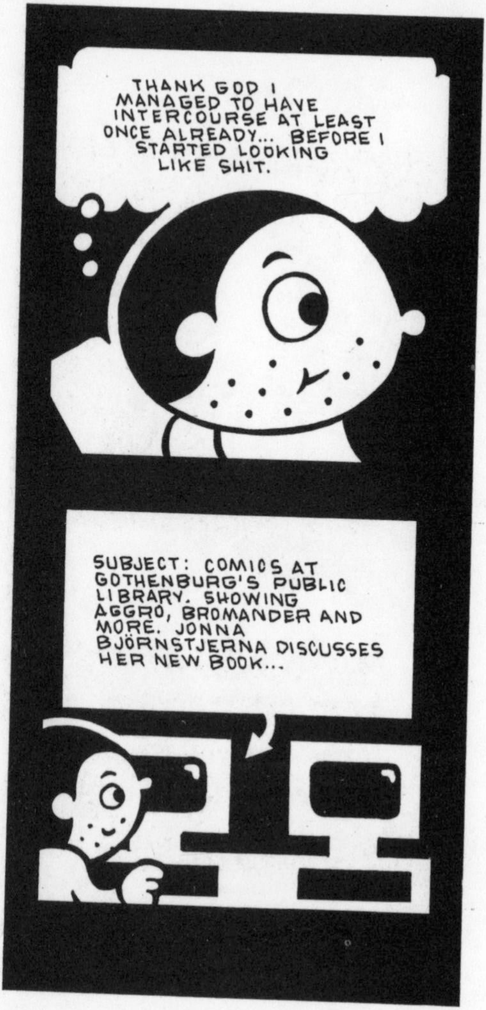

THANK GOD I MANAGED TO HAVE INTERCOURSE AT LEAST ONCE ALREADY... BEFORE I STARTED LOOKING LIKE SHIT.
SUBJECT: COMICS AT GOTHENBURG'S PUBLIC LIBRARY. SHOWING AGGRO, BROMANDER AND MORE. JONNA BJÖRNSTJERNA DISCUSSES HER NEW BOOK...

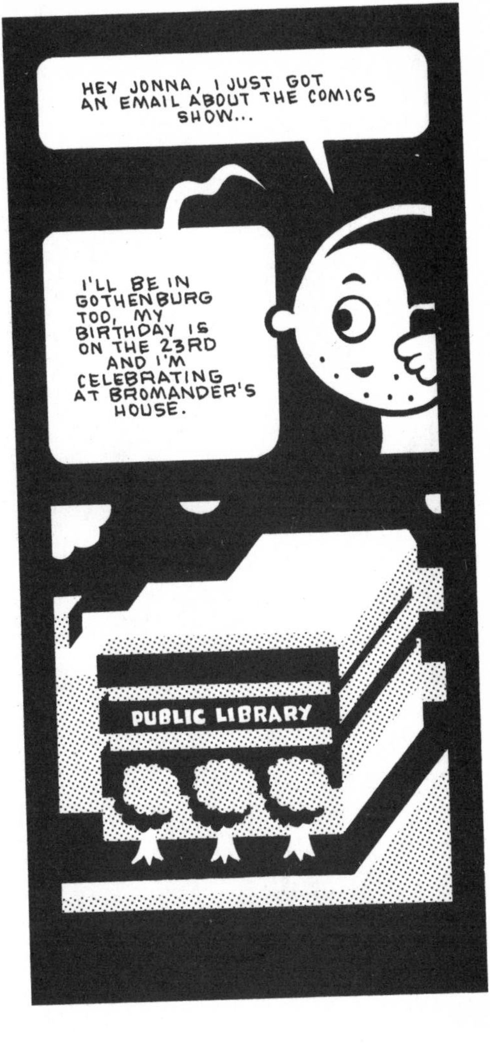
HEY JONNA, I JUST GOT AN EMAIL ABOUT THE COMICS SHOW...
I'LL BE IN GOTHENBURG TOO, MY BIRTHDAY IS ON THE 23RD AND I'M CELEBRATING AT BROMANDER'S HOUSE.
PUBLIC LIBRARY

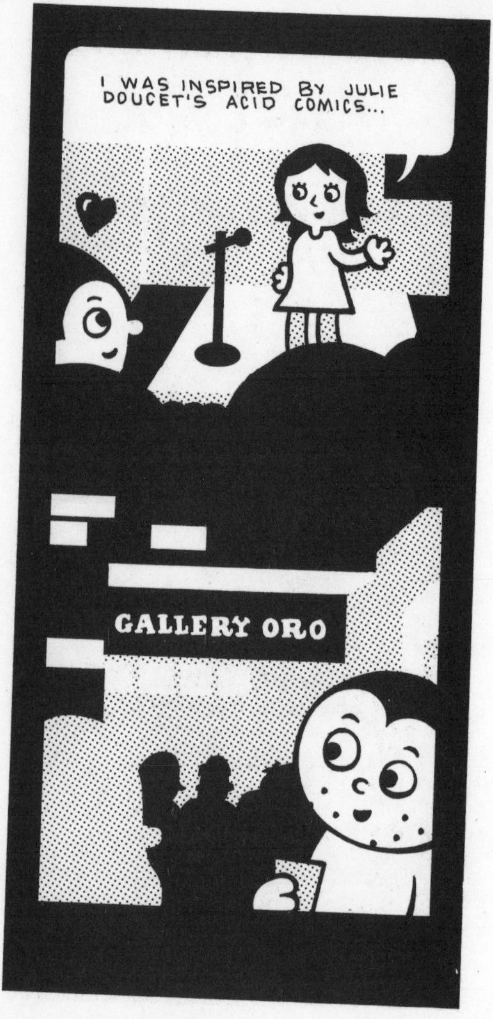
I WAS INSPIRED BY JULIE DOUCET'S ACID COMICS...
GALLERY ORO

YOU LOOK A LITTLE DIFFERENT.
IT'S THE TOUGH VAGABOND LIFESTYLE, YOU KNOW...
AREN'T YOU A LITTLE PUDGIER?
I GAINED LIKE TWO POUNDS A WEEK.

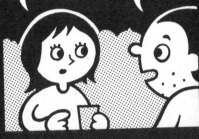

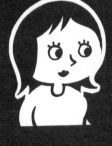

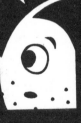

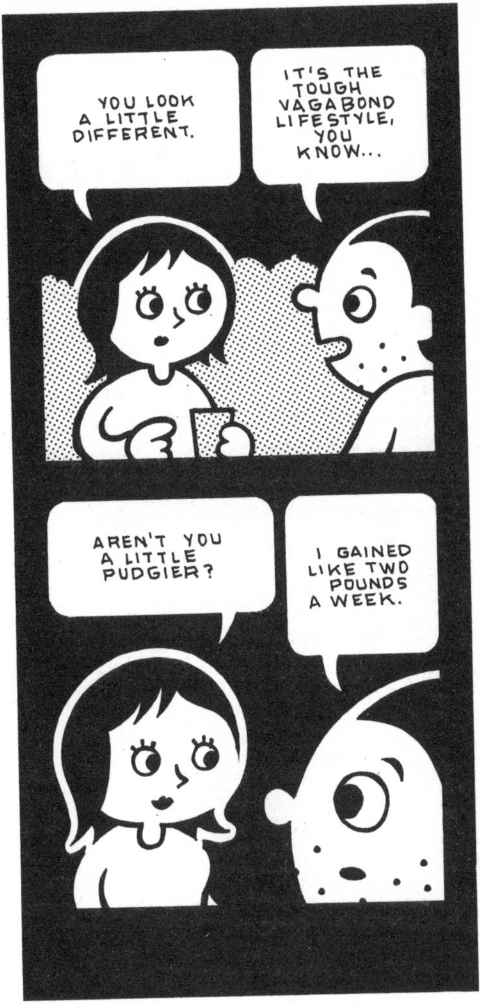

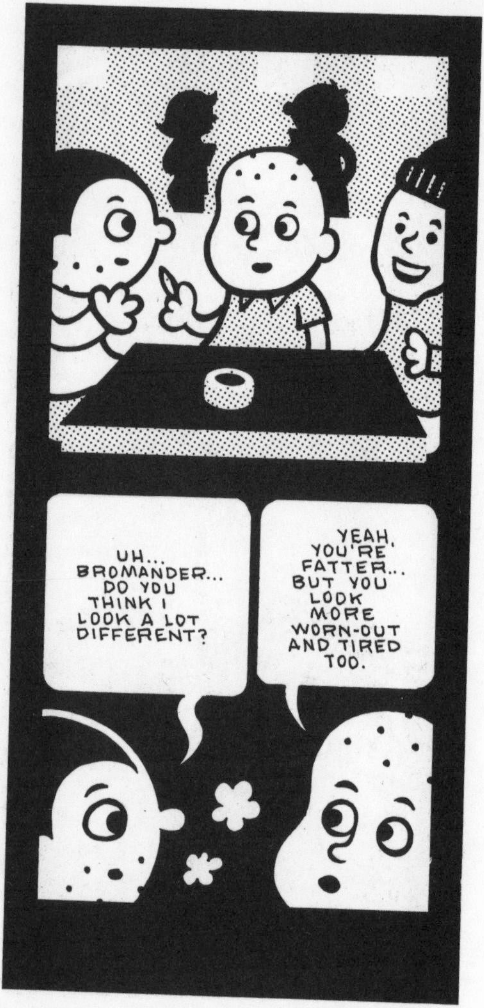
UH... BROMANDER... DO YOU THINK I LOOK A LOT DIFFERENT?
YEAH, YOU'RE FATTER... BUT YOU LOOK MORE WORN-OUT AND TIRED TOO.

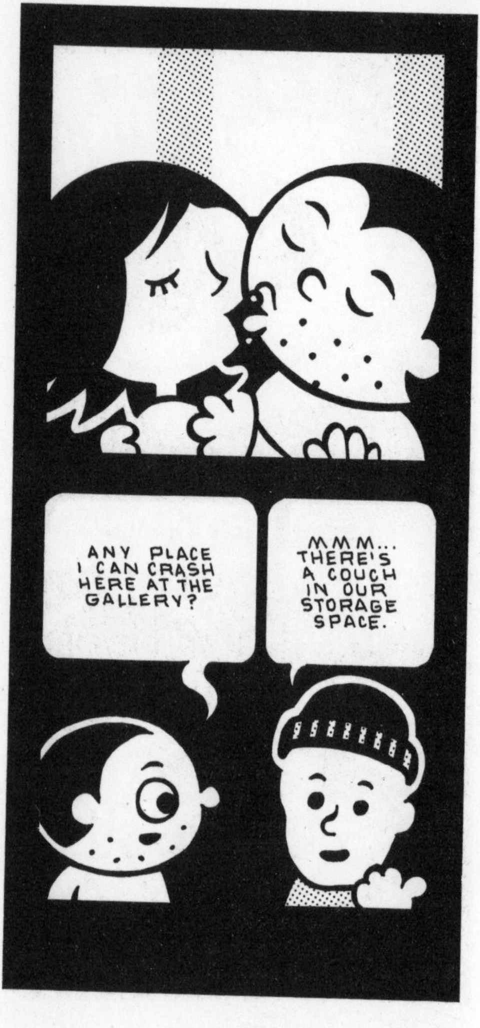
ANY PLACE I CAN CRASH HERE AT THE GALLERY?
MMM... THERE'S A COUCH IN OUR STORAGE SPACE.

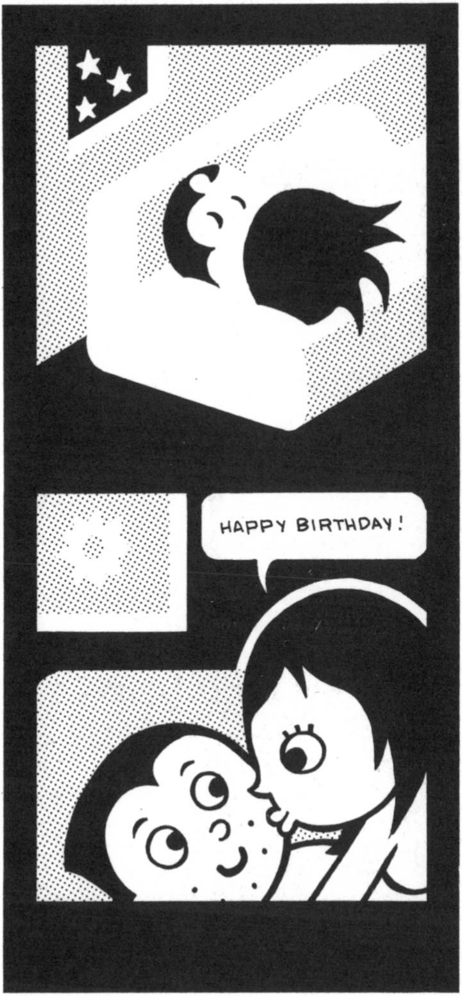
HAPPY BIRTHDAY!

HEY, CHECK IT OUT, THE FRIDGE IS FULL OF BEER.
HOW'D THEY KNOW IT WAS MY BIRTHDAY?

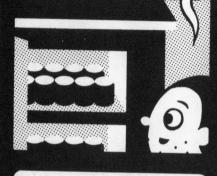

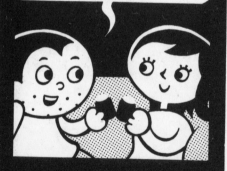

YOU WANNA HIT THE TOWN AND GET ANOTHER DRINK FOR BREAKFAST?
MM-MMM!
BLOODY MARYS

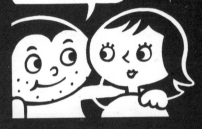

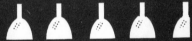

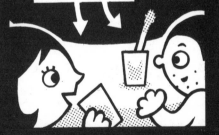

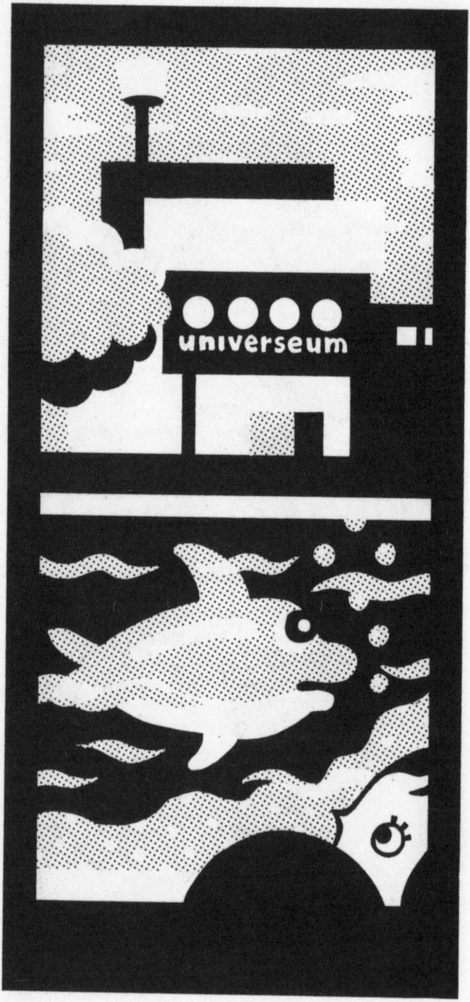
universeum

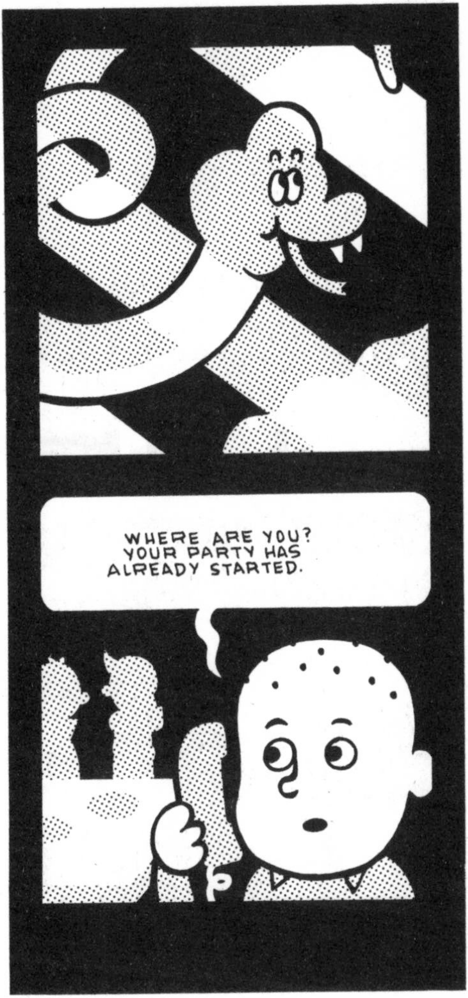
WHERE ARE YOU?
YOUR PARTY HAS
ALREADY STARTED.

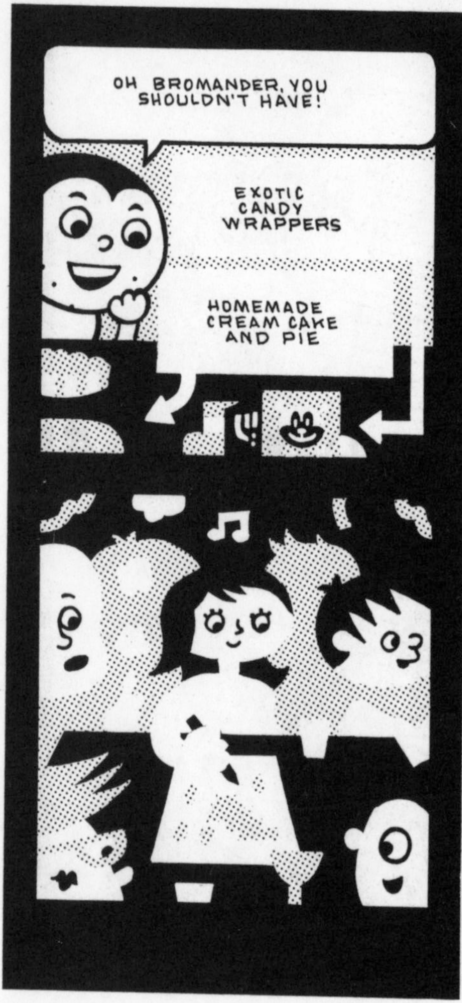
OH BROMANDER, YOU SHOULDN'T HAVE!
EXOTIC CANDY WRAPPERS
HOMEMADE CREAM CAKE AND PIE

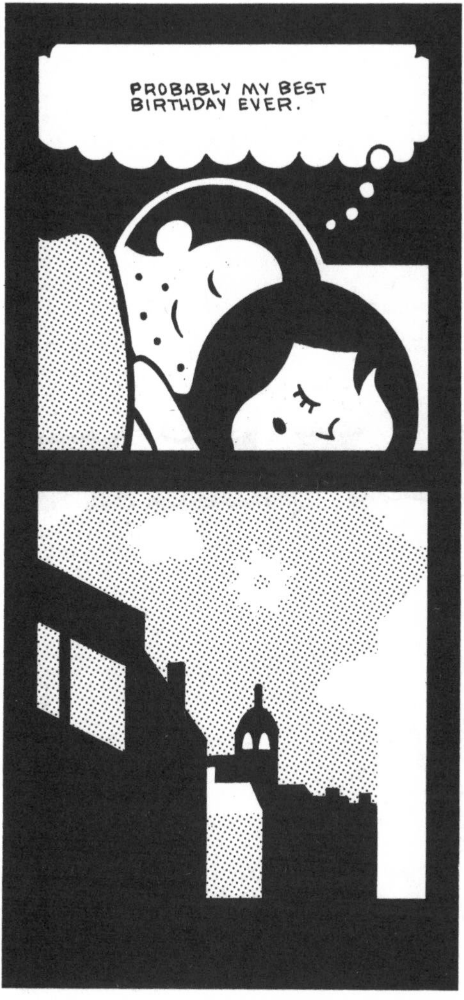
PROBABLY MY BEST BIRTHDAY EVER.

WHO'RE YOU STAYING WITH TODAY?
AGGRO
I DUNNO... BUT IT'S HERE IN GOTHENBURG. WE CAN CHILL FOR A BIT, I'LL CHECK MY PAPERS LATER.

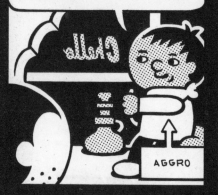

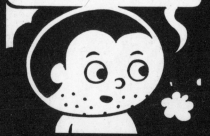

IT'S THE MIDDLE EAST, BITCH.
SO YOU LIKE BEING 29? OLDIE BUT GOLDIE, HUH?
I'M GONNA BE 30. THIS WHOLE TRIP IS ONE BIG IDENTITY CRISIS ON WHEELS.

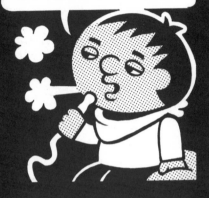

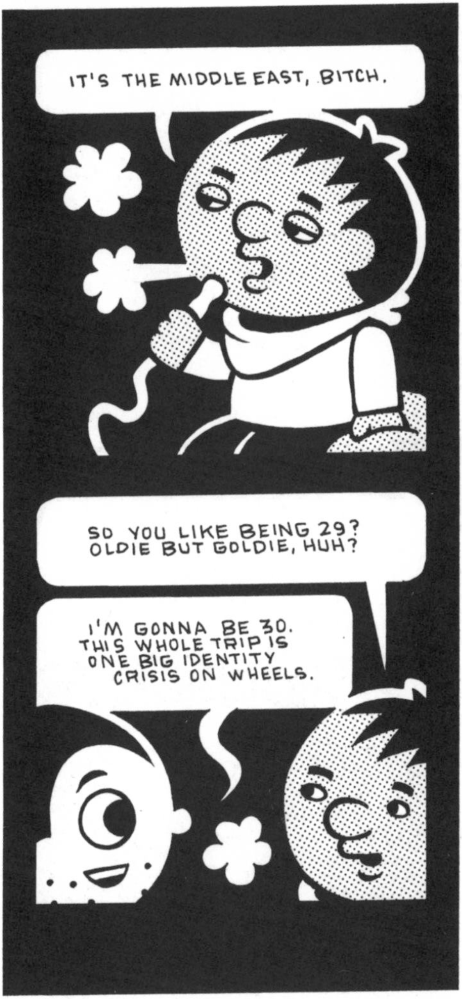

THIS IS MY RUMSPRINGA... YOU KNOW, LIKE WHAT THE AMISH DO. AT SOME POINT I MIGHT HAVE TO SETTLE DOWN, BUT RIGHT NOW IT'S ALL ABOUT BOOZE, DRUGS AND GETTING LAID AS MUCH AS POSSIBLE.

BUT... UH... WHAT ABOUT YOU AND JONNA?

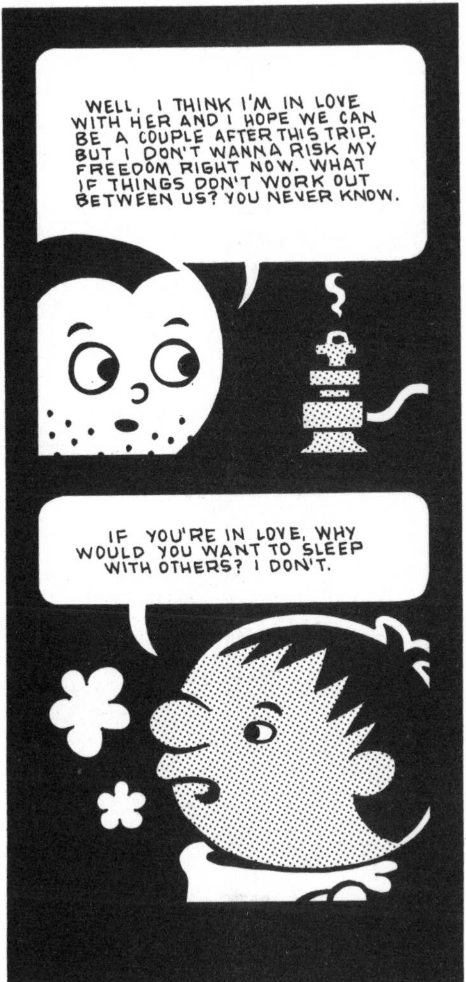
WELL, I THINK I'M IN LOVE WITH HER AND I HOPE WE CAN BE A COUPLE AFTER THIS TRIP. BUT I DON'T WANNA RISK MY FREEDOM RIGHT NOW. WHAT IF THINGS DON'T WORK OUT BETWEEN US? YOU NEVER KNOW.
IF YOU'RE IN LOVE, WHY WOULD YOU WANT TO SLEEP WITH OTHERS? I DON'T.

I'M NOT LIKE THAT. I CAN BE HEAD OVER HEELS FOR SOMEONE AND STILL BE REALLY ATTRACTED TO OTHERS. ONCE I'M IN A RELATIONSHIP I'M HAPPY WITH, I WOULDN'T MESS IT UP BY CHEATING, THOUGH.

BUT... YOU'RE RISKING HER MEETING SOMEONE ELSE WHILE YOU DO THIS.

PSHAW. SOMEONE BETTER THAN ME? DO YOU KNOW WHO I AM?

HEH HEH... DAMN. I SHOULD BE MORE LIKE YOU... AND BE SLUTTIER... BUT I CAN'T. I FALL IN LOVE WITH WHOEVER I SLEEP WITH. I'M PROBABLY EMOTIONALLY DISTURBED.
OR MAYBE I'M THE ONE WHO'S EMOTIONALLY DISTURBED... TO BE ABLE TO SEPARATE THOSE FEELINGS.
HMM...

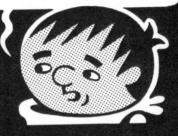

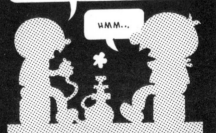

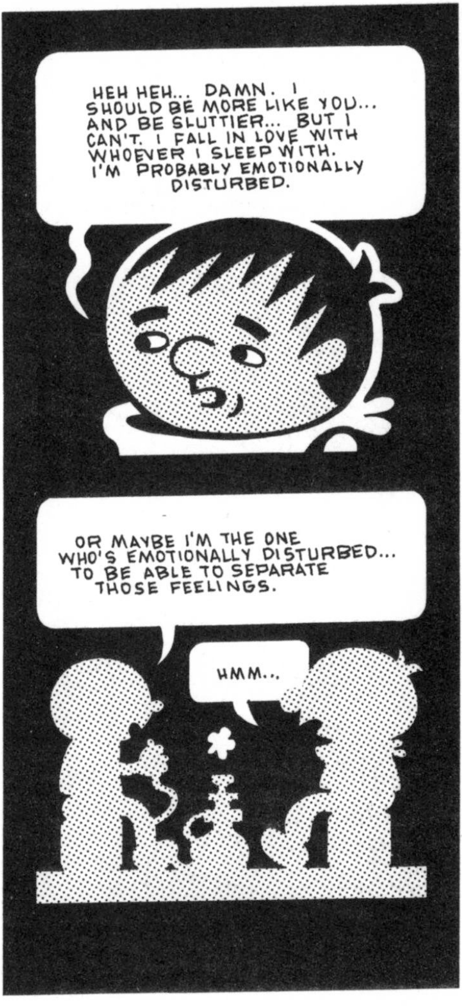

OR NEITHER OF US. HELL, IT'S LIKE WHAT THEY TAUGHT US IN KINDERGARTEN: EVERYBODY IS DIFFERENT.
GOTHENBURG, 3/26 2007. HOST #18: DAVID BERGLUND
NO FREE NEWSPAPERS!
BERGLUND&

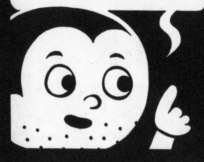

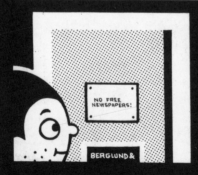

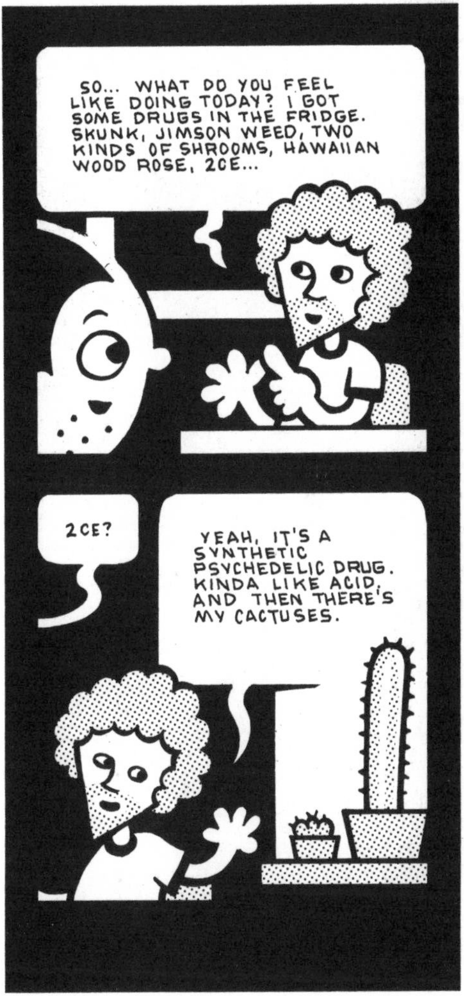
SO... WHAT DO YOU FEEL LIKE DOING TODAY? I GOT SOME DRUGS IN THE FRIDGE. SKUNK, JIMSON WEED, TWO KINDS OF SHROOMS, HAWAIIAN WOOD ROSE, 2CE...
2CE?
YEAH, IT'S A SYNTHETIC PSYCHEDELIC DRUG. KINDA LIKE ACID. AND THEN THERE'S MY CACTUSES.

WOW. MESCALINE CACTUSES... I NEVER TRIED THAT.
YUP. THE BIG ONE IS A SAN PEDRO AND THE SMALL ONES ARE PEYOTE.

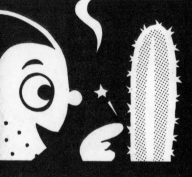

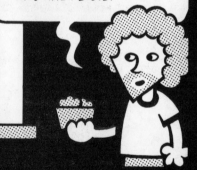

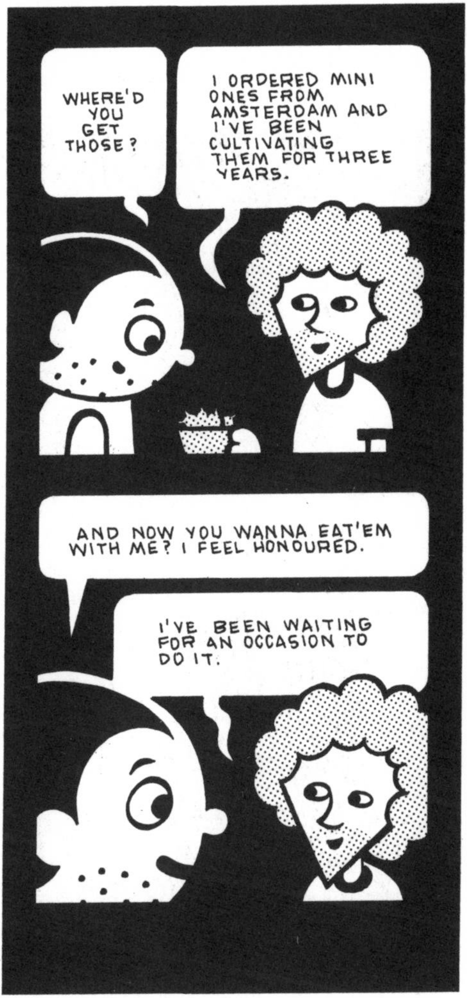
WHERE'D YOU GET THOSE?
I ORDERED MINI ONES FROM AMSTERDAM AND I'VE BEEN CULTIVATING THEM FOR THREE YEARS.
AND NOW YOU WANNA EAT'EM WITH ME? I FEEL HONOURED.
I'VE BEEN WAITING FOR AN OCCASION TO DO IT.

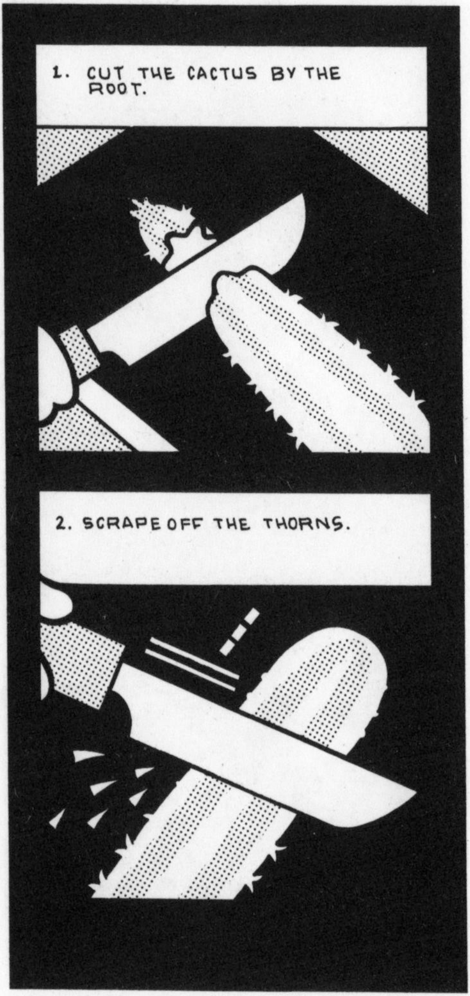
1. CUT THE CACTUS BY THE ROOT.
2. SCRAPE OFF THE THORNS.

3. SLICE.
GOD DAMN THAT'S BITTER!

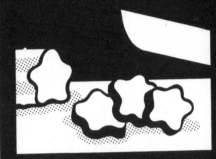

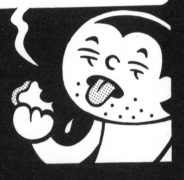

THE INDIANS USED TO EAT THESE IN RITES OF PASSAGE... TO GAIN INSIGHT.
THEY WOULD ALWAYS VOMIT... BUT BY THEN ENOUGH OF THE MESCALINE HAD BEEN ABSORBED BY THEIR SYSTEM TO MAKE THEM HALLUCINATE.

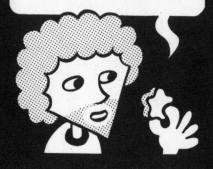

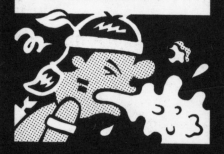

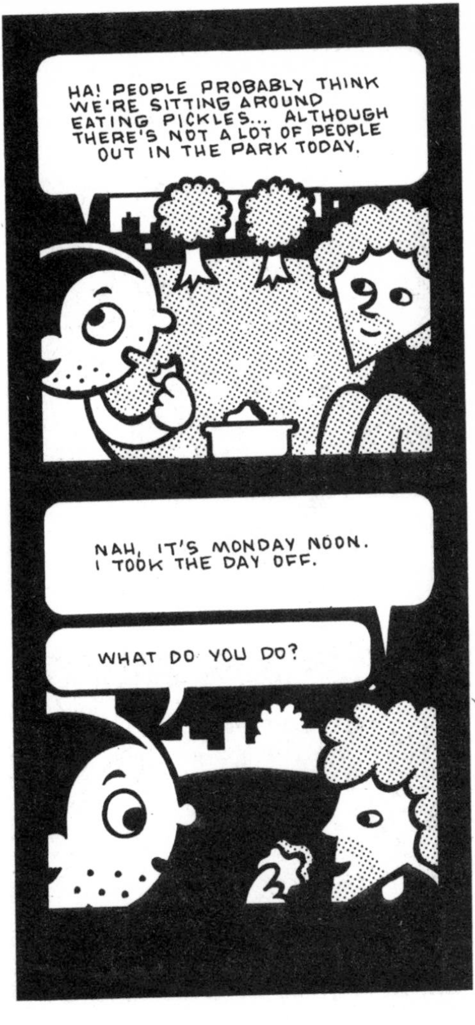
HA! PEOPLE PROBABLY THINK WE'RE SITTING AROUND EATING PICKLES... ALTHOUGH THERE'S NOT A LOT OF PEOPLE OUT IN THE PARK TODAY.
NAH, IT'S MONDAY NOON. I TOOK THE DAY OFF.
WHAT DO YOU DO?

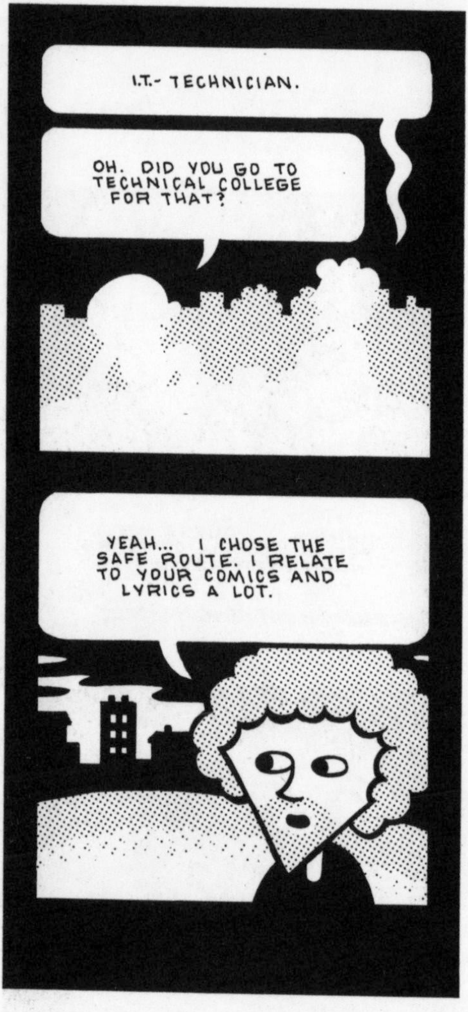
I.T.- TECHNICIAN.
OH. DID YOU GO TO TECHNICAL COLLEGE FOR THAT?
YEAH... I CHOSE THE SAFE ROUTE. I RELATE TO YOUR COMICS AND LYRICS A LOT.

I FEEL LIKE WE'RE THE SAME KIND OF PERSON, ALTHOUGH YOU MADE LESS "SAFE" CHOICES IN LIFE.
HMMM... I GUESS WE'LL SEE IN A COUPLE OF YEARS, WHEN EVERYTHING COMES AROUND, WHO MADE THE RIGHT CHOICE. I MIGHT END UP LIKE BRITNEY SPEARS. COMPLETELY FUCKED OVER BY SHOW BUSINESS.

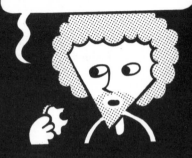

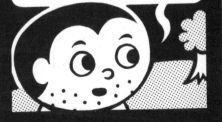

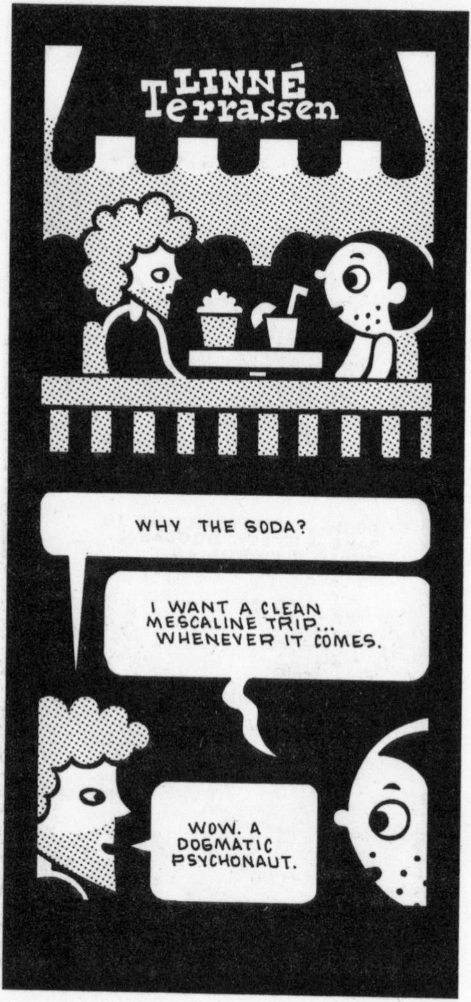
LINNÉ Terrassen
WHY THE SODA?
I WANT A CLEAN MESCALINE TRIP... WHENEVER IT COMES.
WOW. A DOGMATIC PSYCHONAUT.

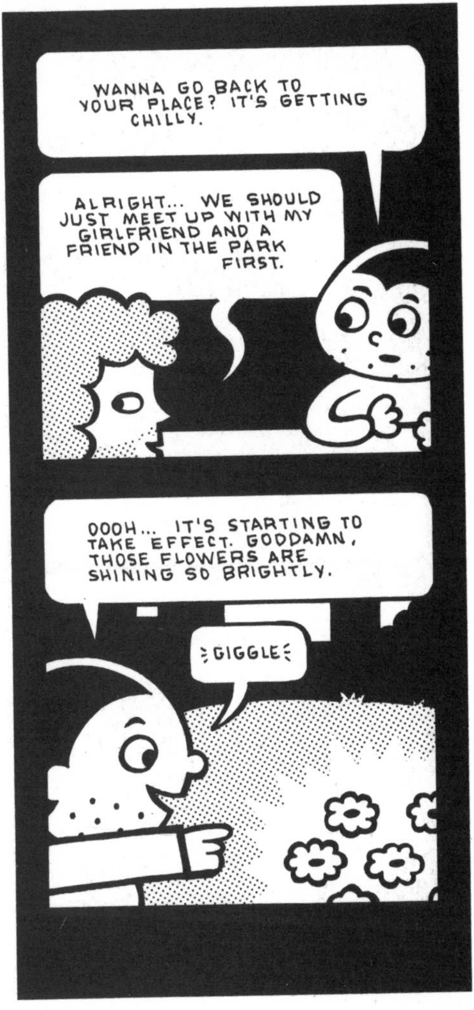
WANNA GO BACK TO YOUR PLACE? IT'S GETTING CHILLY.
ALRIGHT... WE SHOULD JUST MEET UP WITH MY GIRLFRIEND AND A FRIEND IN THE PARK FIRST.
OOOH... IT'S STARTING TO TAKE EFFECT. GODDAMN, THOSE FLOWERS ARE SHINING SO BRIGHTLY.
GIGGLE

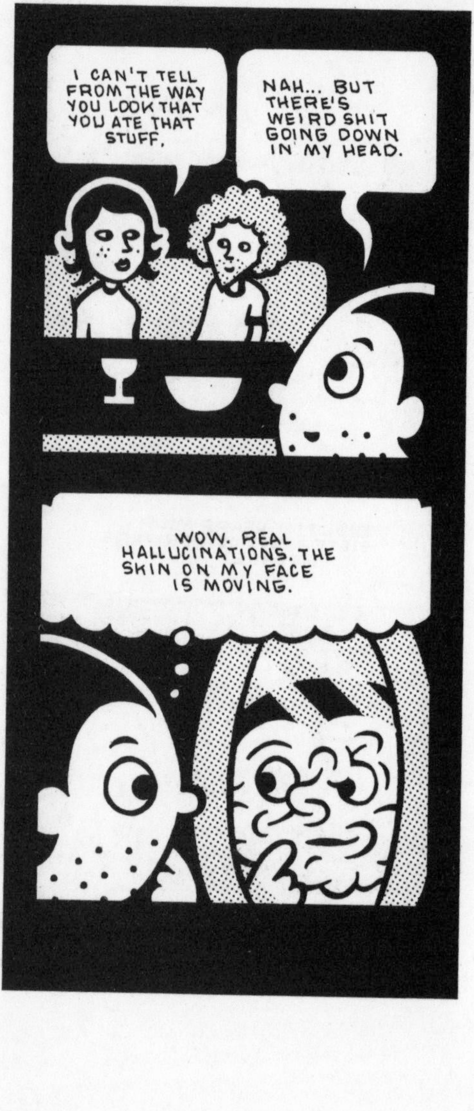
I CAN'T TELL FROM THE WAY YOU LOOK THAT YOU ATE THAT STUFF.
NAH... BUT THERE'S WEIRD SHIT GOING DOWN IN MY HEAD.
WOW. REAL HALLUCINATIONS. THE SKIN ON MY FACE IS MOVING.

OW! THERE'S THORNS ON THE FLOOR!
RIGHT! I HEARD YOUR SISTER GOT HER DRIVERS LICENSE.

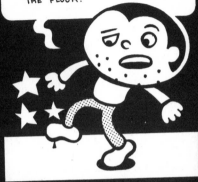

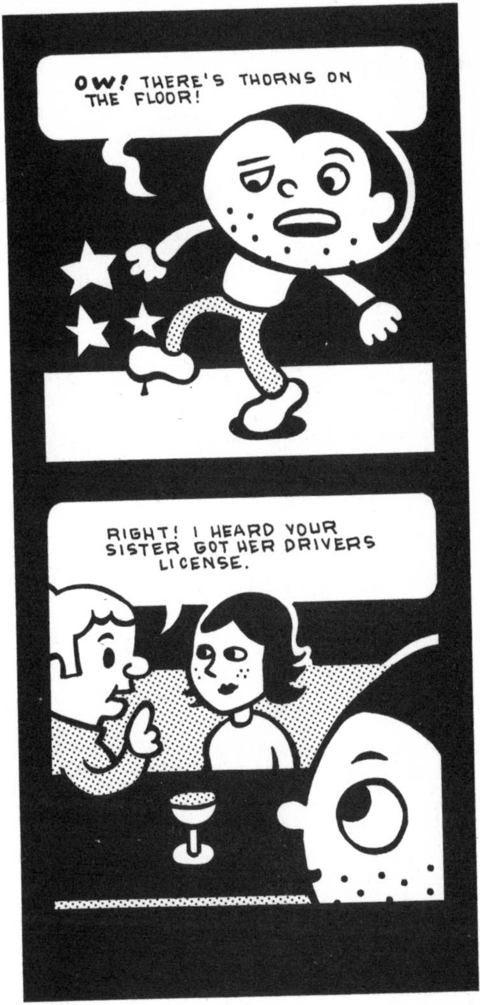

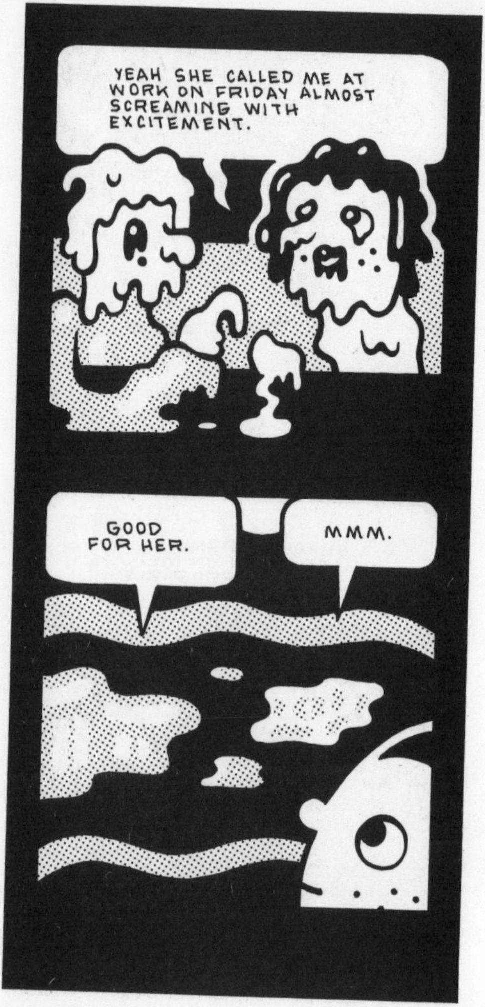
YEAH SHE CALLED ME AT WORK ON FRIDAY ALMOST SCREAMING WITH EXCITEMENT.
GOOD FOR HER.
MMM.

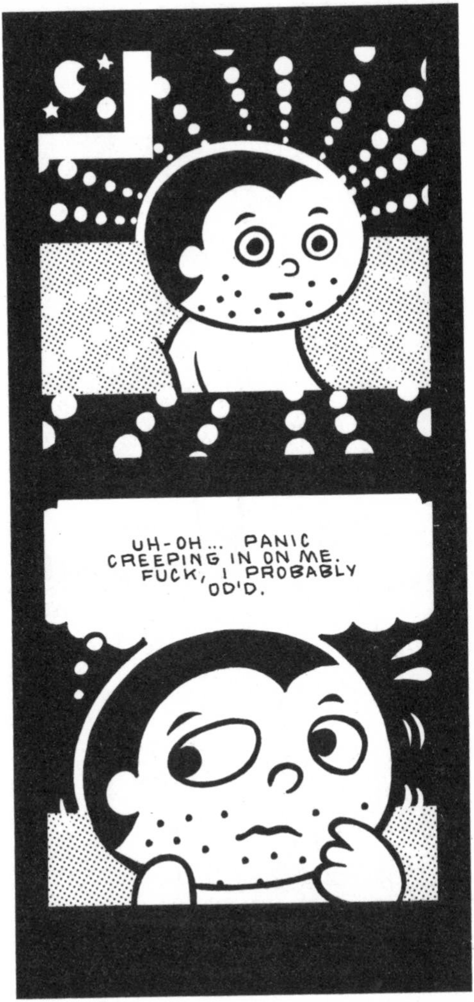
UH-OH... PANIC CREEPING IN ON ME. FUCK, I PROBABLY OD'D.

FUCKING HELL... IT FEELS JUST LIKE WHEN I ATE TOO MUCH PSILOCYBIN SHROOMS IN JANUARY. I PROMISED MYSELF THEN TO AVOID THE WORLD OF THE PSYCHEDELIC IN THE FUTURE. WHAT THE HELL WAS I THINKING JUST **NOW?**

I ENDED UP IN SOME KIND OF SUPER MARIO WORLD AND IT GOT REALLY FREAKY AFTER A WHILE. I WAS STUCK THERE FOR THIRTY-SIX HOURS AND HAD NO CLUE WHO I WAS. THOSE FEELINGS ARE PUSHING IN ON ME AGAIN. WHAT IF I GET STUCK FOREVER AND GO SCHIZO?

SIMON ARE YOU OK? YOU LOOK PASTY.
I-I'M PANICKING OVER HERE. I'M AFRAID OF GOING NUTS FOR REAL.
CAN YOU, FROM STUFF LIKE THAT?

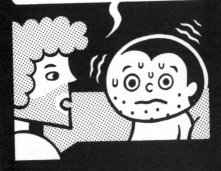

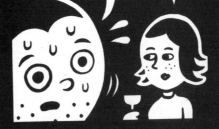

NOT UNHEARD OF. I KNOW OF PEOPLE WHO ENDED UP IN INSTITUTIONS AFTER A BAD TRIP. MY FRIEND JOHANNES NILSSON, WHO WROTE THE BOOK "RECENSION," GOT A CHRIST COMPLEX AFTER EATING ONE TOO MANY SHROOMS. HE THOUGHT HE WAS CHOSEN TO SAVE THE WORLD. HE WAS STUCK IN THAT FOR OVER A YEAR.

HAPPENED TO AN EX OF MY EX AS WELL.

CALM DOWN. YOU DON'T SEEM LIKE THAT KIND OF GUY.

MAYBE NOT, BUT I THINK I HAVE OTHER TENDENCIES THAT AREN'T ENTIRELY HEALTHY.

JOHAN, YOU'RE GOING TO BE A PSYCHOLOGIST RIGHT? HOW DO YOU KNOW IF YOU HAVE A PREDISPOSITION FOR SCHIZOPHRENIA?

I DON'T THINK ANYBODY CAN ANSWER THAT BETTER THAN YOURSELF.

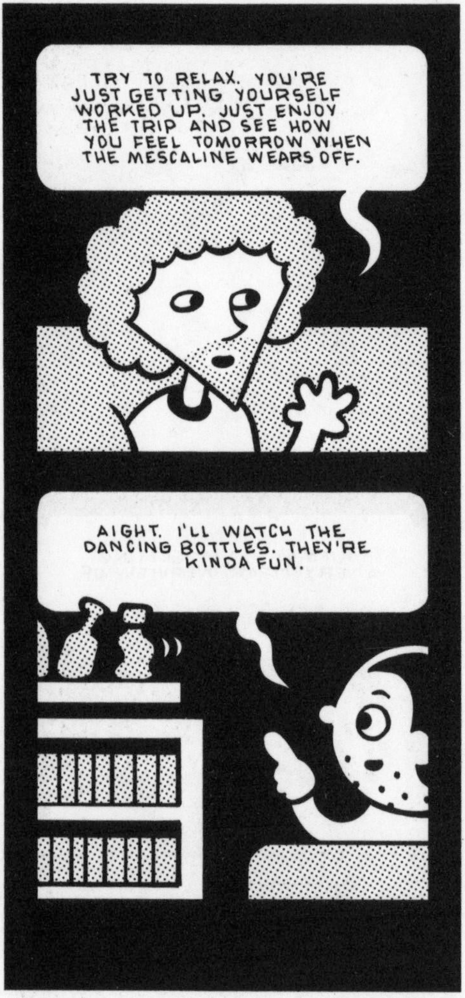
TRY TO RELAX. YOU'RE JUST GETTING YOURSELF WORKED UP. JUST ENJOY THE TRIP AND SEE HOW YOU FEEL TOMORROW WHEN THE MESCALINE WEARS OFF.
AIGHT. I'LL WATCH THE DANCING BOTTLES. THEY'RE KINDA FUN.

HMMM... I'M GETTING A VERY CLEAR OVERVIEW OF MY LIFE RIGHT NOW. MUST BE THE INSIGHT THING.

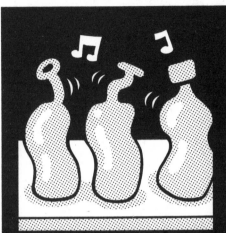

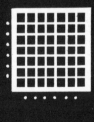

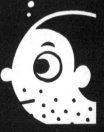

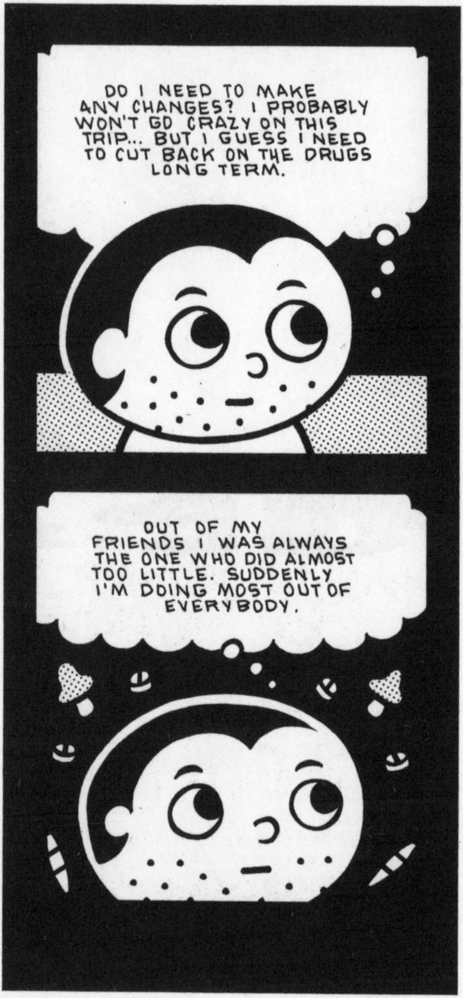
DO I NEED TO MAKE ANY CHANGES? I PROBABLY WON'T GO CRAZY ON THIS TRIP... BUT I GUESS I NEED TO CUT BACK ON THE DRUGS LONG TERM.
OUT OF MY FRIENDS I WAS ALWAYS THE ONE WHO DID ALMOST TOO LITTLE. SUDDENLY I'M DOING MOST OUT OF EVERYBODY.

HA HA... IT'S IRONIC THAT I CAN ONLY HAVE A SERIOUS CONVERSATION WITH MYSELF ABOUT THIS WHEN I'M TRIPPING ON HALLUCINOGENICS.

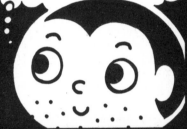

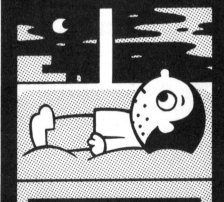

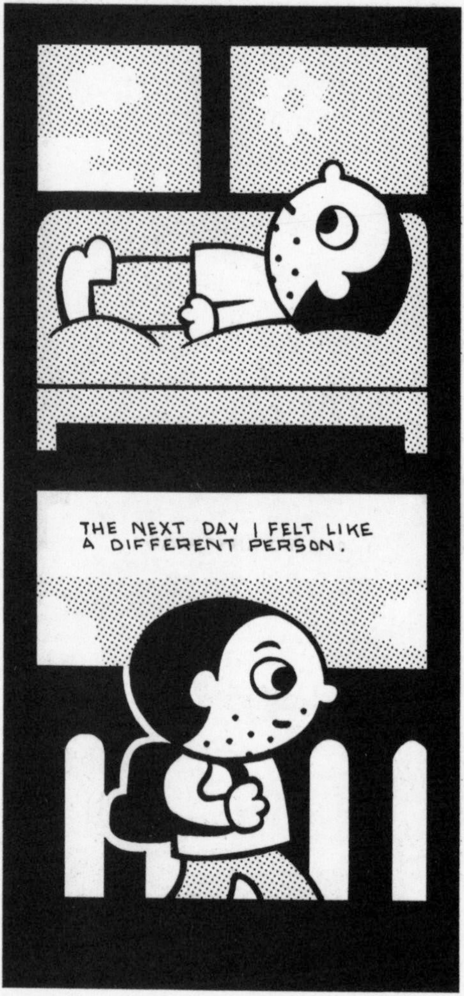
THE NEXT DAY I FELT LIKE A DIFFERENT PERSON.

THE FEELING WAS LIKE WHAT PETER GIBBONS GOT AFTER BEING HYPNOTIZED IN THE MOVIE "OFFICE SPACE." TOTAL MENTAL RELAXATION AND RAVING OPTIMISM.

I CAN DO ANYTHING I WANT. I'LL FIGURE HOW ONE THING LEADS TO ANOTHER... AND THEN, STEP BY STEP TIL I GET WHAT I WANT.

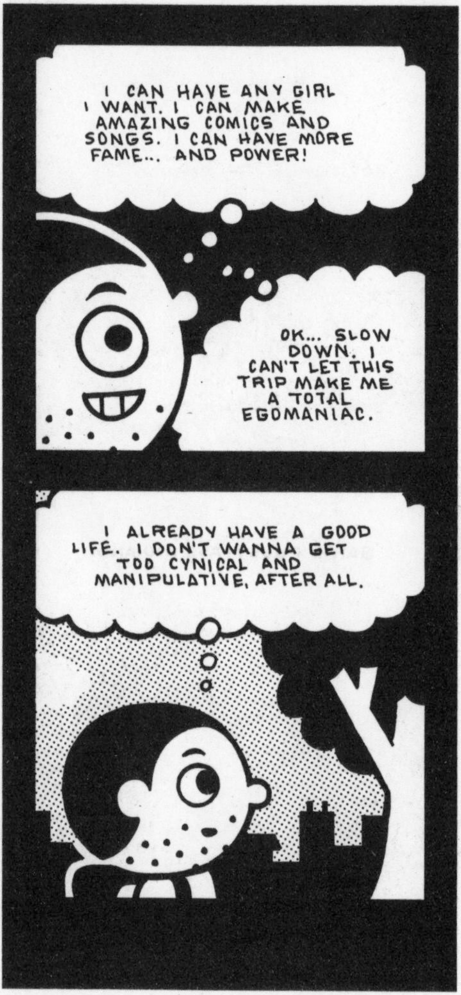
I CAN HAVE ANY GIRL I WANT. I CAN MAKE AMAZING COMICS AND SONGS. I CAN HAVE MORE FAME... AND POWER!
OK... SLOW DOWN. I CAN'T LET THIS TRIP MAKE ME A TOTAL EGOMANIAC.
I ALREADY HAVE A GOOD LIFE. I DON'T WANNA GET TOO CYNICAL AND MANIPULATIVE, AFTER ALL.

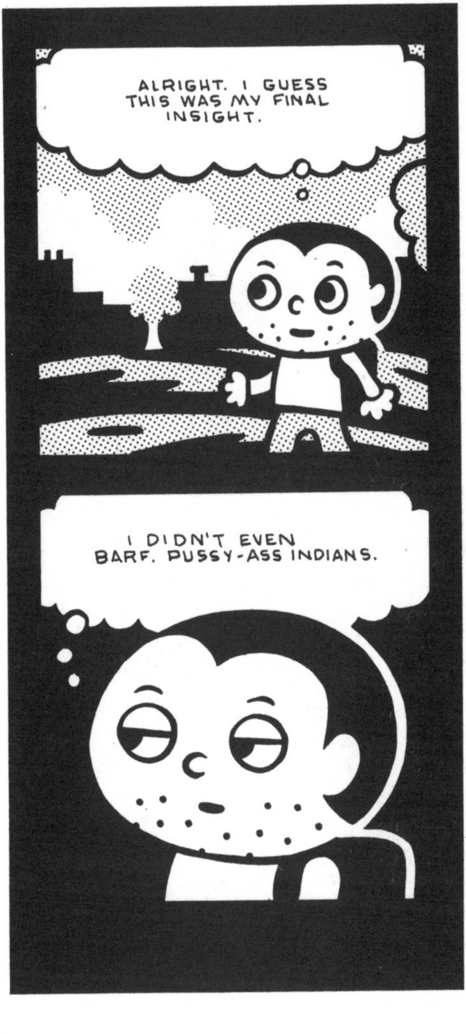
ALRIGHT. I GUESS THIS WAS MY FINAL INSIGHT.
I DIDN'T EVEN BARF. PUSSY-ASS INDIANS.

GOTHENBURG, 3/27 2007.
HOST #19: ASHLEY JONES
HER FRIEND, JENNY
MOM, DON'T YOU WANNA EAT?
WHAT DID YOU MAKE?
SPAGHETTI AND LENTIL STEW.

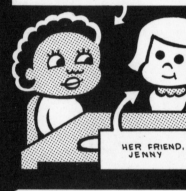

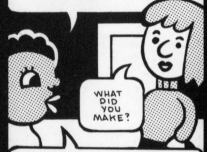

I DON'T THINK I HAVE TIME. GOTTA GO TO WORK.
DAD, ARE YOU EATING WITH US?

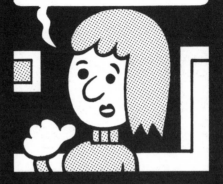

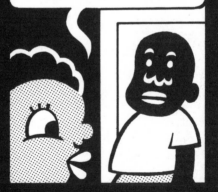

WHAT IS THIS? I DON'T WANNA EAT THIS!
I'M ORDERING PIZZA.
WHAT'S UP TONIGHT THEN?
UH... I'M COMPLETELY BEAT. HOW ABOUT A MOVIE?

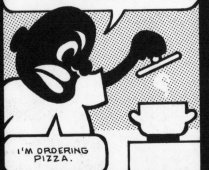

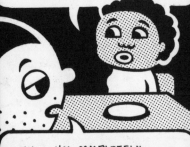

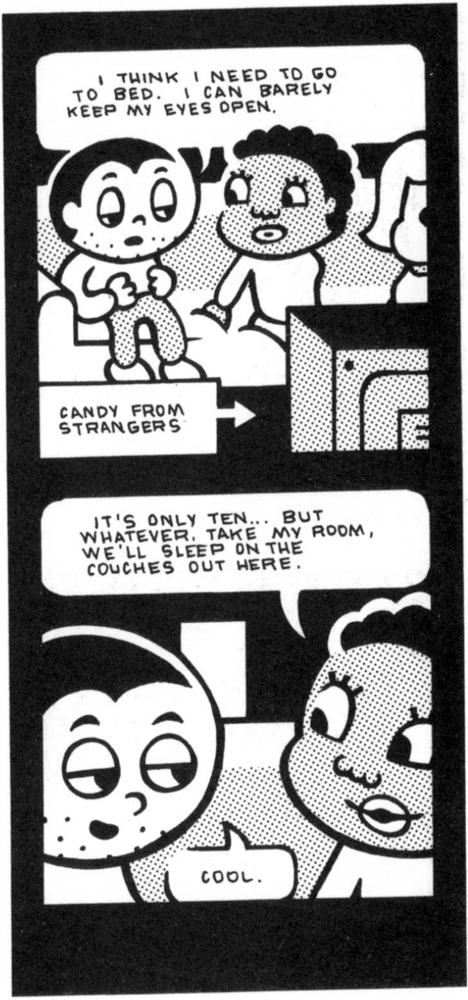
I THINK I NEED TO GO TO BED. I CAN BARELY KEEP MY EYES OPEN.
CANDY FROM STRANGERS
IT'S ONLY TEN... BUT WHATEVER. TAKE MY ROOM, WE'LL SLEEP ON THE COUCHES OUT HERE.
COOL.

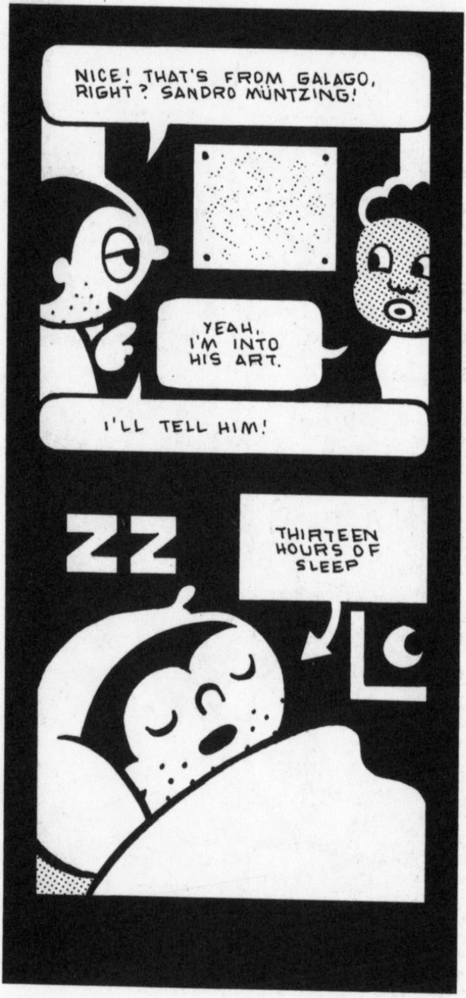
NICE! THAT'S FROM GALAGO, RIGHT? SANDRO MÜNTZING!
YEAH, I'M INTO HIS ART.
I'LL TELL HIM!
ZZ
THIRTEEN HOURS OF SLEEP

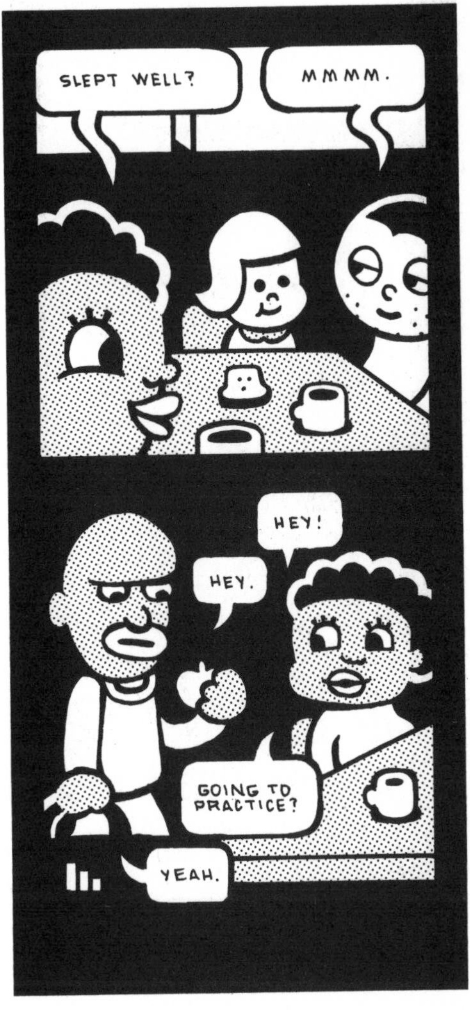
SLEPT WELL?
MMMM.
HEY!
HEY.
GOING TO PRACTICE?
YEAH.

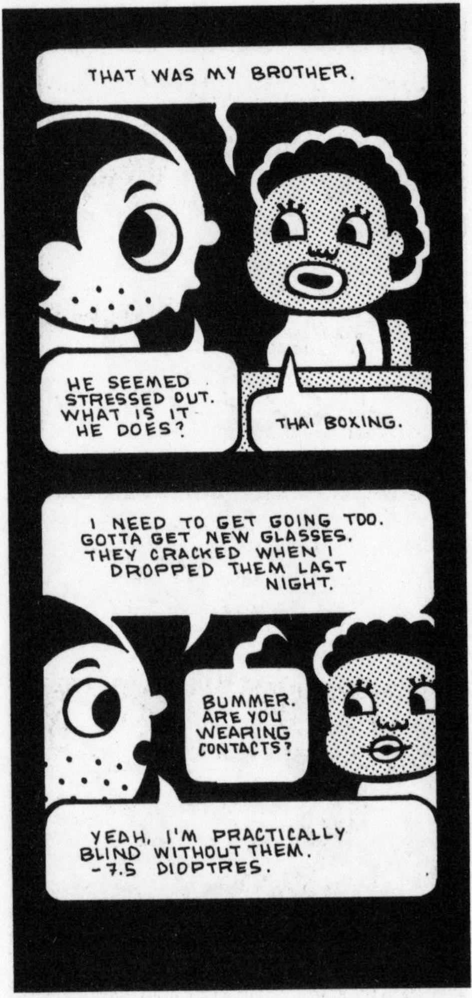
THAT WAS MY BROTHER.
HE SEEMED STRESSED OUT. WHAT IS IT HE DOES?
THAI BOXING.
I NEED TO GET GOING TOO. GOTTA GET NEW GLASSES. THEY CRACKED WHEN I DROPPED THEM LAST NIGHT.
BUMMER. ARE YOU WEARING CONTACTS?
YEAH, I'M PRACTICALLY BLIND WITHOUT THEM. -7.5 DIOPTRES.

I DIDN'T FEEL PARTICULARY DIFFERENT ANYMORE.

THE CACTUS PROBABLY JUST GAVE AN ILLUSION OF INSIGHT. I REMEMBER WHAT I WAS THINKING YESTERDAY, AND SURE, GOOD THOUGHTS. ALTHOUGH THAT'S STUFF I'VE KNOWN ALL ALONG... I GUESS?

MARKARYD, 4/4 2007.
HOST #24: XANIA BOKLUND

HER MOM, KARIN

YOUR DIALECT SOUNDS
LIKE YOU'RE NOT FROM
AROUND HERE...

ME AND XANIA ARE
FROM VÄSTERÅS
ORIGINALLY.

I MET JÖRGEN HERE ONLINE TWO YEARS AGO AND WE MOVED DOWN TO THIS FARM.
I HAVE TWO MORE KIDS IN STOCKHOLM... BUT XANIA CAME WITH. SHE'S ONLY SIXTEEN.

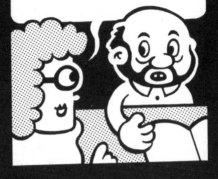

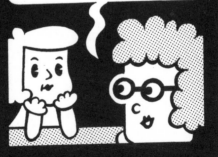

MOVING OUT HERE WAS PERFECT FOR ME... I'VE ALWAYS WANTED TO HAVE OSTRICHES.
I ALWAYS LOVED THEM. I EVEN HAD A TATTOO MADE IN MY YOUNGER DAYS. CHECK IT OUT!

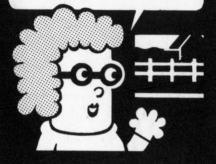

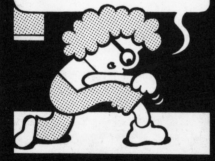

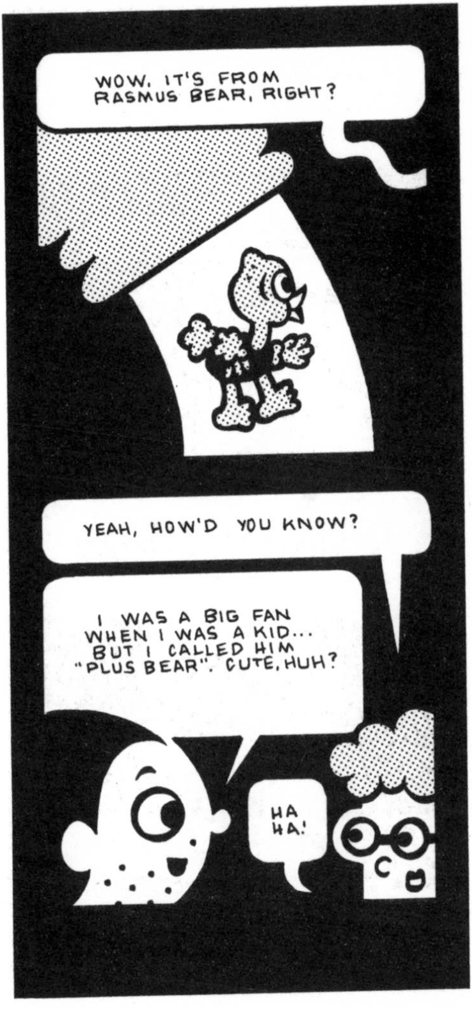
WOW, IT'S FROM RASMUS BEAR, RIGHT?
YEAH, HOW'D YOU KNOW?
I WAS A BIG FAN WHEN I WAS A KID... BUT I CALLED HIM "PLUS BEAR". CUTE, HUH?
HA HA!

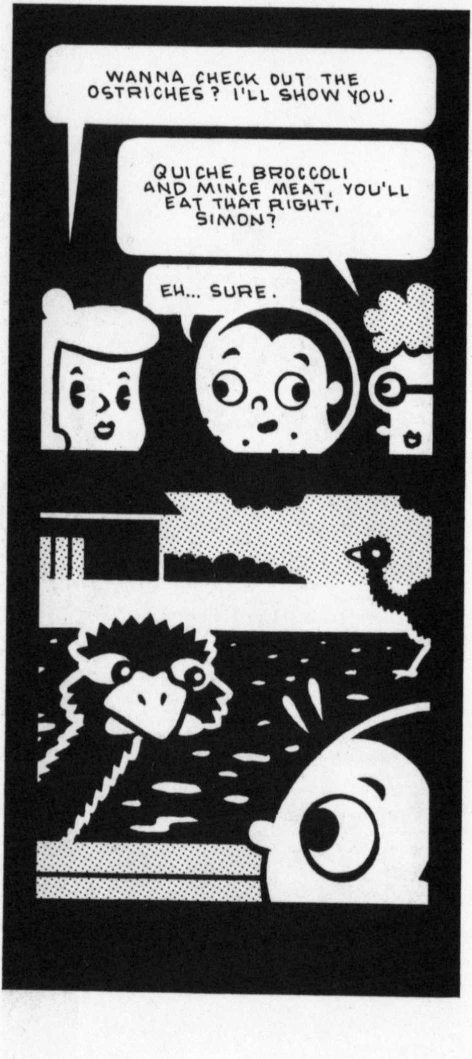
WANNA CHECK OUT THE OSTRICHES? I'LL SHOW YOU.
QUICHE, BROCCOLI AND MINCE MEAT, YOU'LL EAT THAT RIGHT, SIMON?
EH... SURE.

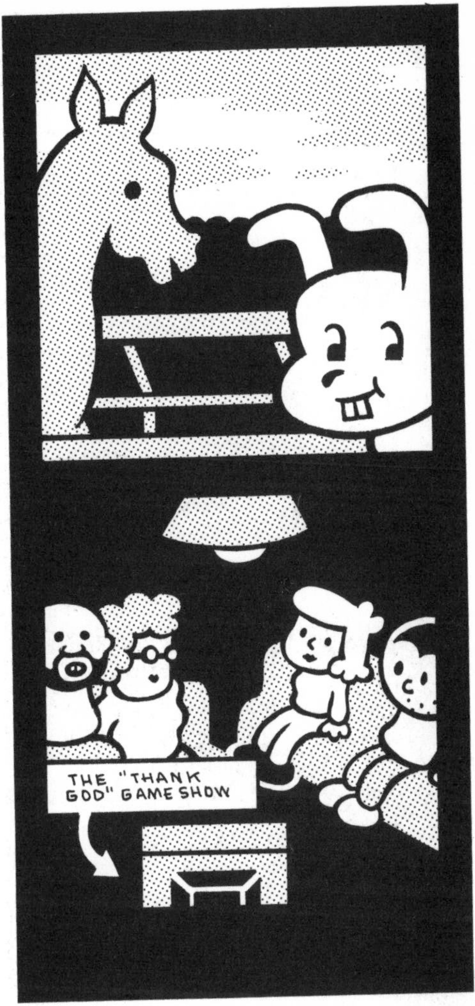
THE "THANK GOD" GAME SHOW

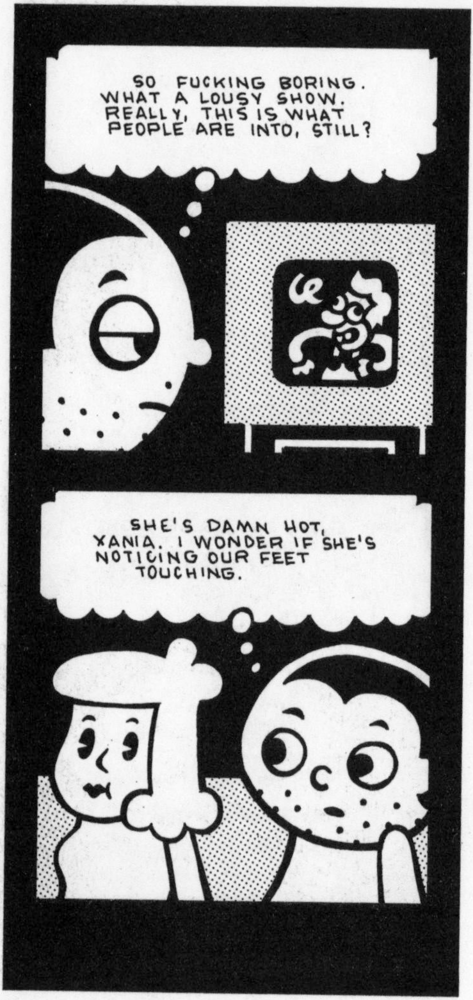
SO FUCKING BORING. WHAT A LOUSY SHOW. REALLY, THIS IS WHAT PEOPLE ARE INTO, STILL?
SHE'S DAMN HOT, XANIA. I WONDER IF SHE'S NOTICING OUR FEET TOUCHING.

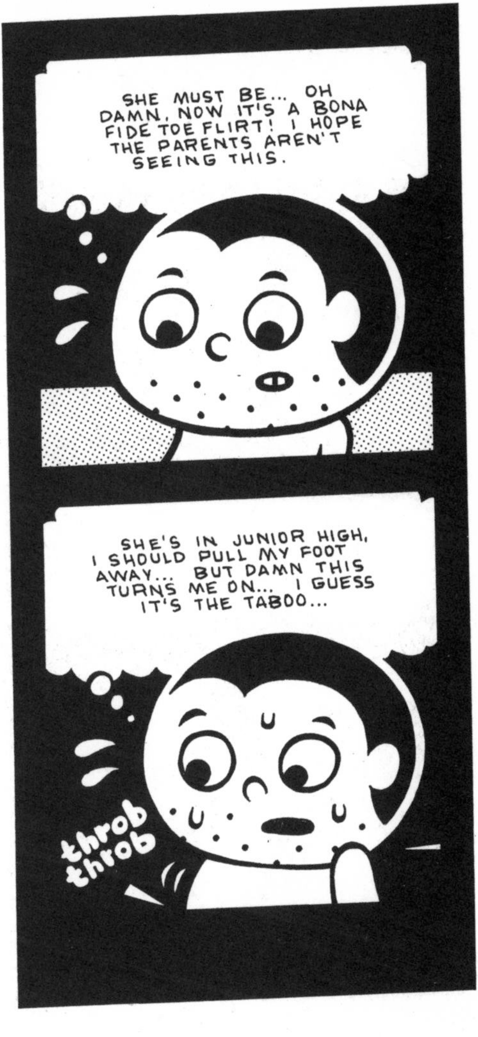
SHE MUST BE... OH DAMN, NOW IT'S A BONA FIDE TOE FLIRT! I HOPE THE PARENTS AREN'T SEEING THIS.
SHE'S IN JUNIOR HIGH, I SHOULD PULL MY FOOT AWAY... BUT DAMN THIS TURNS ME ON... I GUESS IT'S THE TABOO...
throb throb

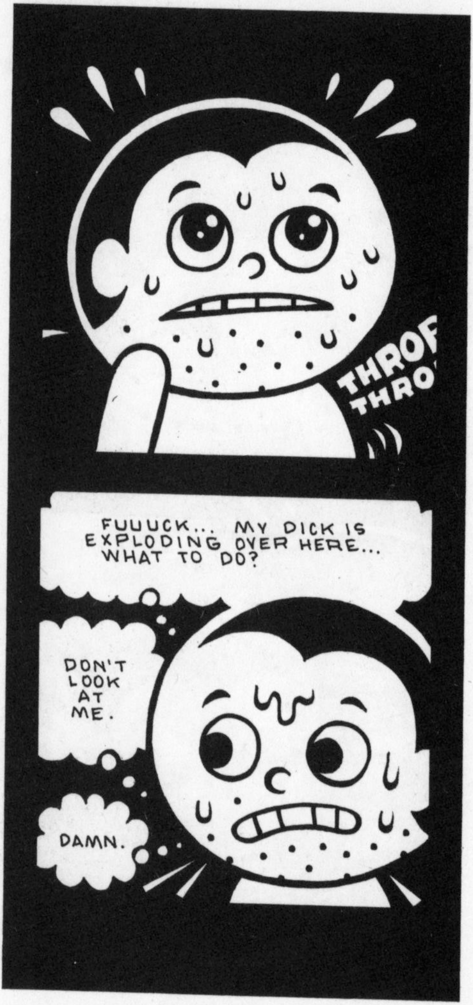
FUUUCK... MY DICK IS EXPLODING OVER HERE... WHAT TO DO?
DON'T LOOK AT ME.
DAMN.

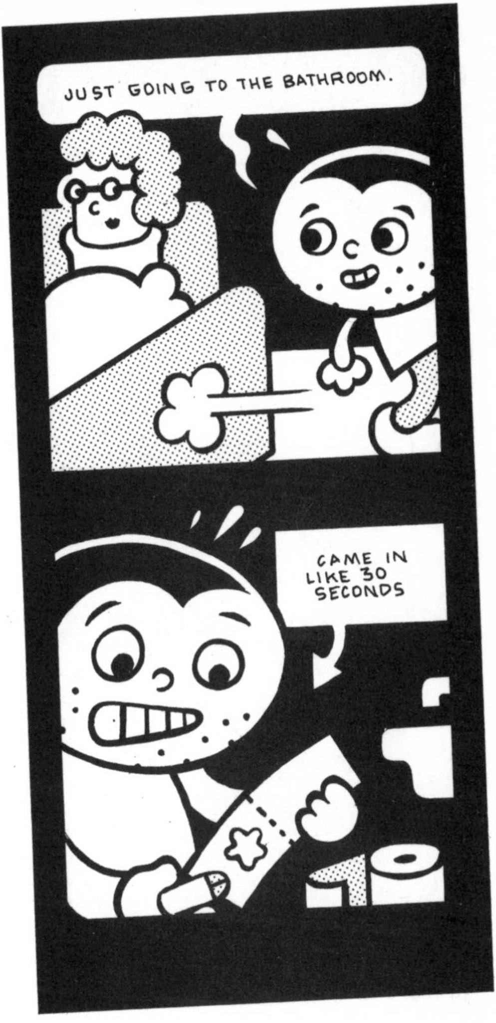
JUST GOING TO THE BATHROOM.
CAME IN LIKE 30 SECONDS

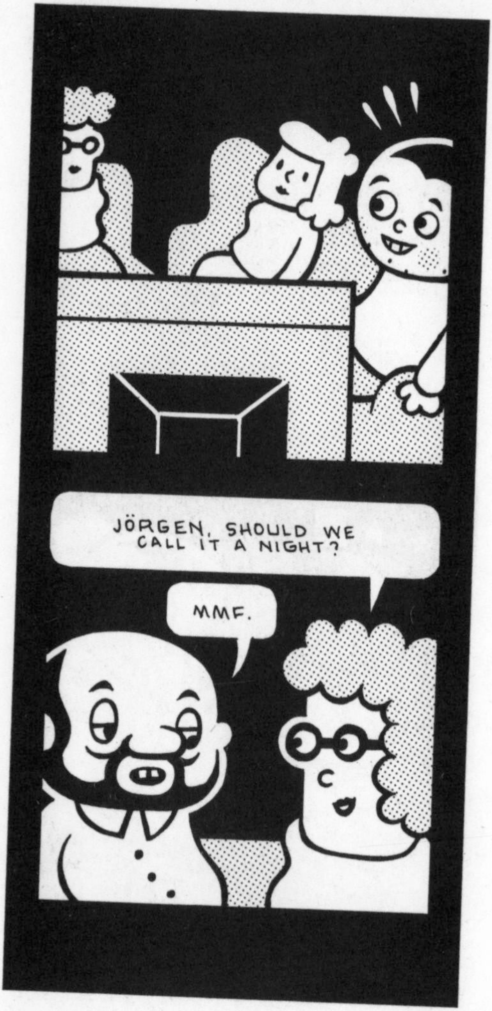
JÖRGEN, SHOULD WE CALL IT A NIGHT?
MMF.

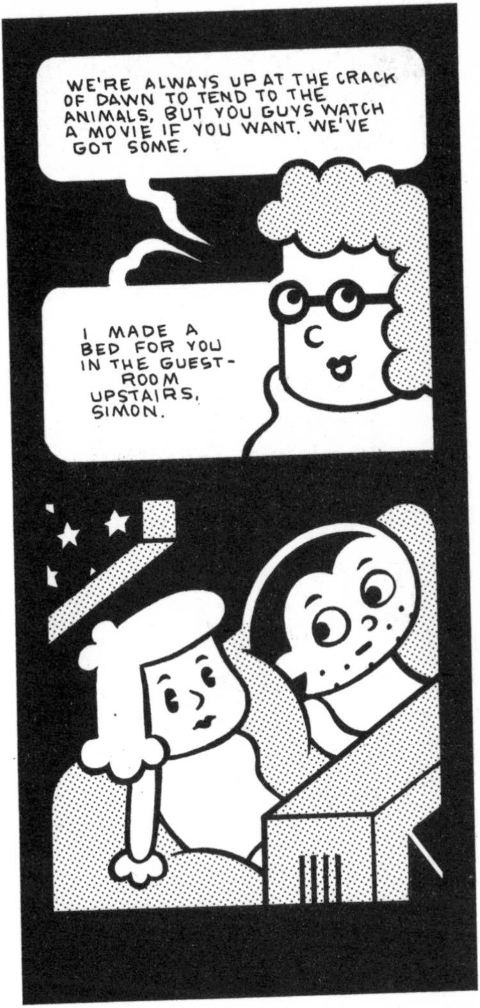
WE'RE ALWAYS UP AT THE CRACK OF DAWN TO TEND TO THE ANIMALS, BUT YOU GUYS WATCH A MOVIE IF YOU WANT. WE'VE GOT SOME.
I MADE A BED FOR YOU IN THE GUEST-ROOM UPSTAIRS, SIMON.

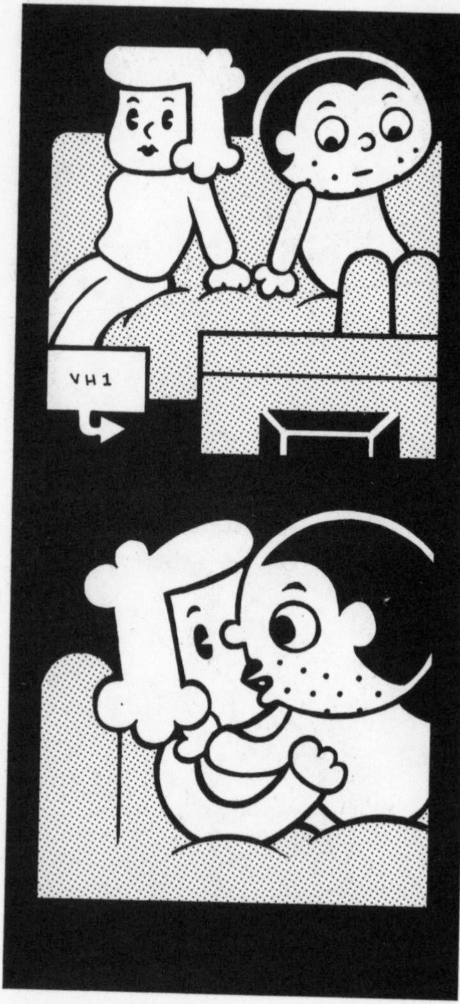
VH1

UMM... I REALLY SHOULDN'T.

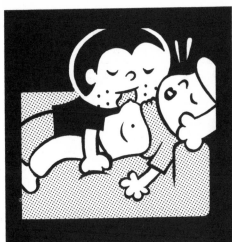

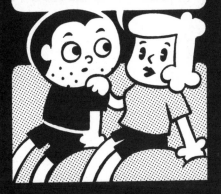

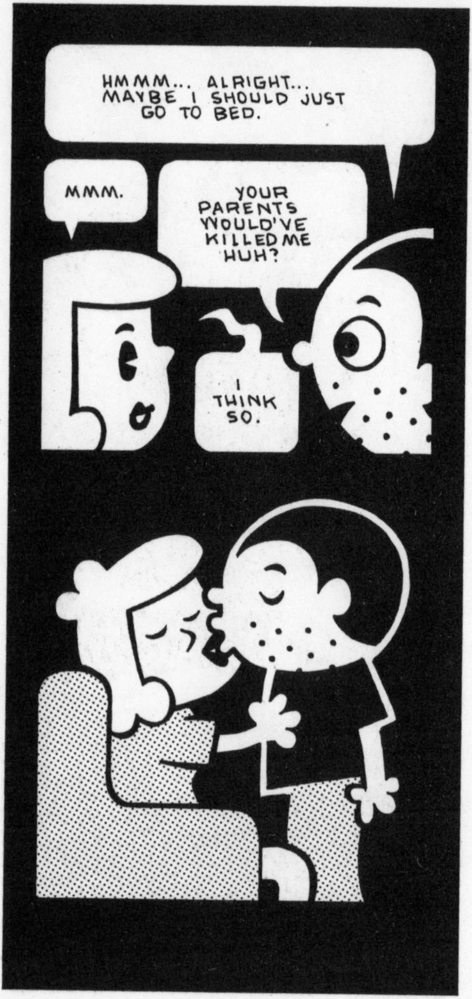
HMMMM... ALRIGHT... MAYBE I SHOULD JUST GO TO BED.
MMM.
YOUR PARENTS WOULD'VE KILLED ME HUH?
I THINK SO.

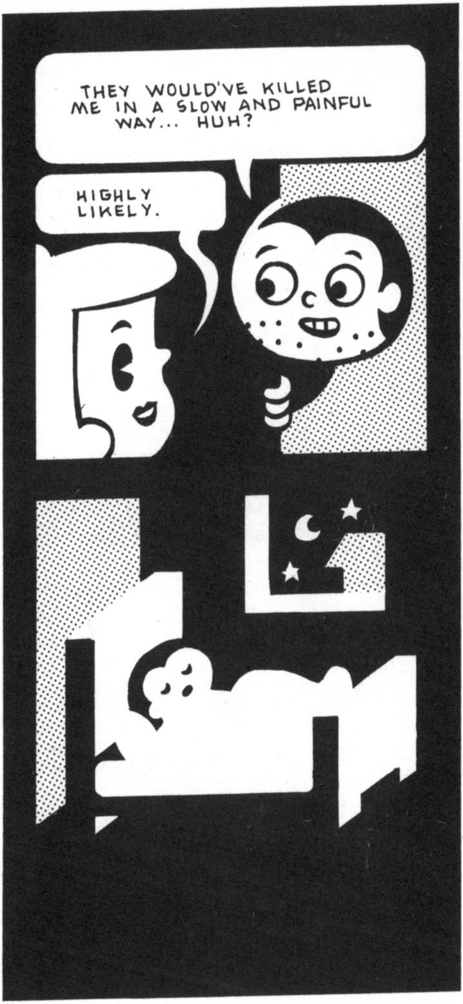
THEY WOULD'VE KILLED ME IN A SLOW AND PAINFUL WAY... HUH?
HIGHLY LIKELY.

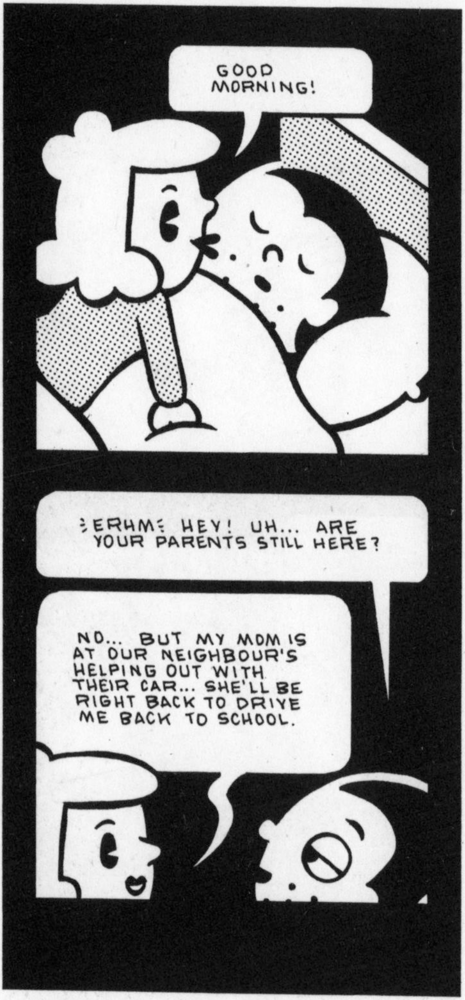
GOOD MORNING!
ERHM HEY! UH... ARE YOUR PARENTS STILL HERE?
NO... BUT MY MOM IS AT OUR NEIGHBOUR'S HELPING OUT WITH THEIR CAR... SHE'LL BE RIGHT BACK TO DRIVE ME BACK TO SCHOOL.

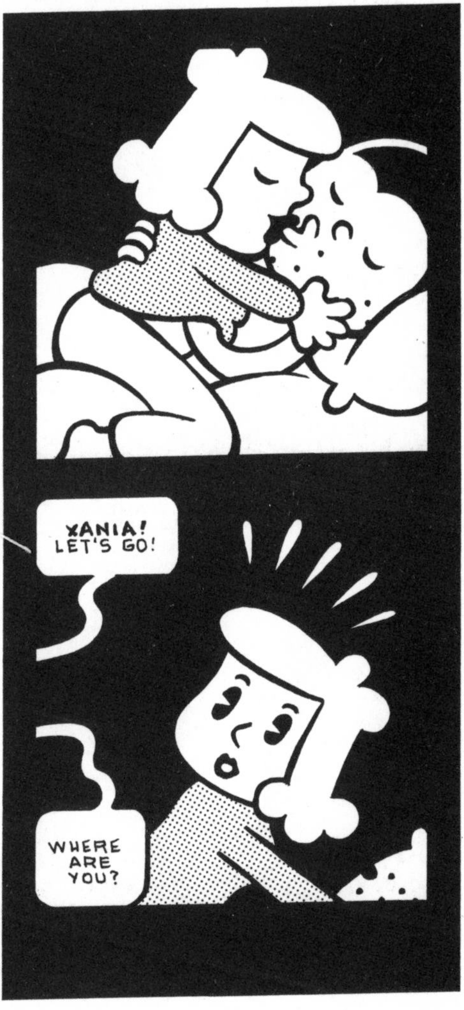
XANIA!
LET'S GO!
WHERE
ARE
YOU?

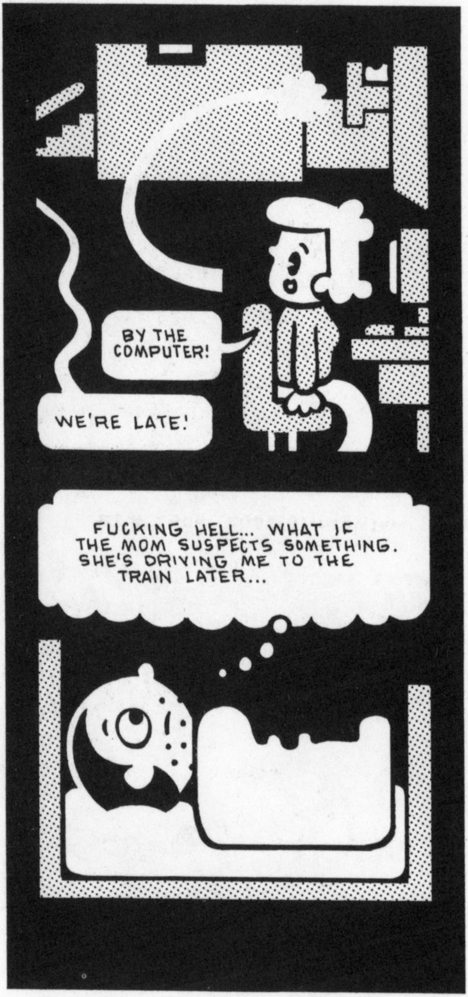

BY THE COMPUTER!
WE'RE LATE!
FUCKING HELL... WHAT IF THE MOM SUSPECTS SOMETHING. SHE'S DRIVING ME TO THE TRAIN LATER...

IT WAS GREAT HAVING YOU, SIMON. YOU'RE WELCOME BACK ANYTIME.
THANKS!
PHEW!
MALMÖ, 4/8 2007. HOST #27: SANDRA DAHLSTRÖM
HEY THIS IS SIMON GÄRDENFORS!
WHAT?

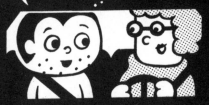

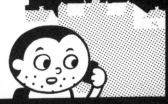

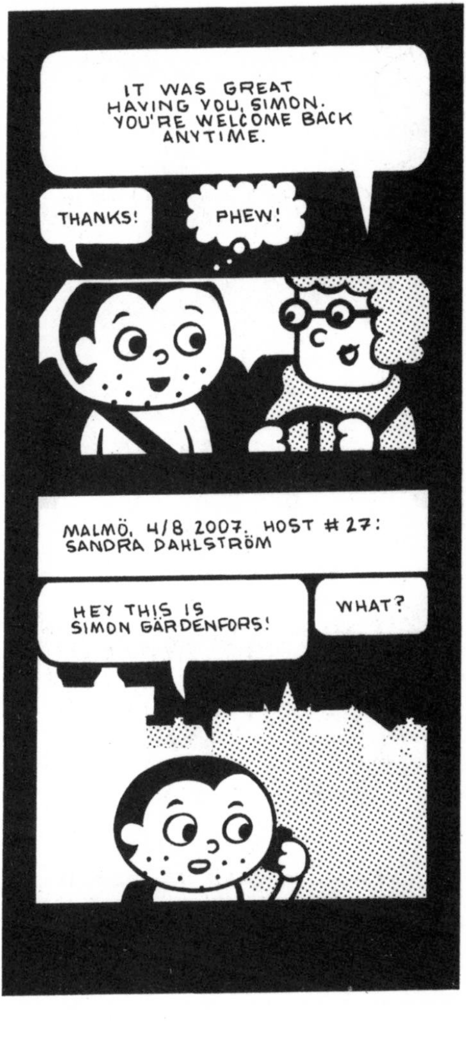

YOU'VE BOOKED FOR ME TO STAY WITH YOU TODAY.

'RIGHT! HEEEY SIMON!

BUT EH... I'M NOT IN MALMÖ RIGHT NOW. I GOT EVICTED. I'M WITH MY MOTHER IN ÖSTERLEN. CLOSE TO BORRBY.

ALRIGHT, WELL I WAS THERE THE DAY BEFORE YESTERDAY. YOU COULD'VE EMAILED ME OR SOMETHING.

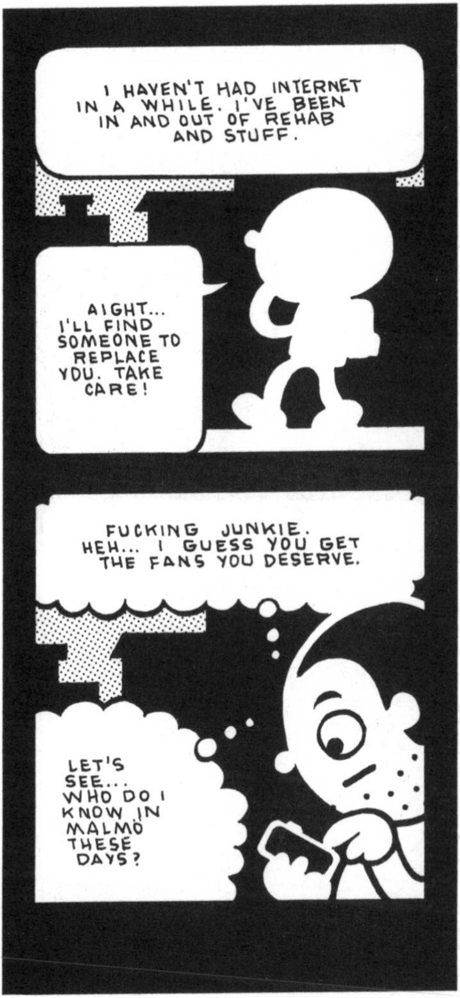
I HAVEN'T HAD INTERNET IN A WHILE. I'VE BEEN IN AND OUT OF REHAB AND STUFF.
AIGHT... I'LL FIND SOMEONE TO REPLACE YOU. TAKE CARE!
FUCKING JUNKIE. HEH... I GUESS YOU GET THE FANS YOU DESERVE.
LET'S SEE... WHO DO I KNOW IN MALMÖ THESE DAYS?

HEY ALBERT! IT'S BEEN A WHILE... ARE YOU COOL WITH ME CRASHING AT YOUR PLACE TONIGHT?

EXCELLENT! I'LL BE RIGHT OVER.

I WAS JUST GETTING IN THE SHOWER. HAVE A SEAT. THIS IS MIRANDA AND VIKTORIA.

I WONDER IF THAT'S ALBERT'S GIRLFRIEND... I HOPE NOT, SHE'S DAMN CUTE. I THINK HE HAS A BLACK GIRLFRIEND THOUGH... THAT'S WHY HE GETS ON MY BACK WHEN I USE THE WORD "NIGGER" IN MY LYRICS.

SO HOW DO YOU GUYS KNOW ALBERT?

HE'S GOING OUT WITH MY SISTER... AND VIKTORIA IS THEIR ROOMMATE.

RIGHT ON.

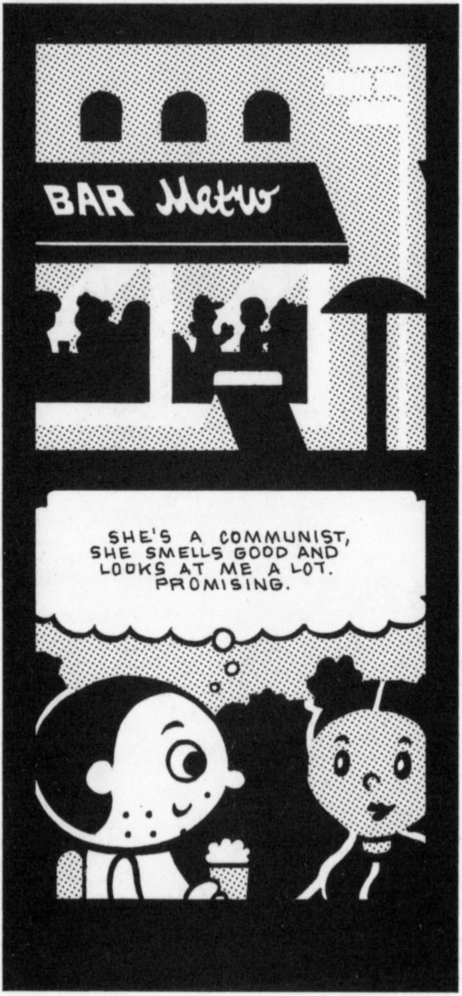
BAR Metro
SHE'S A COMMUNIST, SHE SMELLS GOOD AND LOOKS AT ME A LOT. PROMISING.

WANNA GO TO THE ILLEGAL CLUB BY ST. KNUTS SQUARE? I THINK THEY STAY OPEN 'TIL 5 AM.
DEFINITELY.
GOT I.D.S?
SURE.
WHAT'S THE POINT OF CHECKING ID'S AT AN ILLEGAL CLUB?

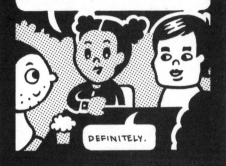

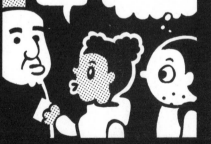

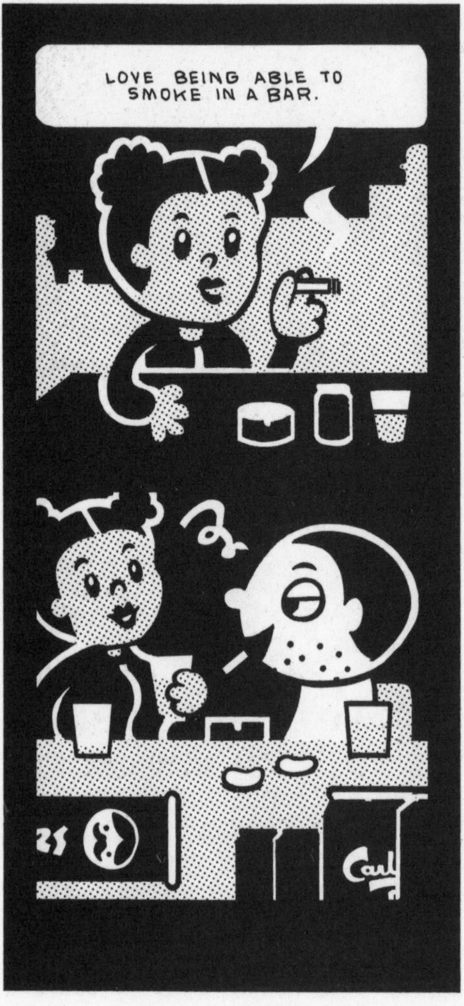
LOVE BEING ABLE TO SMOKE IN A BAR.

GOD, YOU GUYS ARE BORING.

MMM... MAYBE WE SHOULD JUST GO TO MY PLACE.
EH... HOLD ON.

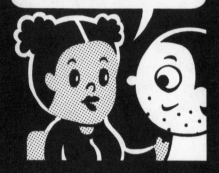

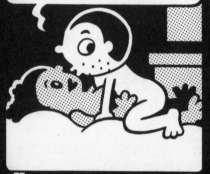

DAMN IT. PENIS GOES LIMP THE MINUTE IT TOUCHES THE RUBBER. BEING DRUNK OFF YOUR ASS AND WEARING A CONDOM JUST DOESN'T WORK.

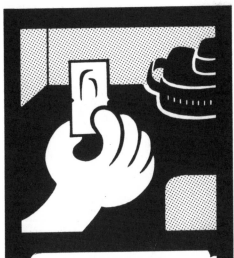

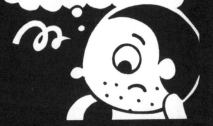

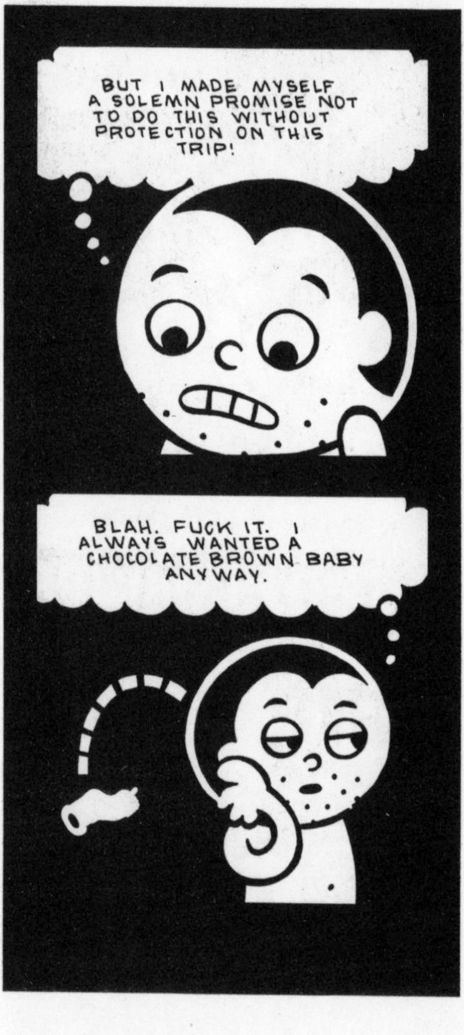
BUT I MADE MYSELF A SOLEMN PROMISE NOT TO DO THIS WITHOUT PROTECTION ON THIS TRIP!
BLAH. FUCK IT. I ALWAYS WANTED A CHOCOLATE BROWN BABY ANYWAY.

NNNGH!
A COUPLE OF DAYS LATER.
bibi-bibi-biPP

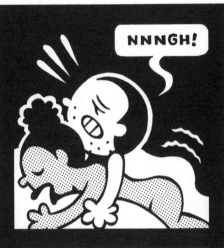

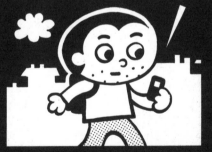

MY NAME IS SINDRA AND I WORK FOR LOCAL T.V. WE READ ABOUT YOUR "120 DAYS OF SIMON" PROJECT AND WE'D LIKE TO DO A SHOW.

NICE!

WOULD YOU BE OK WITH IF WE TAGGED ALONG AND FILMED WHILE YOU STAY WITH A FAMILY?

ALRIGHT... BUT CAN WE DO THIS WHEN IT'S SOMEONE I ALREADY KNOW? OTHERWISE IT MIGHT GET A LITTLE AWKWARD.

...BUT WE'D LOVE IT IF IT WAS WITH STRANGERS.
ALRIGHT. I'LL ASK SOME FAMILY.
WHY THE HELL DID I AGREE TO DO THAT?

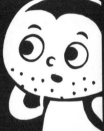

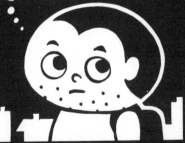

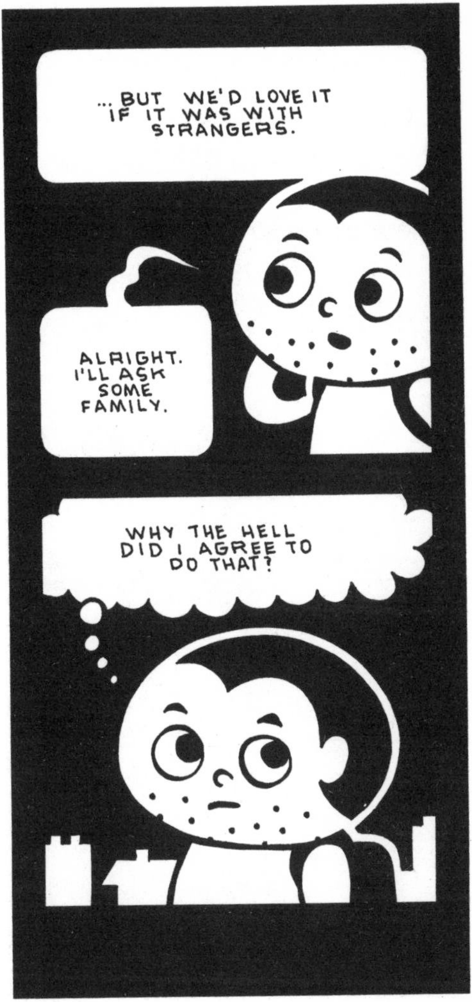

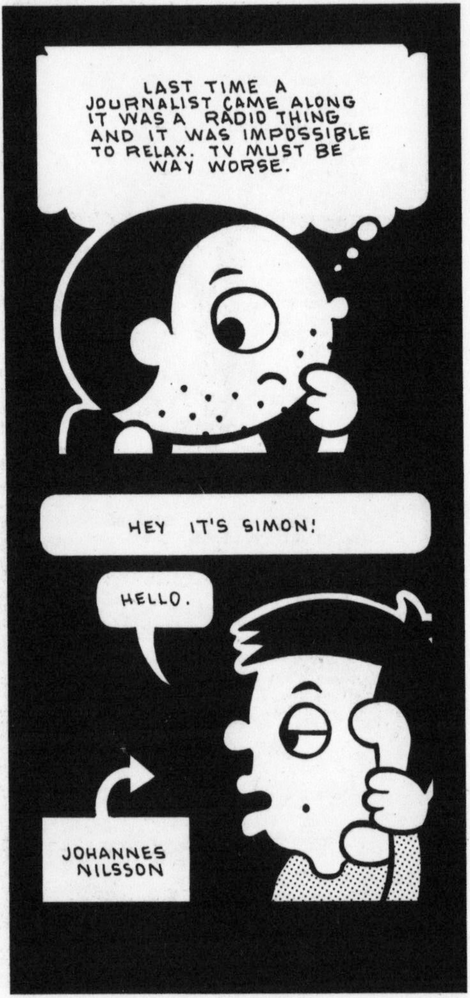
LAST TIME A JOURNALIST CAME ALONG IT WAS A RADIO THING AND IT WAS IMPOSSIBLE TO RELAX. TV MUST BE WAY WORSE.
HEY IT'S SIMON!
HELLO.
JOHANNES NILSSON

TV WANTS TO FILM ME WHEN I STAY WITH SOMEONE I'VE NEVER MET BEFORE. WHEN I COME OVER THERE CAN WE PRETEND WE DON'T KNOW EACH OTHER?

SURE, THAT COULD BE FUN. I'LL PRETEND TO BE INTO ASATRU OR SOMETHING.

HAHA SEE YOU IN SKÅNE IN TWO WEEKS THEN.

SURE. WHERE ARE YOU NOW?

MALMÖ... HEADING TO GOTHENBURG.

GOTHENBURG, 4/14 2007.

HEY BJÖRN! I'M IN GOTHENBURG.

AGAIN? DIDN'T YOU JUST GET OUT OF HERE?

YEAH... BUT WE JUST GOT A GIG WITH LAS PALMAS AT THAT CLUB RESPEKT. THE SHOW'S TONIGHT.

SO... BROMANDER SAID YOUR APARTMENT'S EMPTY.

YEAH... YOU CAN HAVE THE KEYS IF YOU WANNA. I'M REDECORATING SO I'M MOSTLY AT STINA'S HOUSE.
HELLO MONEY, WHASSUP? WE'RE GONNA SOUND CHECK.

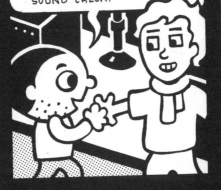

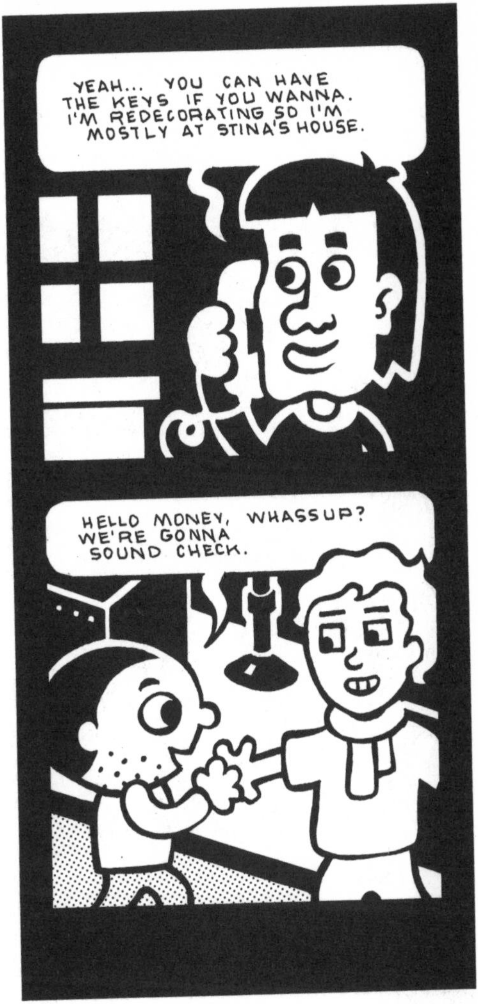

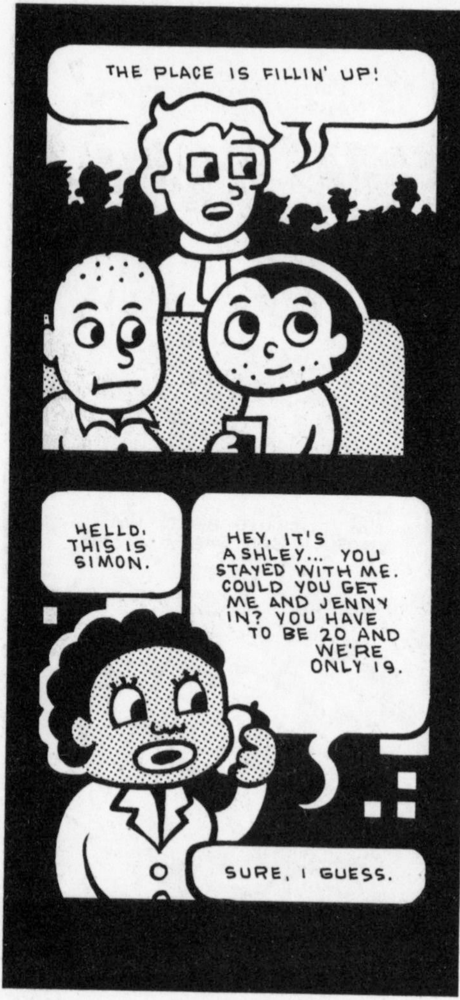
THE PLACE IS FILLIN' UP!
HELLO. THIS IS SIMON.
HEY, IT'S ASHLEY... YOU STAYED WITH ME. COULD YOU GET ME AND JENNY IN? YOU HAVE TO BE 20 AND WE'RE ONLY 19.
SURE, I GUESS.

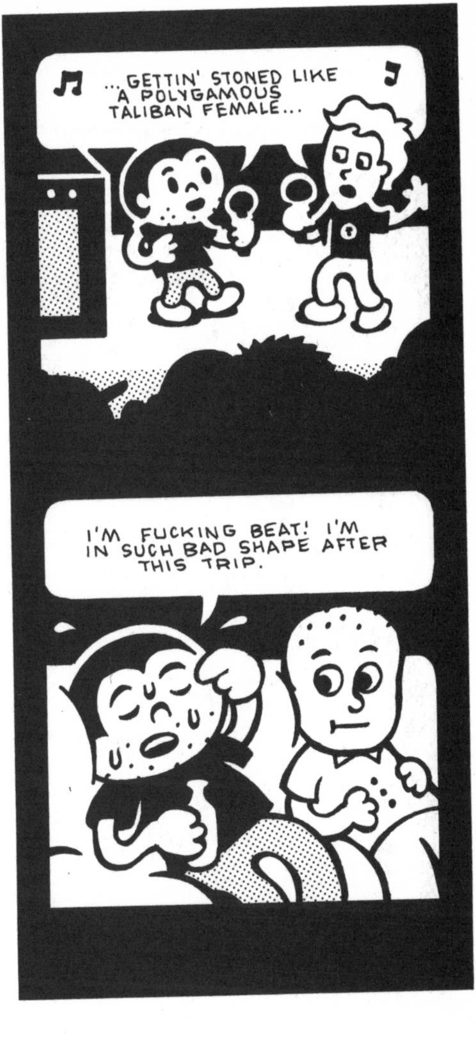
...GETTIN' STONED LIKE A POLYGAMOUS TALIBAN FEMALE...
I'M FUCKING BEAT! I'M IN SUCH BAD SHAPE AFTER THIS TRIP.

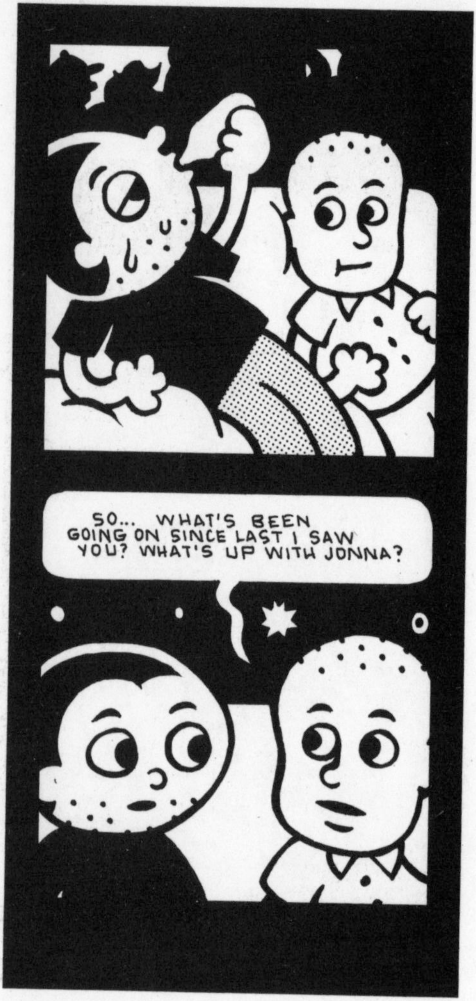
SO... WHAT'S BEEN GOING ON SINCE LAST I SAW YOU? WHAT'S UP WITH JONNA?

NOTHING MUCH... I BARELY HEAR FROM HER ANYMORE. WE USED TO BE ON THE PHONE ALL THE TIME.
I THINK SHE GOT A LITTLE FED UP WITH ME.
I'VE BEEN TALKING MORE TO MELINA LATELY. YOU KNOW, SODA'S SISTER. WE KINDLED SOME SORT OF ROMANCE BEFORE I TOOK OFF.
OH NO.

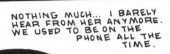

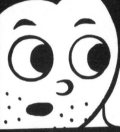

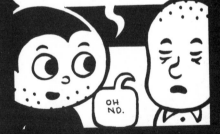

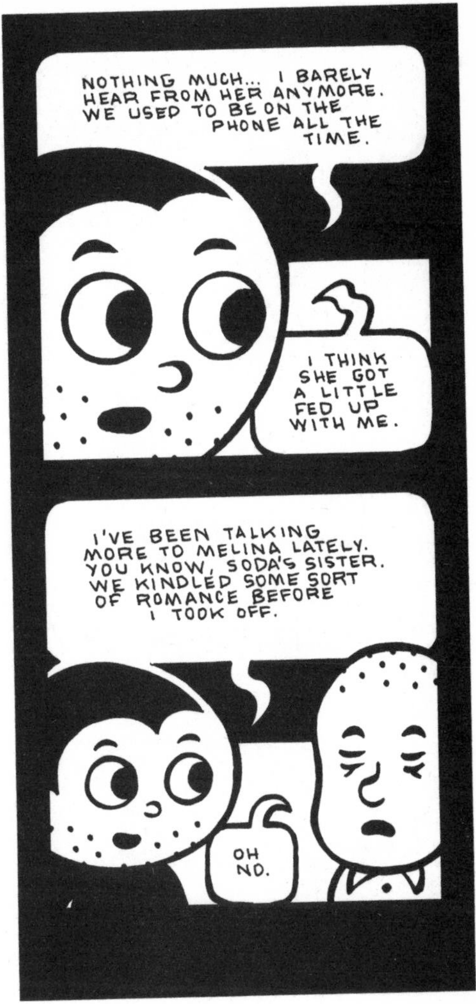

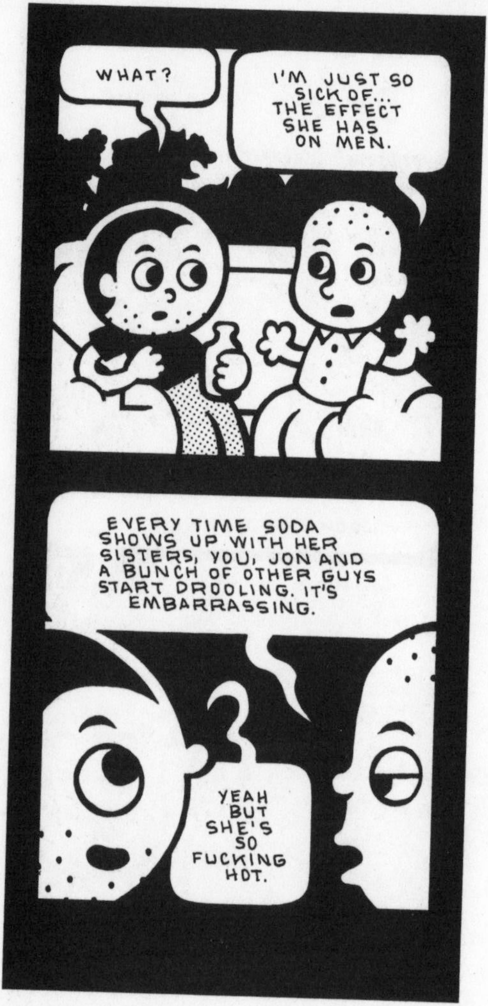
WHAT?
I'M JUST SO SICK OF... THE EFFECT SHE HAS ON MEN.
EVERY TIME SODA SHOWS UP WITH HER SISTERS, YOU, JON AND A BUNCH OF OTHER GUYS START DROOLING. IT'S EMBARRASSING.
YEAH BUT SHE'S SO FUCKING HOT.

SHE LOOKS LIKE MOLLY RINGWALD, BUT EVEN SEXIER.
LOOKS... PFFF!
NOT JUST THAT... SHE'S COOL. SHE'S KIND OF "I WANNA BE BAD," STUDIES LITERATURE AND HAS ASPERGERS.
ALRIGHT, YOU GOT ME. SOUNDS PRETTY DAMN AWESOME ACTUALLY.

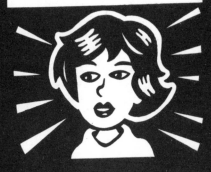

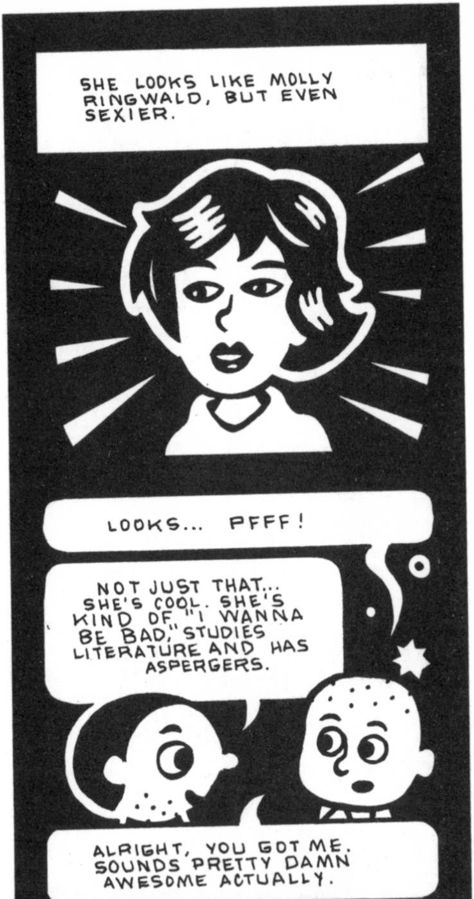

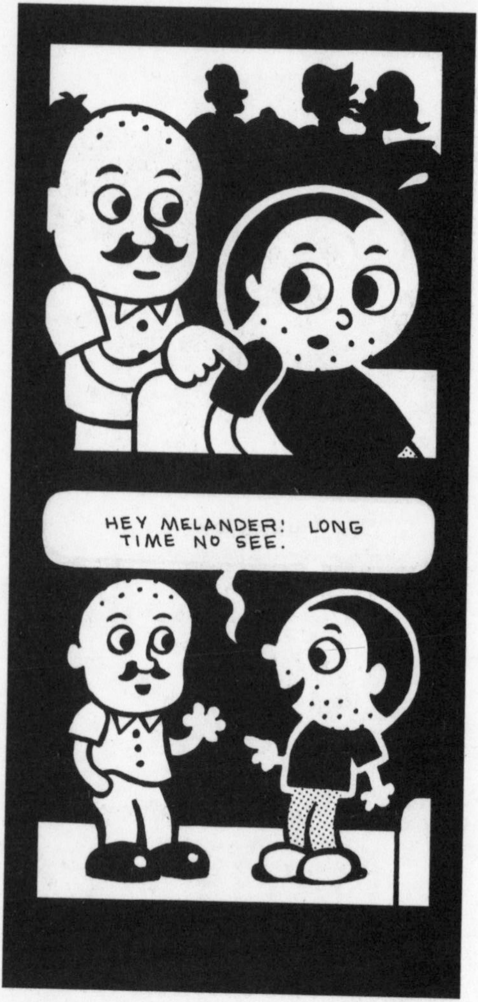
HEY MELANDER! LONG TIME NO SEE.

HEY THERE YOU! WANNA GO INTO A STALL AND DO SOME LINES?
SURE THING!
EH... HANG ON!

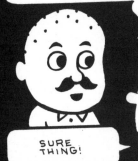

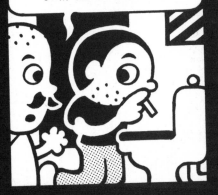

YOU CAN HAVE THE BLOW ON ONE CONDITION... DON'T PUT IT IN YOUR BOOK.

WHY?

I DON'T WANT MY PARENTS TO KNOW I DO HEAVY SHIT.

THAT'S COOL. I'LL PUT A BLUR OVER YOUR FACE OR SOMETHING.

SNORT!

WE'RE HEADED TO THE KOLONI-PARTY AT BERGRUM 211. WANNA COME?
SURE. JENNY, YOU UP FOR IT?

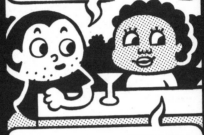

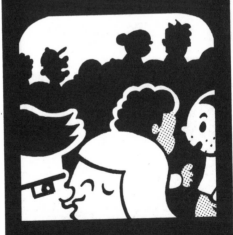

WANNA GO TO WIESELGRENSPLATSEN? I'M BORROWING BJÖRN AHLÉNS APARTMENT.
ALRIGHT.

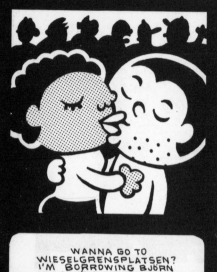

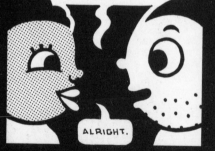

DO YOU KNOW YOUR WAY THERE? THOUGHT YOU SAID YOU'VE GOT NO SENSE OF DIRECTION.
I LIVED ON HISINGEN FOR FOUR MONTHS IN 2003, SO I THINK I'M GOOD. BESIDES, I WAS AT BJÖRN'S PLACE LAST WEEK.

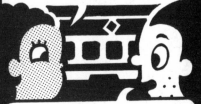

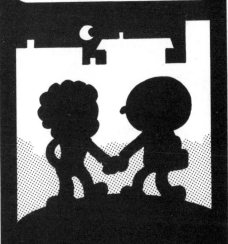

DO YOU THINK A LOT OF PEOPLE SIGNED UP FOR THIS TO GET INTO YOUR PANTS?
I DUNNO. EH... WAS THAT YOUR ORIGINAL PLAN?
MMM... BUT THEN I GOT KINDA NERVOUS WHEN YOU REPLIED.

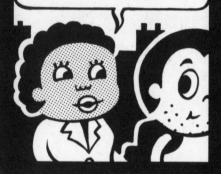

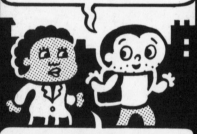

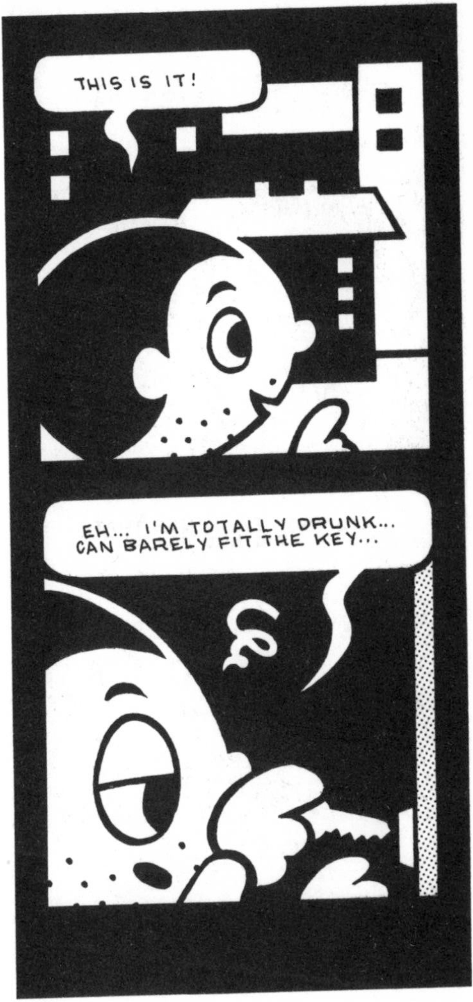
THIS IS IT!
EH... I'M TOTALLY DRUNK... CAN BARELY FIT THE KEY...

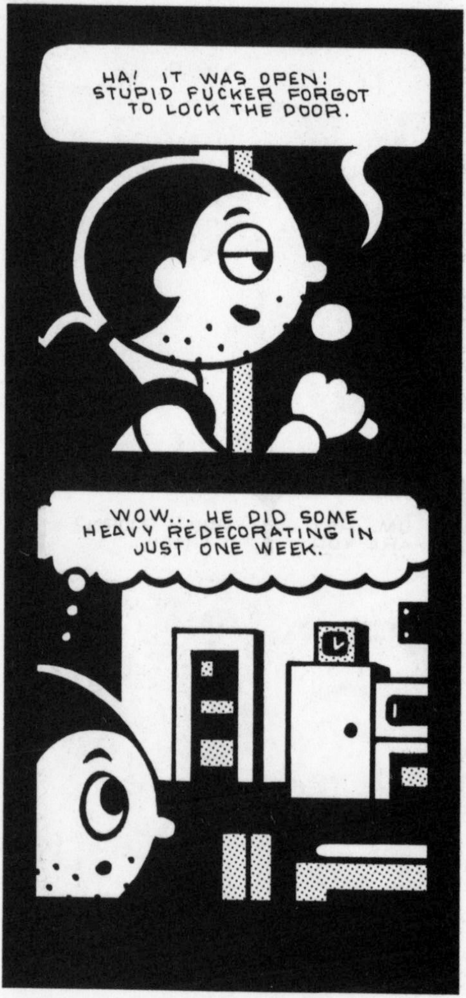
HA! IT WAS OPEN! STUPID FUCKER FORGOT TO LOCK THE DOOR.
WOW... HE DID SOME HEAVY REDECORATING IN JUST ONE WEEK.

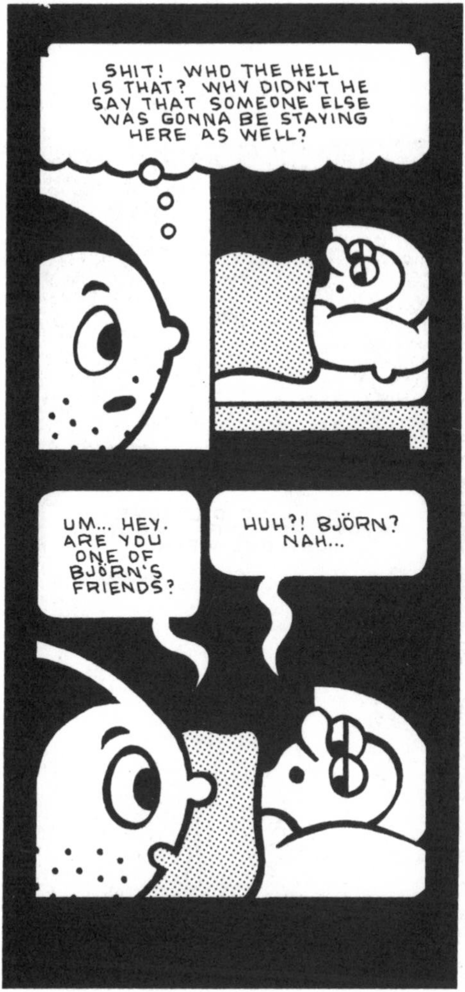
SHIT! WHO THE HELL IS THAT? WHY DIDN'T HE SAY THAT SOMEONE ELSE WAS GONNA BE STAYING HERE AS WELL?
UM... HEY. ARE YOU ONE OF BJÖRN'S FRIENDS?
HUH?! BJÖRN? NAH...

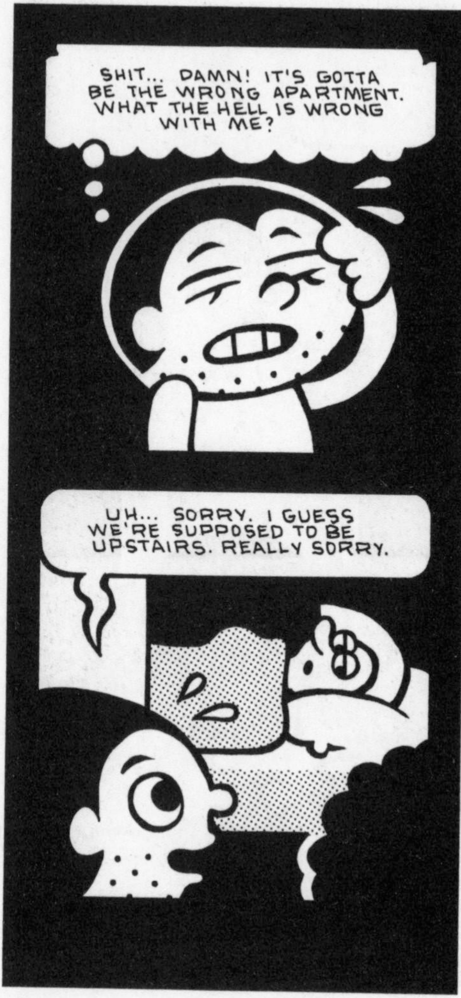
SHIT... DAMN! IT'S GOTTA BE THE WRONG APARTMENT. WHAT THE HELL IS WRONG WITH ME?
UH... SORRY. I GUESS WE'RE SUPPOSED TO BE UPSTAIRS. REALLY SORRY.

FUCKING HELL THAT WAS AWKWARD.
ALRIGHT... LOOK IT SAYS "AHLÉN" ON THE DOOR.

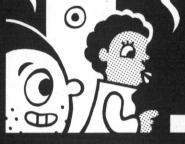

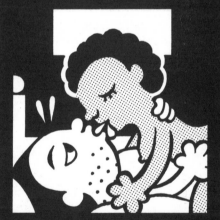

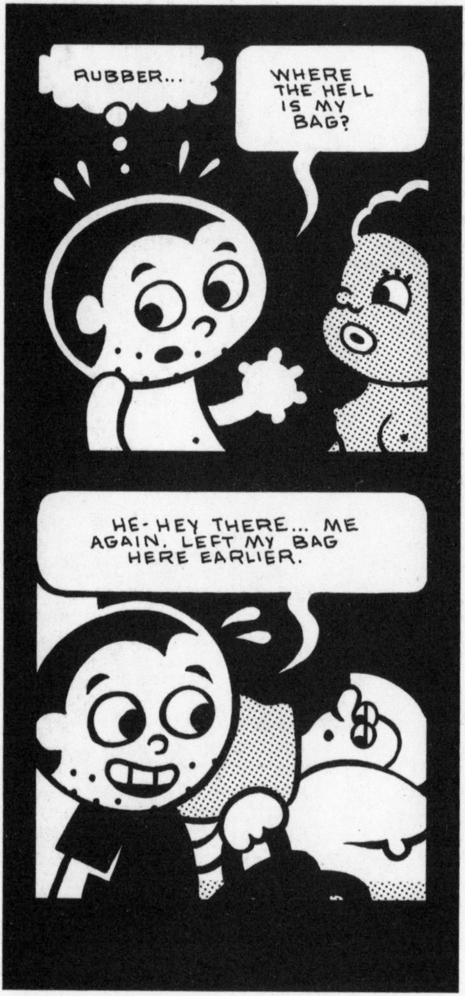
RUBBER...
WHERE THE HELL IS MY BAG?
HE-HEY THERE... ME AGAIN. LEFT MY BAG HERE EARLIER.

NO PROTECTION, AFTER ALL.

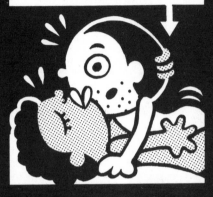

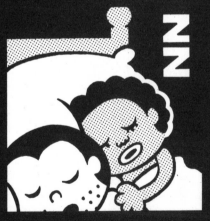

OOOW... MY HEAD IS THROBBING! WHAT TIME IS IT?
FOUR MISSED CALLS. THANK GOD I PUT IT ON SILENT...
031 AREA CODE. MUST BE BJÖRN WANTING HIS KEYS BACK.

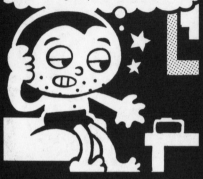

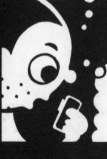

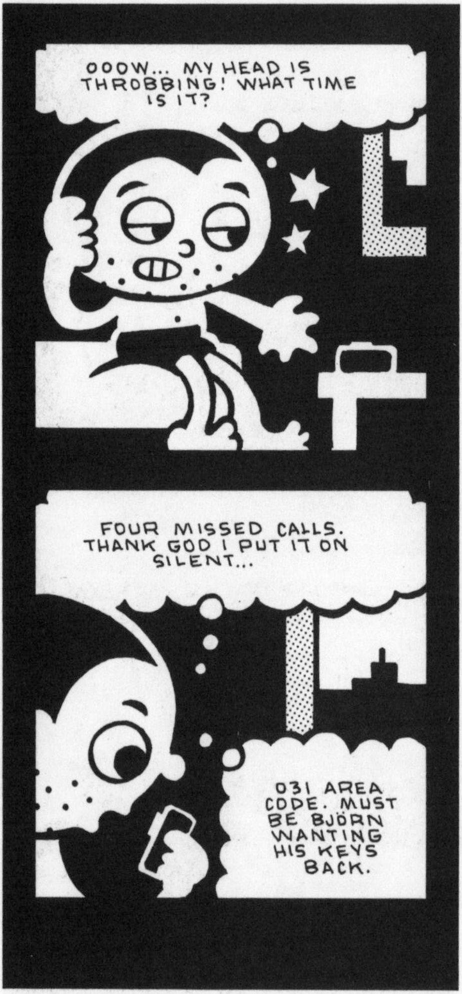

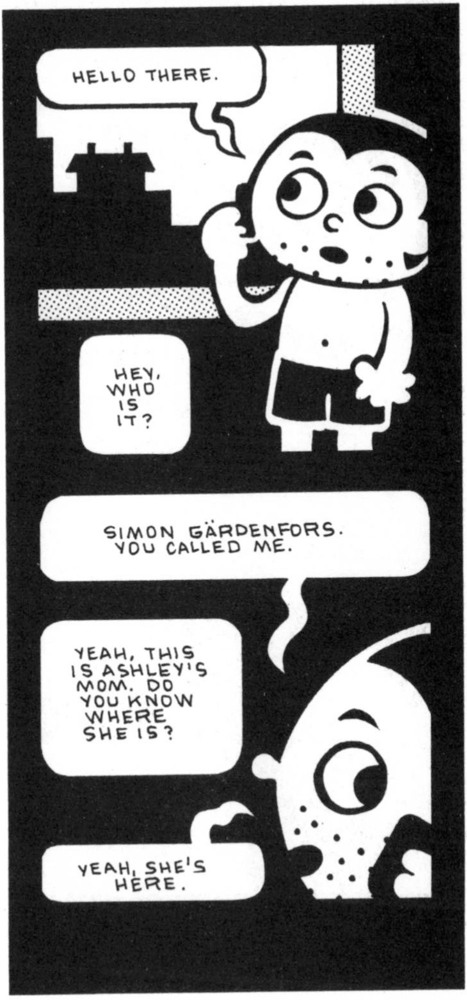
HELLO THERE.
HEY, WHO IS IT?
SIMON GÄRDENFORS. YOU CALLED ME.
YEAH, THIS IS ASHLEY'S MOM. DO YOU KNOW WHERE SHE IS?
YEAH, SHE'S HERE.

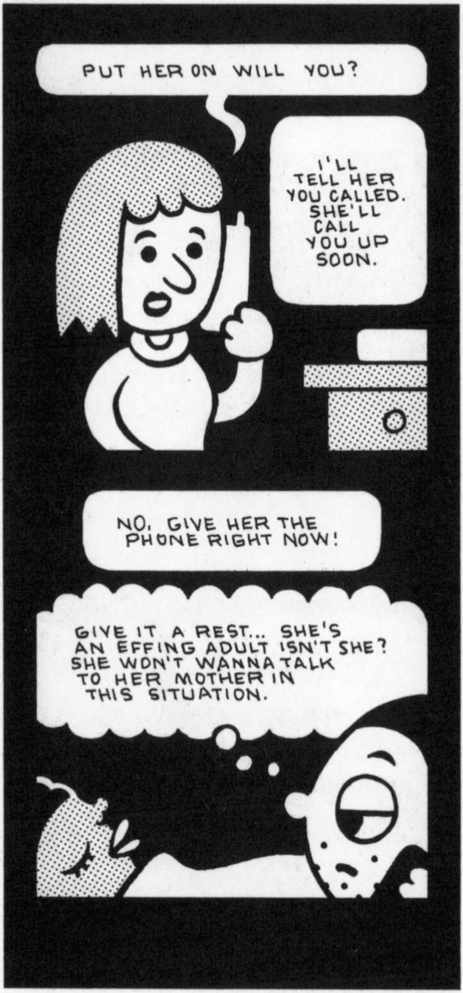
PUT HER ON WILL YOU?
I'LL TELL HER YOU CALLED. SHE'LL CALL YOU UP SOON.
NO. GIVE HER THE PHONE RIGHT NOW!
GIVE IT A REST... SHE'S AN EFFING ADULT ISN'T SHE? SHE WON'T WANNA TALK TO HER MOTHER IN THIS SITUATION.

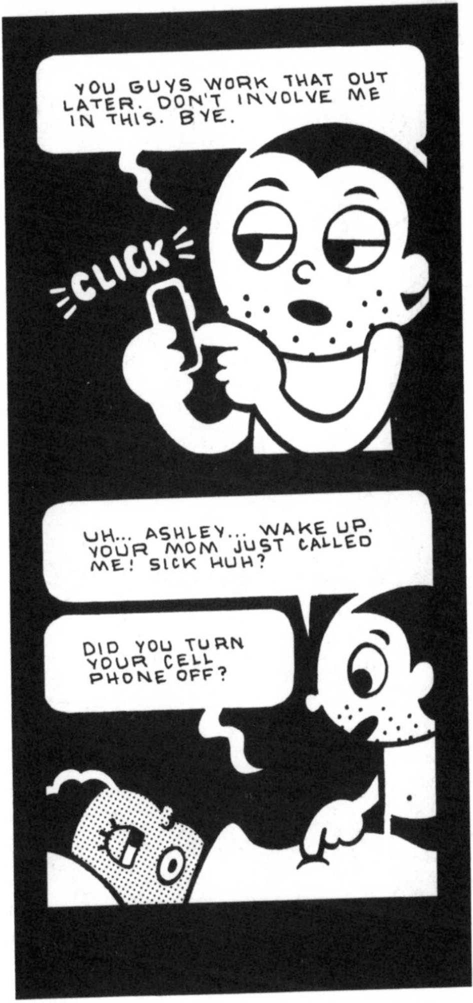
YOU GUYS WORK THAT OUT LATER. DON'T INVOLVE ME IN THIS. BYE.
CLICK
UH... ASHLEY... WAKE UP. YOUR MOM JUST CALLED ME! SICK HUH?
DID YOU TURN YOUR CELL PHONE OFF?

MMM... I GUESS I SHOULD TURN IT BACK ON.
RIIING!
OOPS.

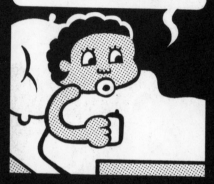

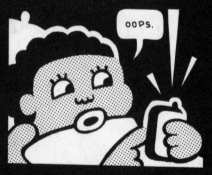

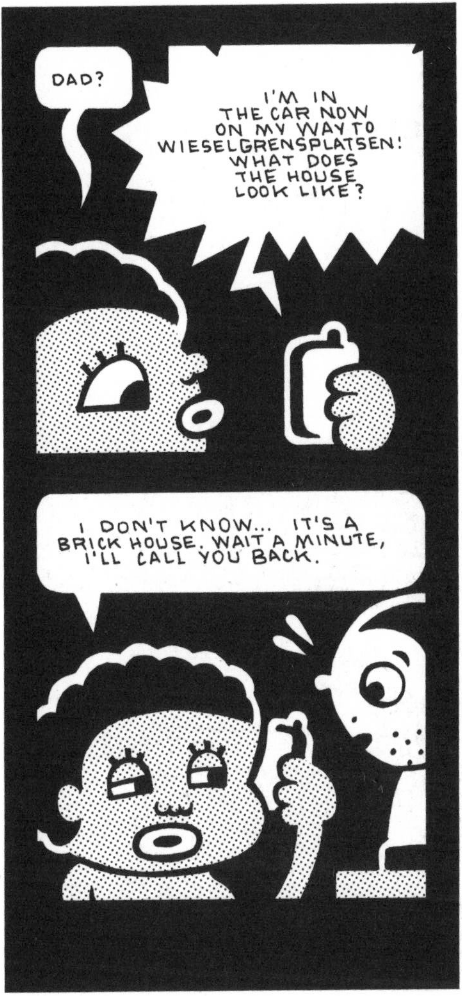
DAD?
I'M IN THE CAR NOW ON MY WAY TO WIESELGRENSPLATSEN! WHAT DOES THE HOUSE LOOK LIKE?
I DON'T KNOW... IT'S A BRICK HOUSE. WAIT A MINUTE, I'LL CALL YOU BACK.

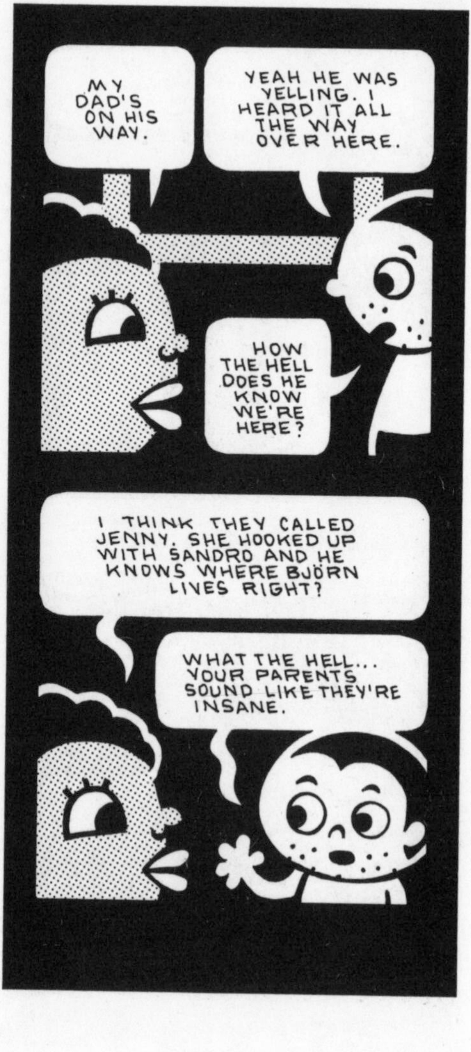
MY DAD'S ON HIS WAY.
YEAH HE WAS YELLING. I HEARD IT ALL THE WAY OVER HERE.
HOW THE HELL DOES HE KNOW WE'RE HERE?
I THINK THEY CALLED JENNY. SHE HOOKED UP WITH SANDRO AND HE KNOWS WHERE BJÖRN LIVES RIGHT?
WHAT THE HELL... YOUR PARENTS SOUND LIKE THEY'RE INSANE.

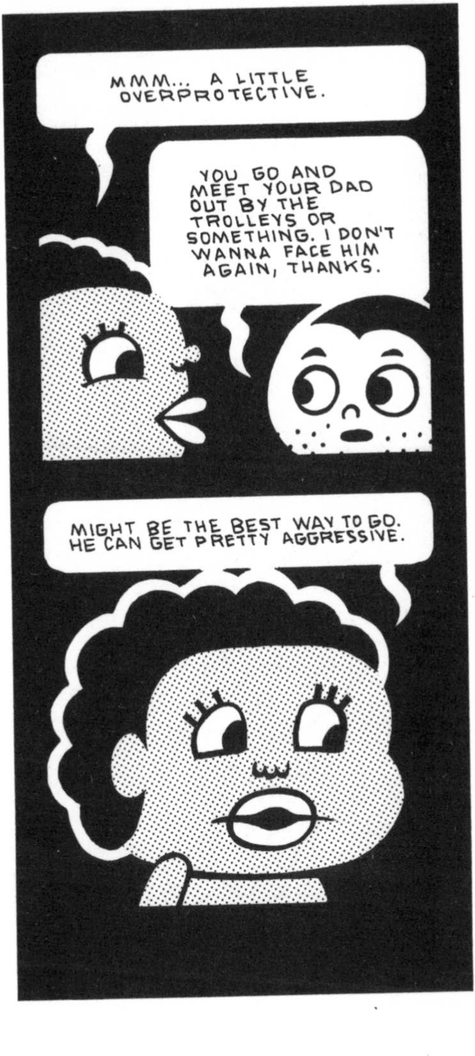
MMM... A LITTLE OVERPROTECTIVE.
YOU GO AND MEET YOUR DAD OUT BY THE TROLLEYS OR SOMETHING. I DON'T WANNA FACE HIM AGAIN, THANKS.
MIGHT BE THE BEST WAY TO GO. HE CAN GET PRETTY AGGRESSIVE.

BUH BYE.
DAMN, THAT WAS WEIRD. BUT PRETTY FUNNY.
GOTTA HIT THE ROAD MYSELF. BACK TO SKÅNE.

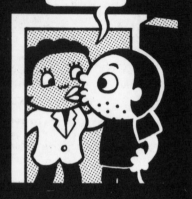

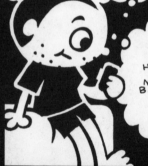

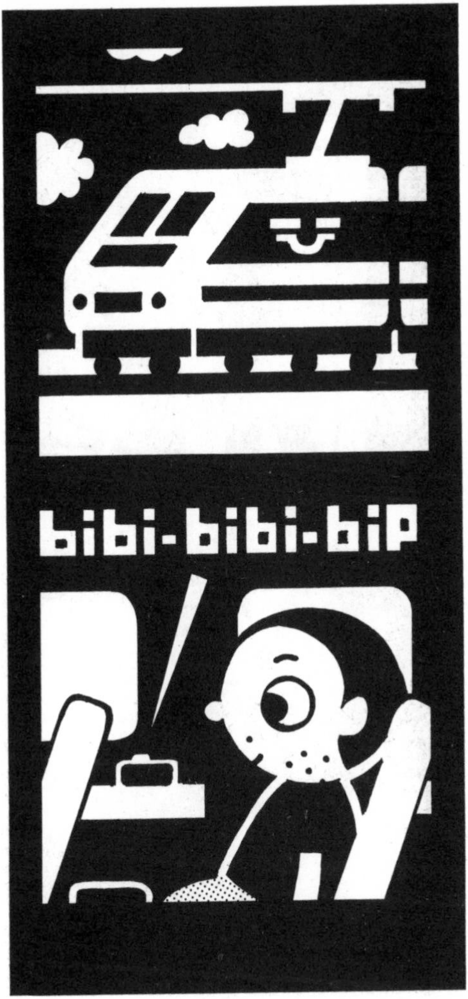
bibi-bibi-bip

THIS IS SIMON SPEAKING.
THIS IS ASHLEY'S BROTHER.
SIIIGH.
WHERE YOU AT?
ON THE TRAIN, HEADING TO SKÅNE.

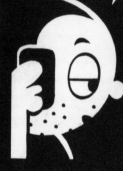

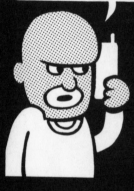

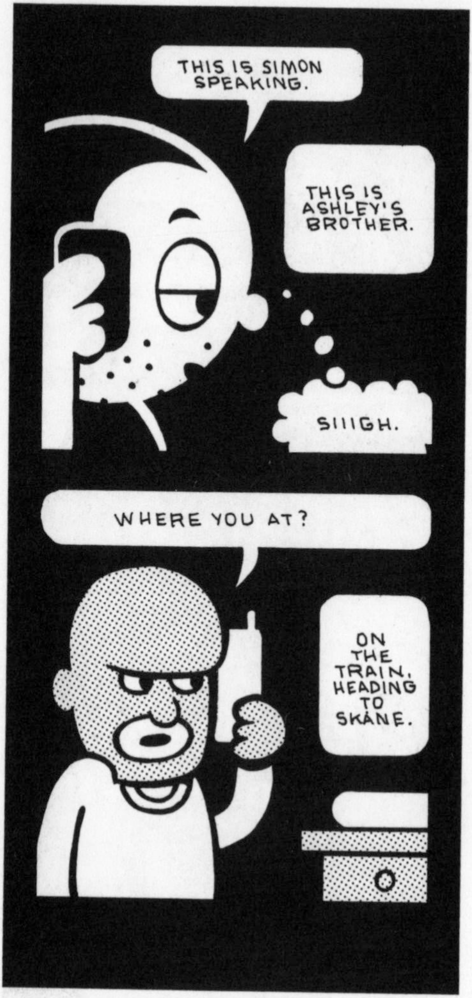

WHY DONTCHA COME OVER AND WE CAN TALK ABOUT THIS?

HUH? TALK ABOUT WHAT?

YOU KNOW WHERE WE LIVE. JUST COME OVER AND WE'LL WORK IT OUT.

UHM, LOOK. I'M NOT GONNA TAKE THE TRAIN BACK TO GOTHENBURG. WHAT DO YOU WANNA TALK ABOUT?

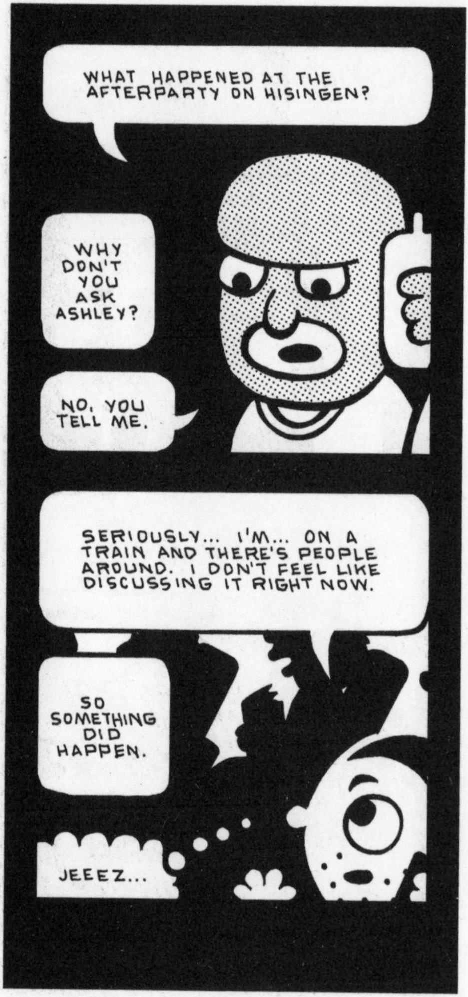
WHAT HAPPENED AT THE AFTERPARTY ON HISINGEN?
WHY DON'T YOU ASK ASHLEY?
NO, YOU TELL ME.
SERIOUSLY... I'M... ON A TRAIN AND THERE'S PEOPLE AROUND. I DON'T FEEL LIKE DISCUSSING IT RIGHT NOW.
SO SOMETHING DID HAPPEN.
JEEEZ...

WHERE IN SKÅNE ARE YOU HEADED?
ARE YOU KNOWLEDGEABLE ON SOUTH SWEDISH GEOGRAPHY?
FUNNY BOY, EH? YOU SHOW YOUR MUG IN GOTHENBURG AGAIN AND WE'LL HAVE YOUR ASS, GET IT? YOU'RE DONE FOR!
LOOK, I DIDN'T DO ANYTHING BAD TO YOUR SISTER. JUST CHILL, OK.

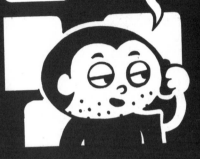

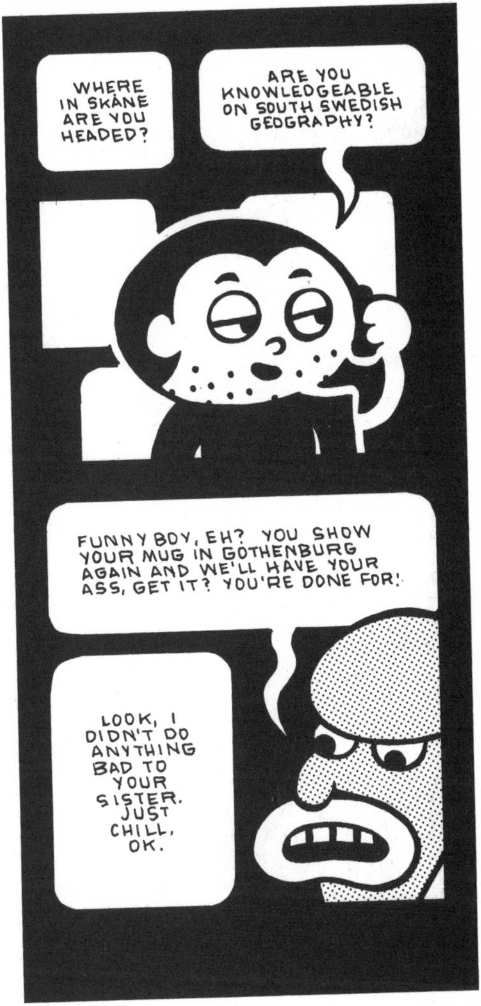

YOU DIDN'T EVEN LET HER TALK TO HER MOTHER WHEN SHE CALLED! MY MOTHER WAS CRYING... YOU HEAR ME? I'M GONNA KILL YOU... I SWEAR I'M GONNA KILL YOU!
YOU KNOW THAT KIND OF THREAT IS A CRIMINAL OFFENCE RIGHT?
YOU KNOW WHAT? I DON'T GIVE A FUCK. I HAVE A FRIEND HERE WHO WANTS TO TELL YOU SOMETHING...

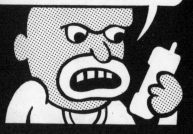

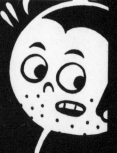

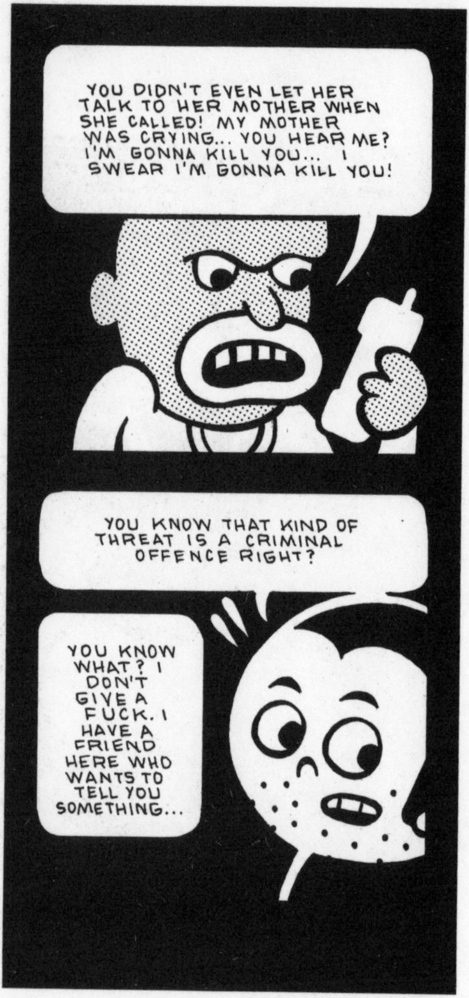

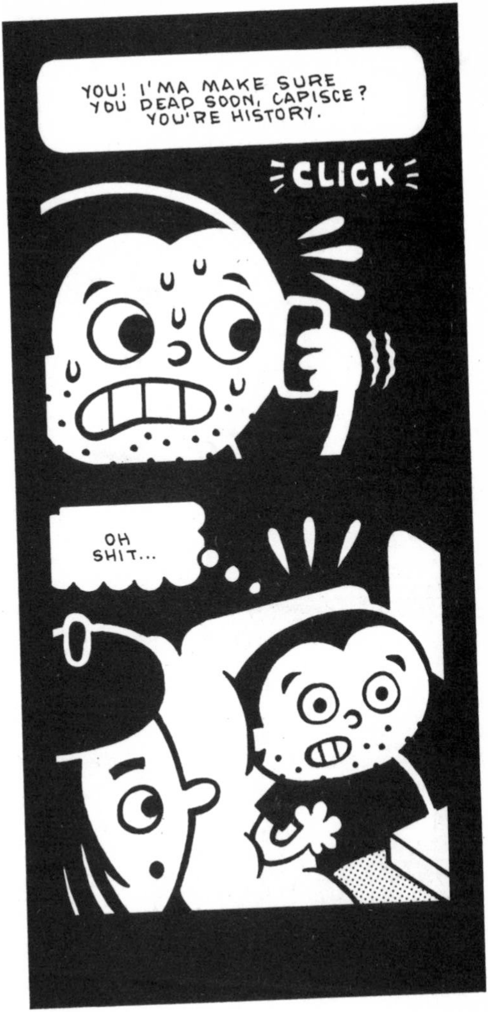
YOU! I'MA MAKE SURE YOU DEAD SOON, CAPISCE? YOU'RE HISTORY.
CLICK
OH SHIT...

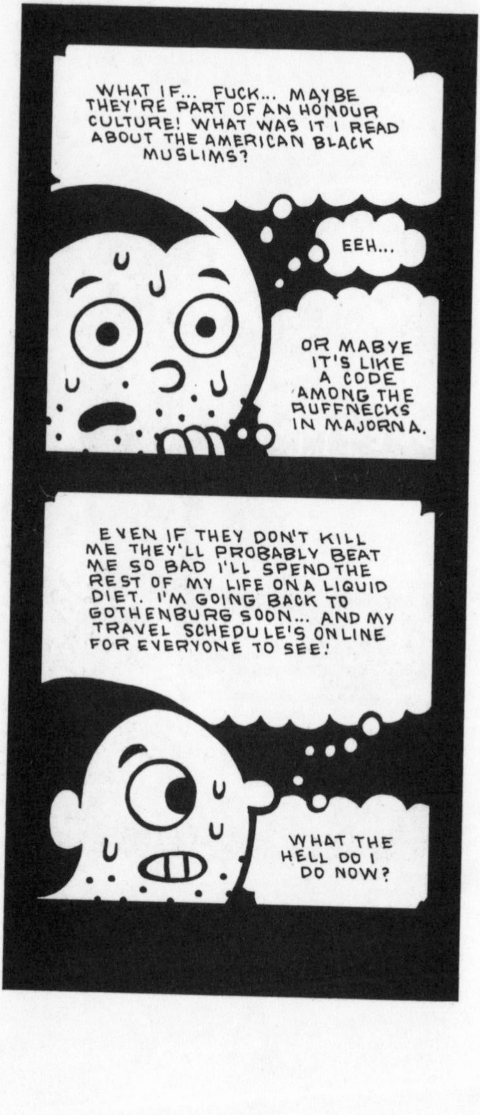
WHAT IF... FUCK... MAYBE THEY'RE PART OF AN HONOUR CULTURE! WHAT WAS IT I READ ABOUT THE AMERICAN BLACK MUSLIMS?
EEH...
OR MABYE IT'S LIKE A CODE AMONG THE RUFFNECKS IN MAJORNA.
EVEN IF THEY DON'T KILL ME THEY'LL PROBABLY BEAT ME SO BAD I'LL SPEND THE REST OF MY LIFE ON A LIQUID DIET. I'M GOING BACK TO GOTHENBURG SOON... AND MY TRAVEL SCHEDULE'S ONLINE FOR EVERYONE TO SEE!
WHAT THE HELL DO I DO NOW?

VITABY, 4/19 2007. HOST # 34: JOHANNES NILSSON
I'M SINDRA AND THIS IS ANDERS, WHO'LL BE FILMING.
SVT
SO WHAT DO YOU KNOW ABOUT THIS FAMILY?
NOT MUCH.
SVT

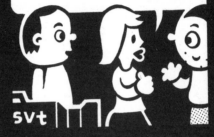

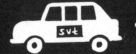

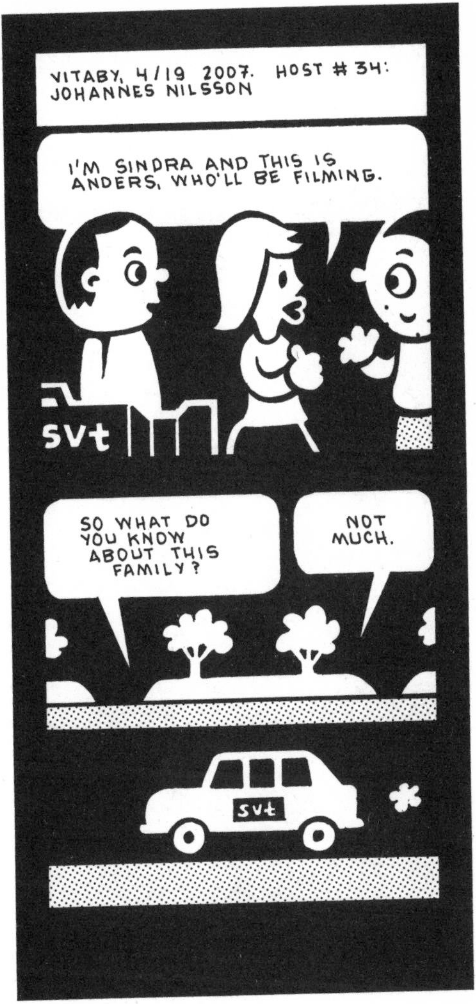

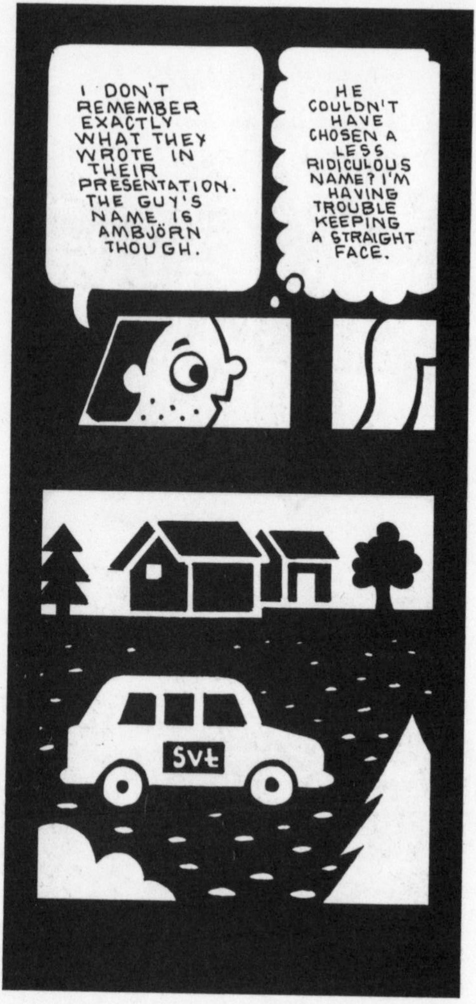
I DON'T REMEMBER EXACTLY WHAT THEY WROTE IN THEIR PRESENTATION. THE GUY'S NAME IS AMBJÖRN THOUGH.
HE COULDN'T HAVE CHOSEN A LESS RIDICULOUS NAME? I'M HAVING TROUBLE KEEPING A STRAIGHT FACE.
Svt

ALRIGHT, I'LL FILM YOU KNOCKING ON THE DOOR. JUST DON'T LOOK INTO THE CAMERA.
SIMON!
I'M AMBJÖRN. WELCOME.

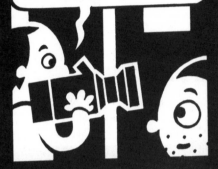

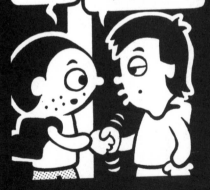

I'M ANNA AND THIS IS SELMA.
OK. LET'S DO ANOTHER TAKE. DIFFERENT ANGLE THIS TIME... AND MAKE IT LIKE YOU'RE SAYING YOUR HELLOS THE FIRST TIME, AGAIN.

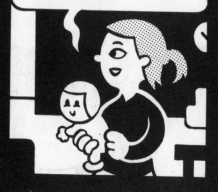

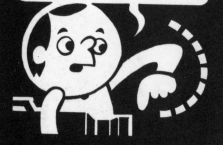

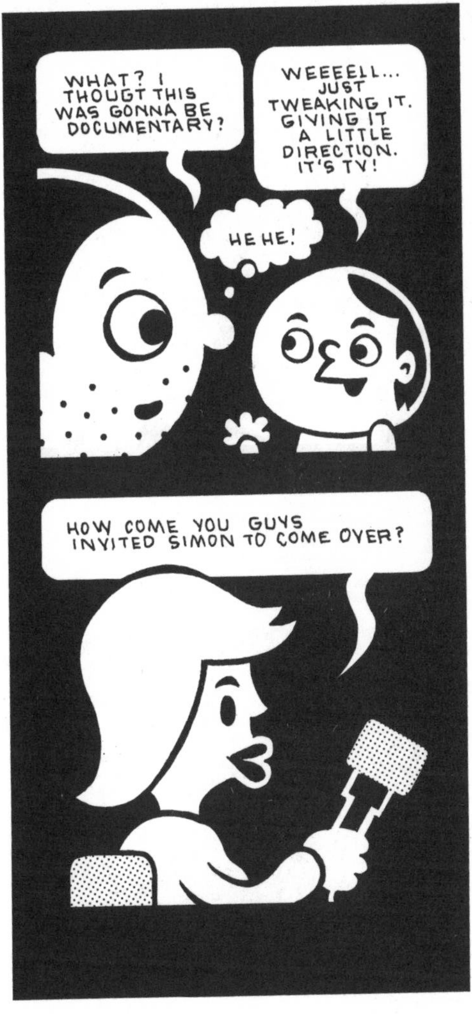
WHAT? I THOUGT THIS WAS GONNA BE DOCUMENTARY?
WEEEEELL... JUST TWEAKING IT. GIVING IT A LITTLE DIRECTION. IT'S TV!
HE HE!
HOW COME YOU GUYS INVITED SIMON TO COME OVER?

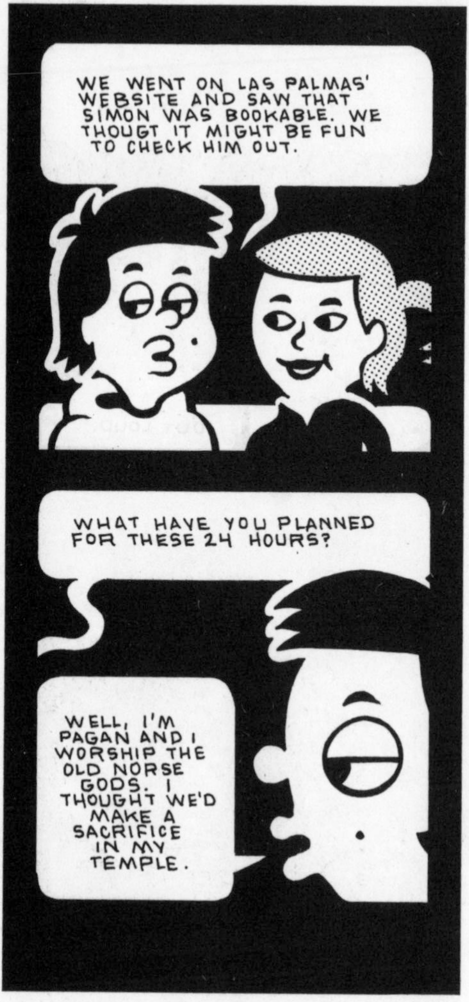
WE WENT ON LAS PALMAS' WEBSITE AND SAW THAT SIMON WAS BOOKABLE. WE THOUGT IT MIGHT BE FUN TO CHECK HIM OUT.
WHAT HAVE YOU PLANNED FOR THESE 24 HOURS?
WELL, I'M PAGAN AND I WORSHIP THE OLD NORSE GODS. I THOUGHT WE'D MAKE A SACRIFICE IN MY TEMPLE.

HEHEH, I'LL BE DAMNED. JOHANNES IS REALLY GETTING INTO THIS!
DON'T LAUGH OUT LOUD.
WHAT DOES THAT MEAN EXACTLY, TO MAKE A SACRIFICE?
HE'LL SACRIFICE SOMETHING THAT'S IMPORTANT TO HIM. TO HIS GOD OF CHOICE.

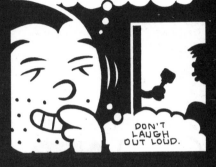

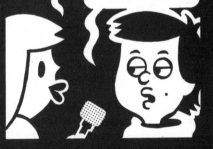

I'D SUGGEST BRAGE, THE GOD OF ART, SO HIS COMIC COMES OUT GOOD.

MAYBE SOMETHING TO NJORD AS WELL... SO IT CREATES RICHES.

I'VE CHOSEN TO SACRIFICE A PAIR OF UNDERWEAR. THEY MEAN A LOT TO ME BECAUSE I DON'T HAVE MANY LAUNDRY OPPORTUNITIES WHILE TRAVELLING. I SACRIFICE THEM TO BRAGE.

AND I'LL SACRIFICE A SOCK TO NJORD... SO THE BOOK GETS GOOD SALES.

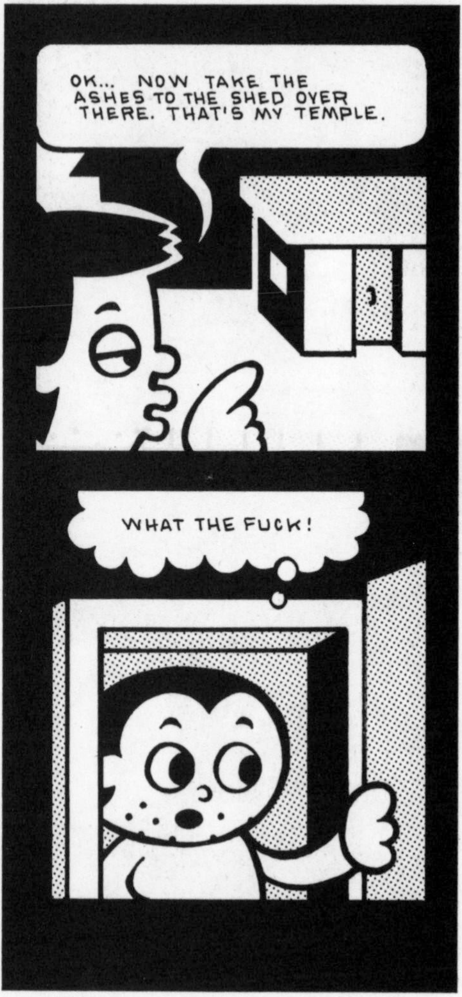
OK... NOW TAKE THE ASHES TO THE SHED OVER THERE. THAT'S MY TEMPLE.
WHAT THE FUCK!

SHIT... THAT LOOKS LIKE A HUMAN SKULL!

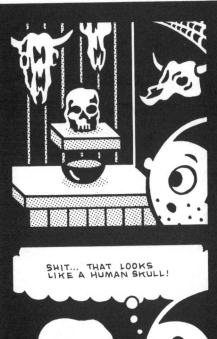

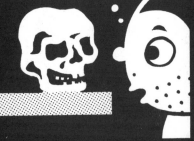

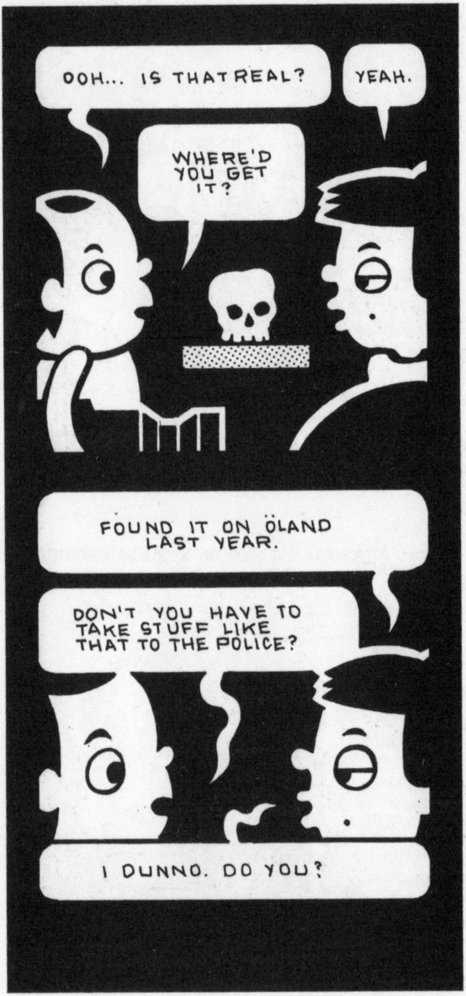
OOH... IS THAT REAL?
YEAH.
WHERE'D YOU GET IT?
FOUND IT ON ÖLAND LAST YEAR.
DON'T YOU HAVE TO TAKE STUFF LIKE THAT TO THE POLICE?
I DUNNO. DO YOU?

UHM... I'LL PUT THE ASHES ON THE ALTAR THEN. SHOULD I SAY SOMETHING?
IF YOU LIKE.
ALRIGHT... A SOCK FOR NJORD AND UNDERWEAR FOR BRAGE THEN.

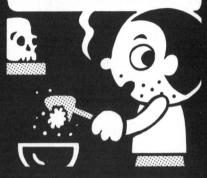

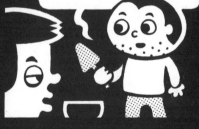

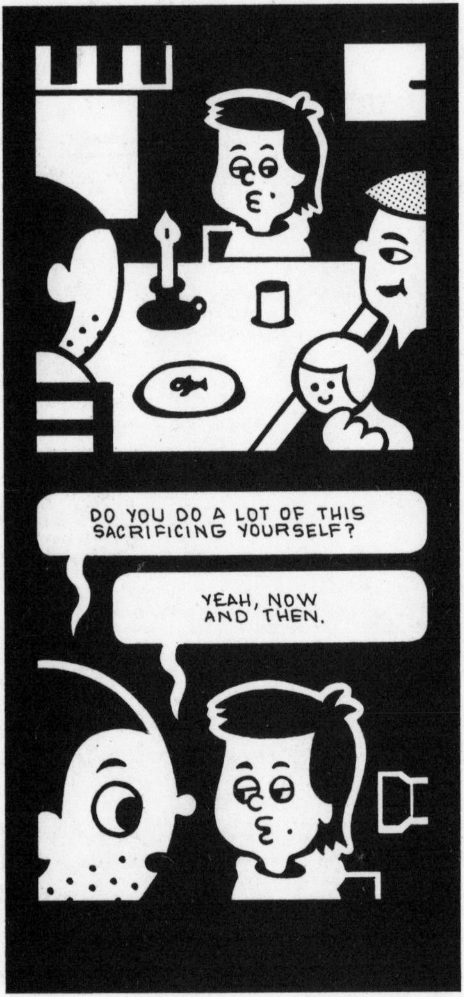
DO YOU DO A LOT OF THIS SACRIFICING YOURSELF?
YEAH, NOW AND THEN.

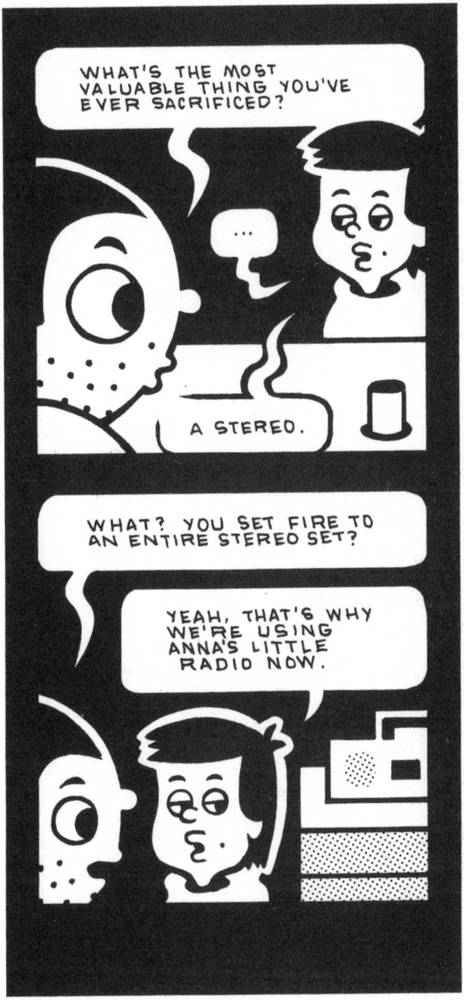
WHAT'S THE MOST VALUABLE THING YOU'VE EVER SACRIFICED?
...
A STEREO.
WHAT? YOU SET FIRE TO AN ENTIRE STEREO SET?
YEAH, THAT'S WHY WE'RE USING ANNA'S LITTLE RADIO NOW.

WHOA... WHAT GOD DID YOU SACRIFICE IT TO?
FREY... THE GOD OF FERTILITY.
DONE HIS HOMEWORK
THAT'S HOW WE GOT SELMA!
A-BOBO-GAGA

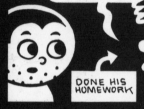

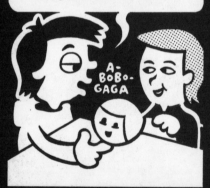

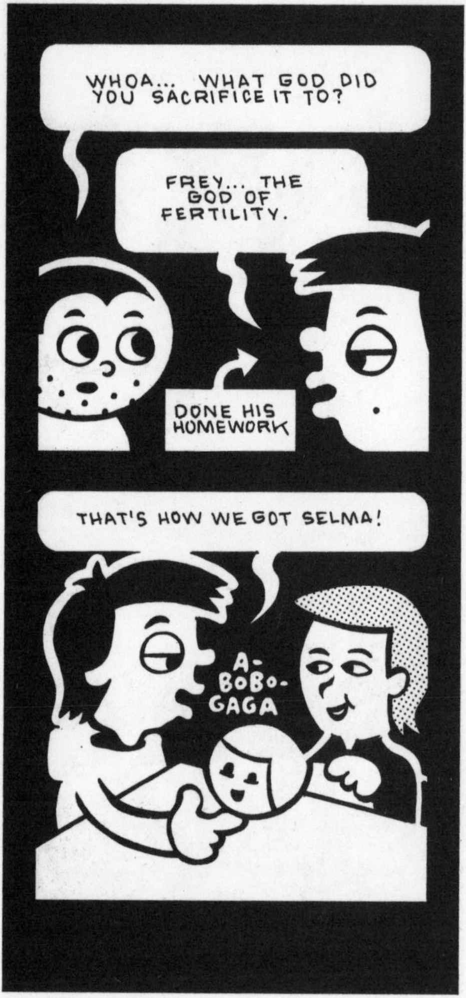

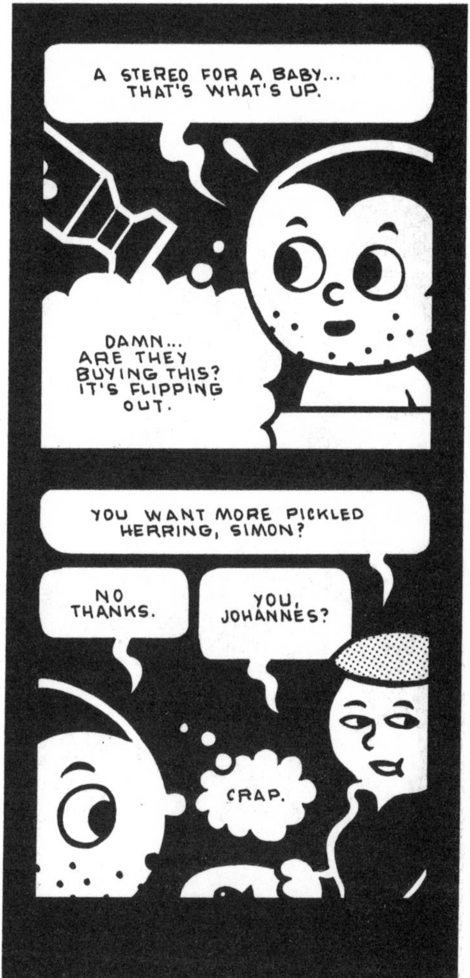
A STEREO FOR A BABY...
THAT'S WHAT'S UP.
DAMN... ARE THEY BUYING THIS? IT'S FLIPPING OUT.
YOU WANT MORE PICKLED HERRING, SIMON?
NO THANKS.
YOU, JOHANNES?
CRAP.

ER... NO.

WHY'D YOU CALL AMBJÖRN JOHANNES?

HE... STARTED CALLING HIMSELF AMBJÖRN WHEN HE GOT INTO ASATRU.

I'M NOT PART OF THE RELIGION MYSELF... SO I HAVEN'T REALLY ACCEPTED THE NAME YET, I GUESS.

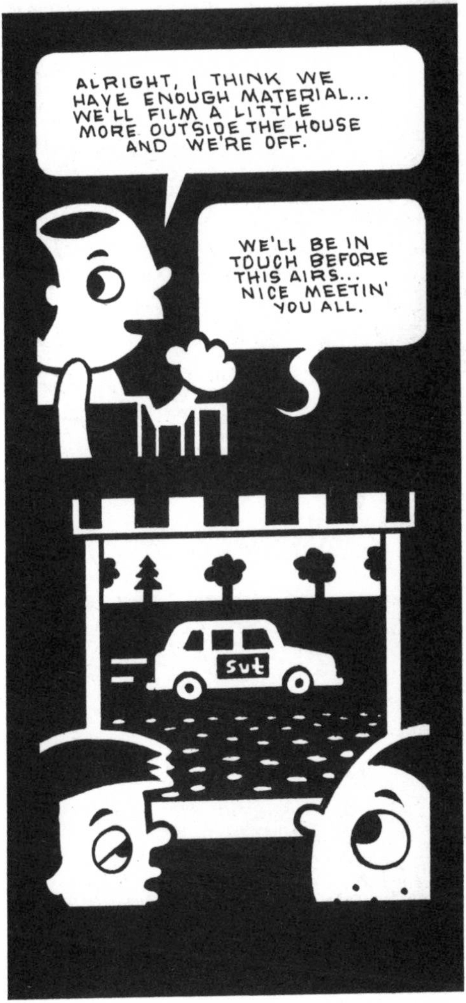
ALRIGHT, I THINK WE HAVE ENOUGH MATERIAL... WE'LL FILM A LITTLE MORE OUTSIDE THE HOUSE AND WE'RE OFF.
WE'LL BE IN TOUCH BEFORE THIS AIRS... NICE MEETIN' YOU ALL.
SUT

BWAA HA HA HA!!
DAMN... DO YOU THINK THEY BOUGHT IT? THEY SEEMED SKEPTICAL.

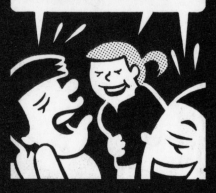

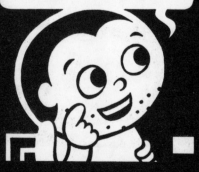

WE'LL SEE. YOU MADE A NICE SAVE AFTER SAYING THE "WRONG" NAME.
THANKS. HMM... I THINK IT'LL WORK.
I ALMOST FREAKED OUT WHEN I SAW THE SKULLS IN THE SHED. WHERE THE HELL DID YOU GET THOSE?

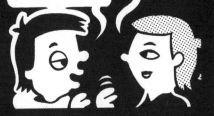

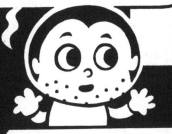

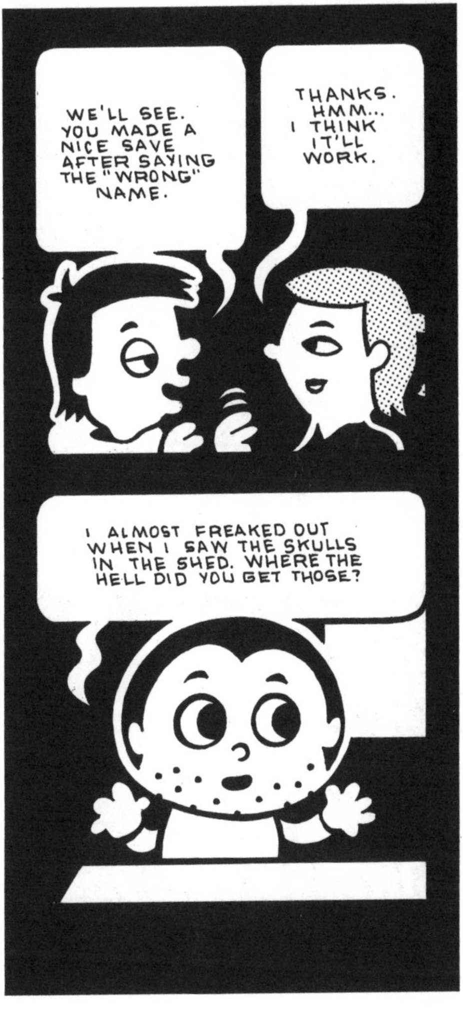

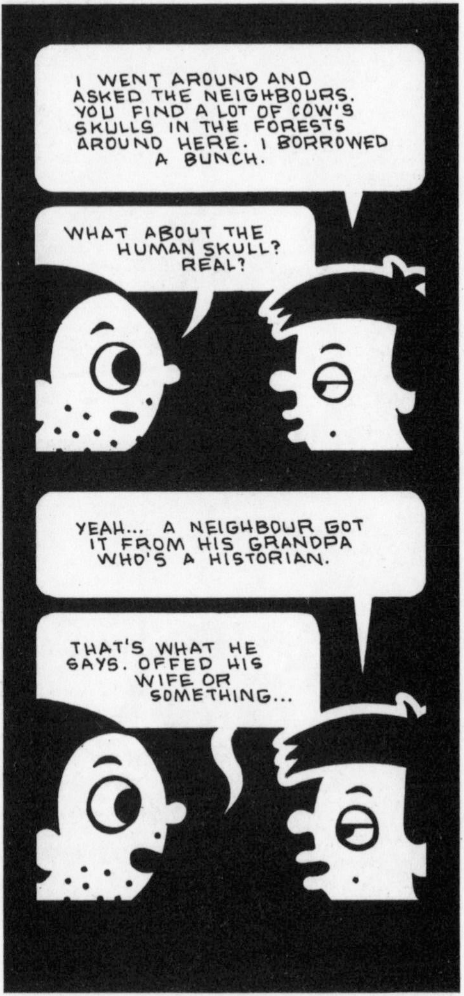
I WENT AROUND AND ASKED THE NEIGHBOURS. YOU FIND A LOT OF COW'S SKULLS IN THE FORESTS AROUND HERE. I BORROWED A BUNCH.
WHAT ABOUT THE HUMAN SKULL? REAL?
YEAH... A NEIGHBOUR GOT IT FROM HIS GRANDPA WHO'S A HISTORIAN.
THAT'S WHAT HE SAYS. OFFED HIS WIFE OR SOMETHING...

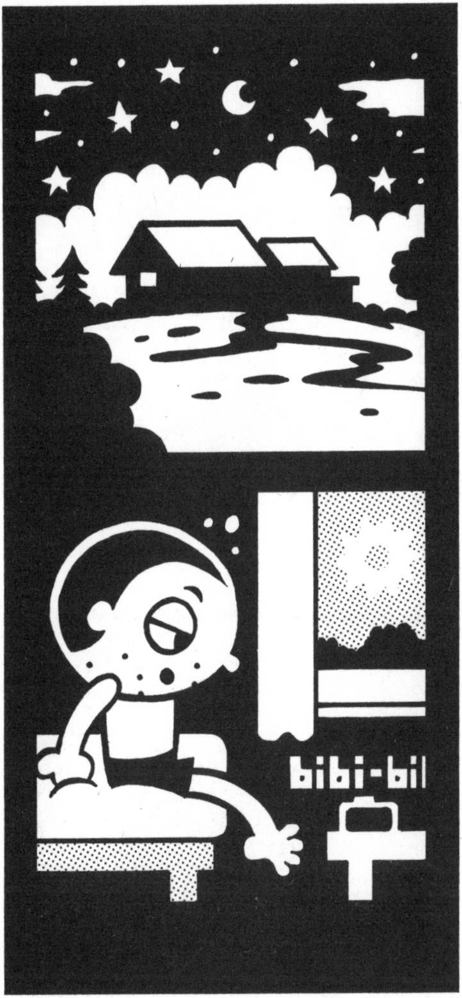
bibi-bil

HEY SIMON! THIS IS SINDRA FROM TV. WE LEFT A LITTLE SUDDENLY YESTERDAY.
WE LOOKED THROUGH THE STUFF WE FILMED AND IT'S KINDA... EXTREME.

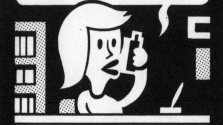

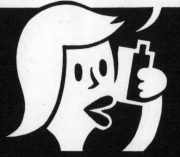

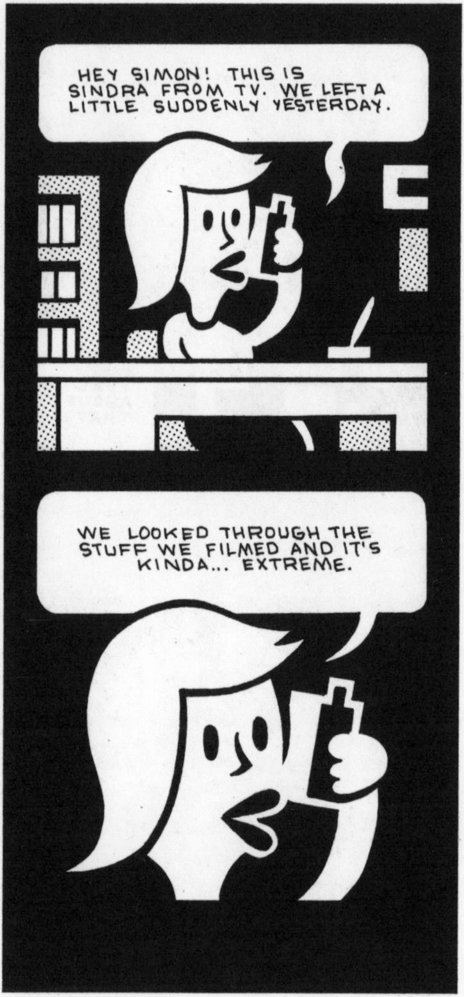

I THINK IT'S EXTREME IN A GOOD WAY THOUGH... SO WE WANNA SHOW IT.
HOW'D YOU FEEL ABOUT THAT?
IT'S COOL WITH ME. IT WAS STRANGE... BUT INTERESTING.

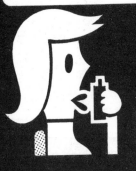

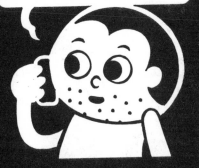

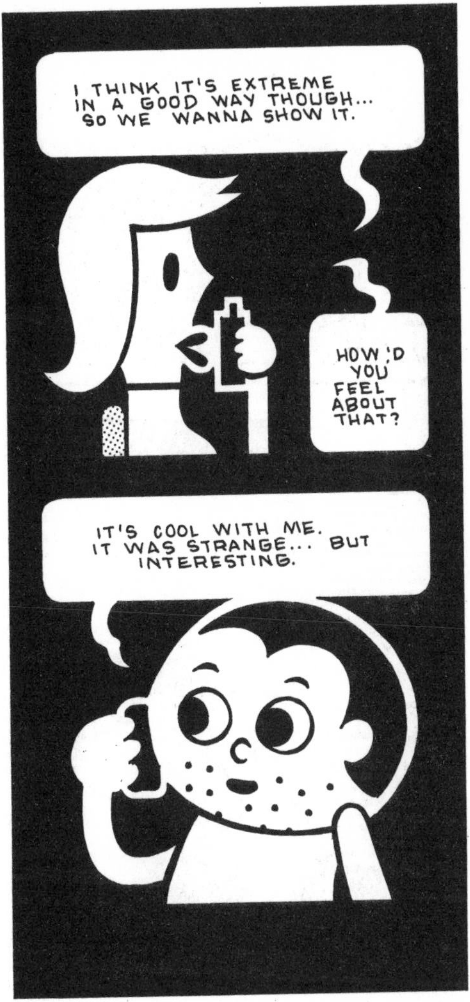

MMM... BUT WE'LL EDIT OUT THE SKULL PART. IT WOULD'VE BEEN... A LITTLE MUCH.
OK. JUST LET ME KNOW WHEN IT'S GONNA BE ON.
TV JUST CALLED.
OH. WHAT'S UP?

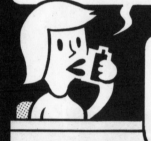

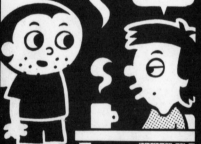

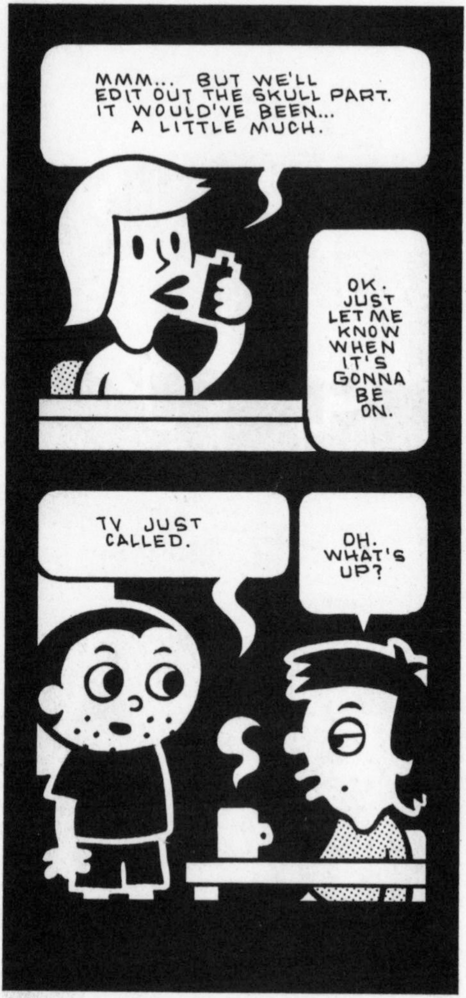

THEY SAID THEY'D AIR IT BUT EDIT OUT THE SKULL. IT'S "TOO MUCH" APPARENTLY.
HA HA THAT'S PRETTY NEGLIGENT. I MEAN, THEY DON'T HAVE A CLUE WHERE I GOT IT.

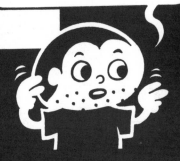

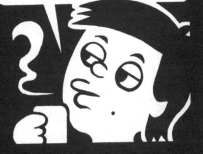

I COULD'VE KILLED A GUY AND GOTTEN AWAY WITH IT DESPITE TV FILMING PARTS OF THE BODY.
THEY'RE JUST GLAD TO HAVE A GOOD SHOW.
THEY WON'T HAVE THE ENERGY TO TAKE THIS TO THE COPS. THEY'LL CENSOR IT AND IT WON'T BE THEIR PROBLEM ANYMORE.
?

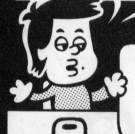

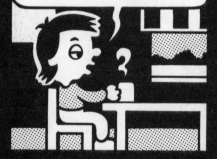

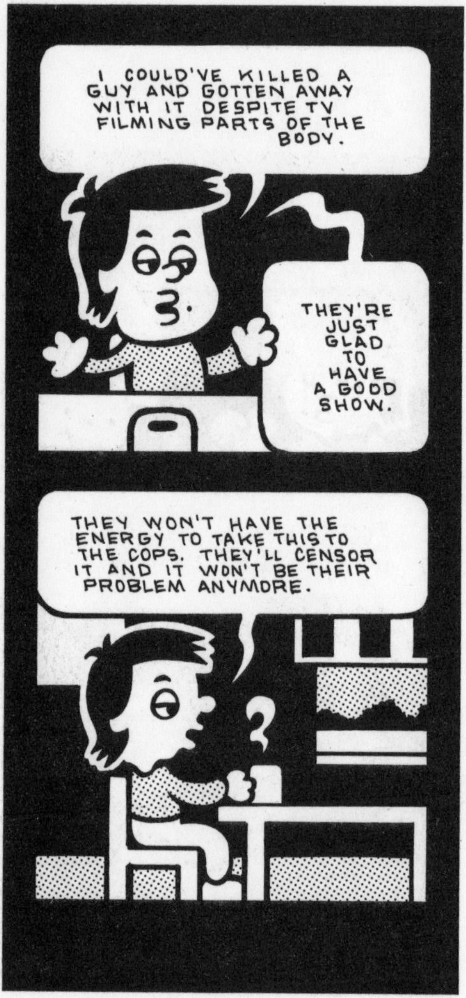

ALTHOUGH YOU NEVER KNOW. A POLICE INSPECTOR MIGHT COME A-KNOCKIN' NEXT WEEK.
I GUESS STATE-CONTROLLED TELEVISION SHOULD HAVE A DUTY TO REPORT SOMETHING LIKE THIS.
HMMM... IF THEY DON'T DO ANYTHING YOU'LL HAVE A TABLOID STORY FOR YOUR BOOK RELEASE:
"SWEDISH TV IGNORED POSSIBLE MURDER!"

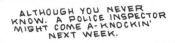

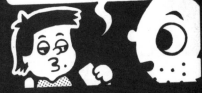

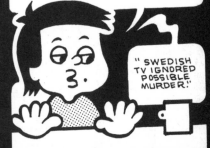

HA HA! HARD NOT TO FEEL LIKE A TOTAL ÜBERMENSCH WHEN YOU'VE GOT THE MEDIA MANIPULATED LIKE THAT!

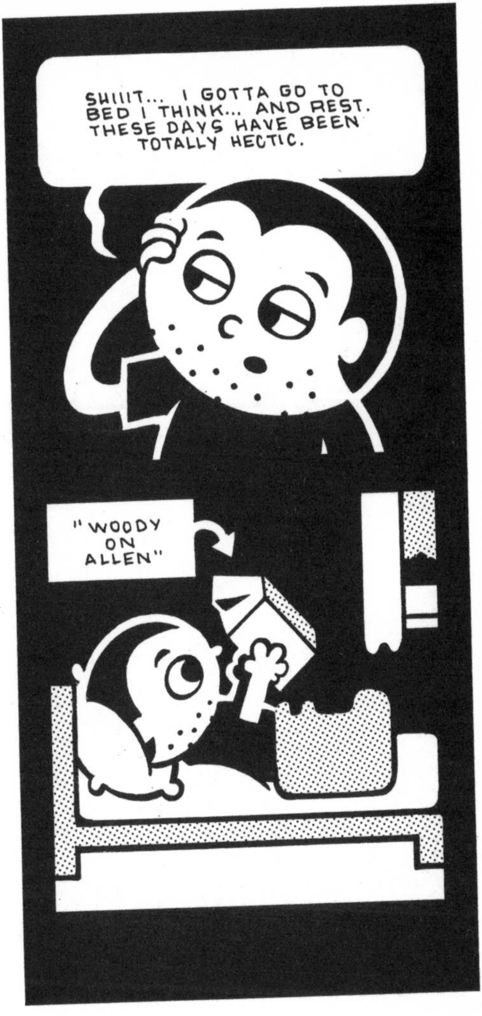
SHIIIT... I GOTTA GO TO BED I THINK... AND REST. THESE DAYS HAVE BEEN TOTALLY HECTIC.
"WOODY ON ALLEN"

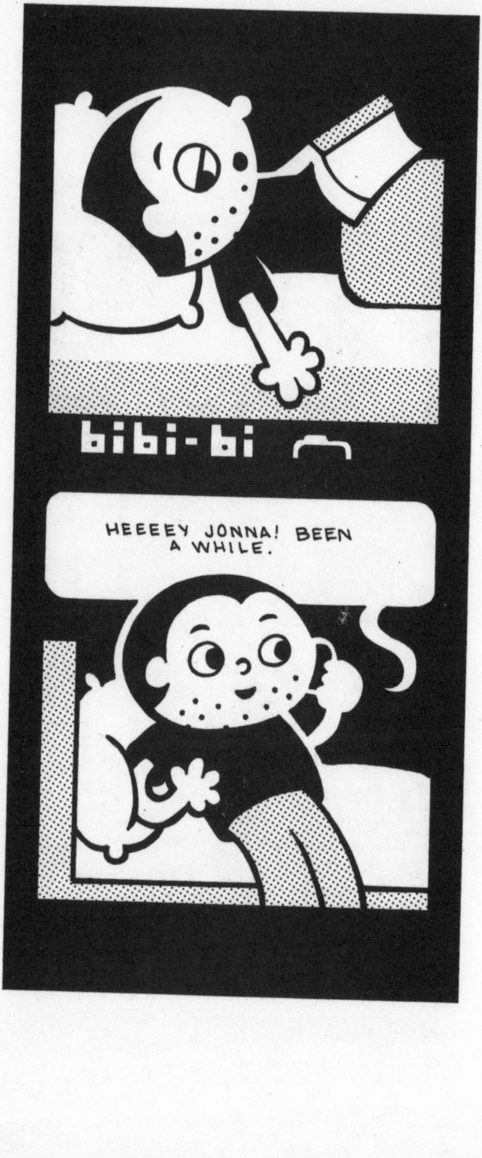
bibi-bi
HEEEEY JONNA! BEEN A WHILE.

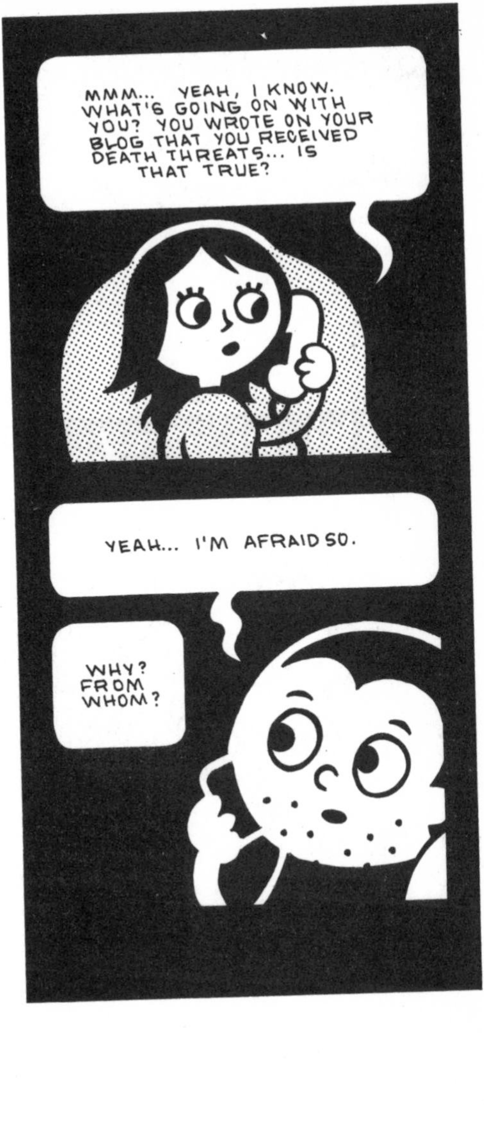
MMM... YEAH, I KNOW. WHAT'S GOING ON WITH YOU? YOU WROTE ON YOUR BLOG THAT YOU RECEIVED DEATH THREATS... IS THAT TRUE?
YEAH... I'M AFRAID SO.
WHY? FROM WHOM?

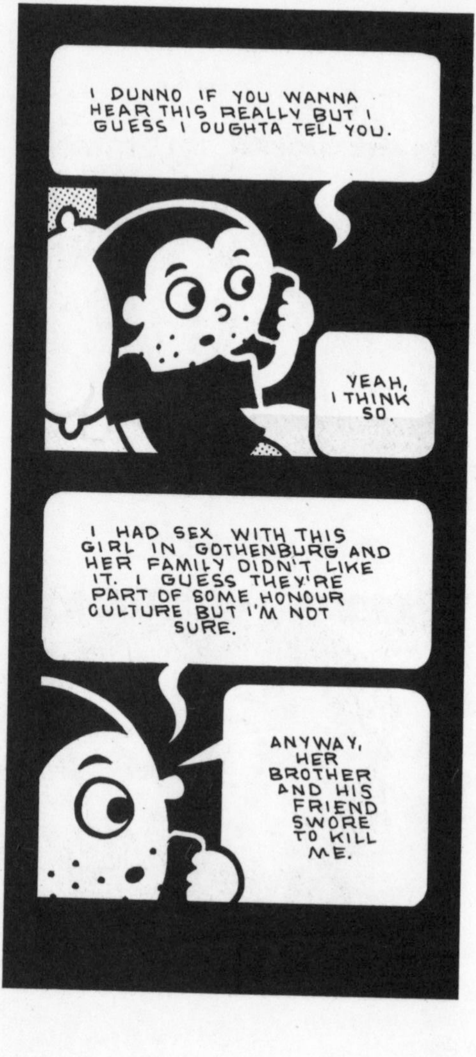
I DUNNO IF YOU WANNA HEAR THIS REALLY BUT I GUESS I OUGHTA TELL YOU.
YEAH, I THINK SO.
I HAD SEX WITH THIS GIRL IN GOTHENBURG AND HER FAMILY DIDN'T LIKE IT. I GUESS THEY'RE PART OF SOME HONOUR CULTURE BUT I'M NOT SURE.
ANYWAY, HER BROTHER AND HIS FRIEND SWORE TO KILL ME.

DAMN, THAT'S SCARY. WHAT'RE YOU GONNA DO?
I DUNNO. I GOTTA TALK TO HER AND FIGURE OUT HOW SERIOUS THIS IS.
IS IT DIFFICULT FOR YOU TO HEAR THIS?

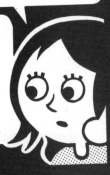

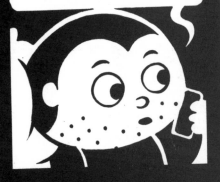

UHMMM... SPEAKING OF THE SEEING OTHERS THING...
YEAH?
I FEEL LIKE I SHOULD TELL YOU... I'VE STARTED SEEING THIS GUY.

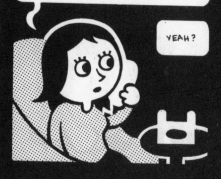

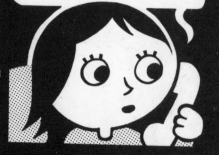

I'VE BEEN WITH OTHERS SINCE YOU'VE BEEN AWAY... BUT THEY FELT LIKE PASTIMES WHILE I WAITED FOR YOU.
I SHOULD TELL YOU THAT THIS GUY IS MORE THAN A PASTIME.

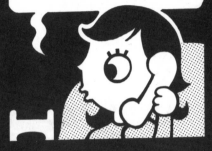

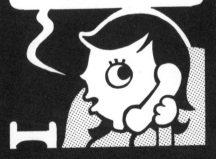

WHAT? YOU'RE IN LOVE?
I THINK I'M FALLING FOR HIM, YEAH.
SHIT.

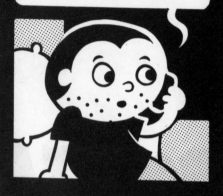

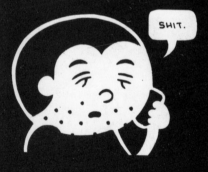

ARGGHH... WELL, I GUESS I'VE GOT MYSELF TO BLAME FOR THIS.
YEAH... I DON'T KNOW WHAT TO SAY TO THAT, I MEAN, YOU DO.

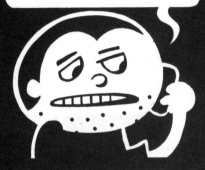

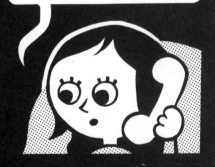

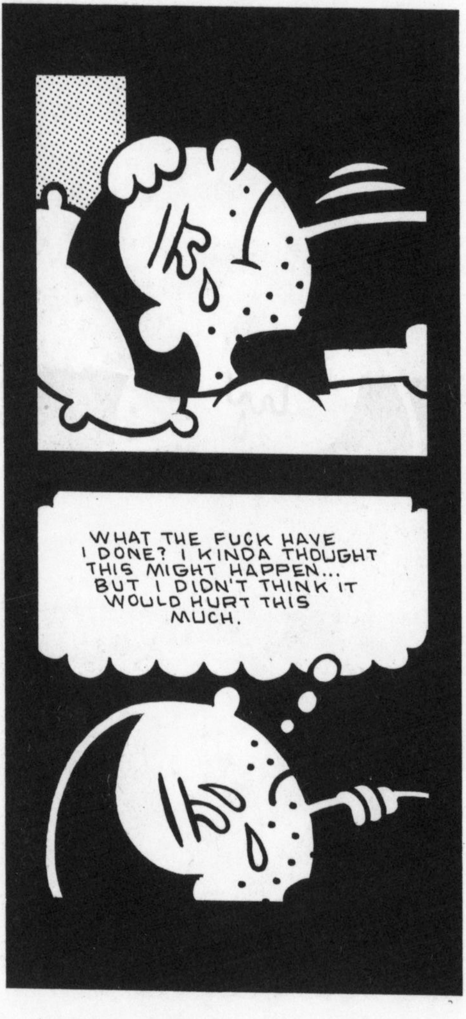
WHAT THE FUCK HAVE I DONE? I KINDA THOUGHT THIS MIGHT HAPPEN... BUT I DIDN'T THINK IT WOULD HURT THIS MUCH.

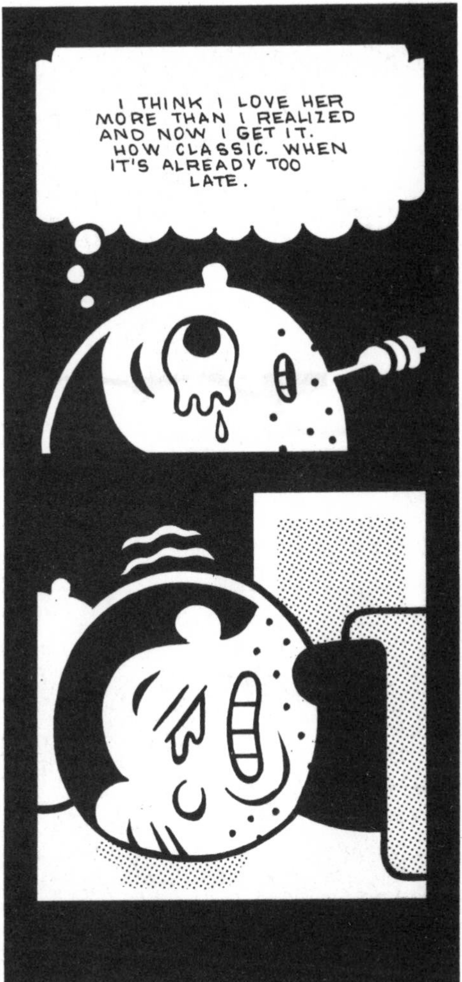
I THINK I LOVE HER MORE THAN I REALIZED AND NOW I GET IT. HOW CLASSIC. WHEN IT'S ALREADY TOO LATE.

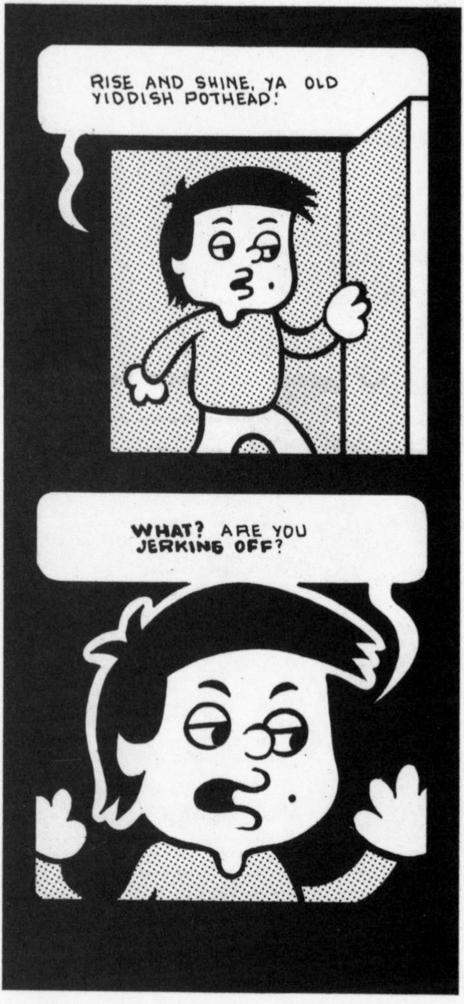
RISE AND SHINE, YA OLD YIDDISH POTHEAD!
WHAT? ARE YOU JERKING OFF?

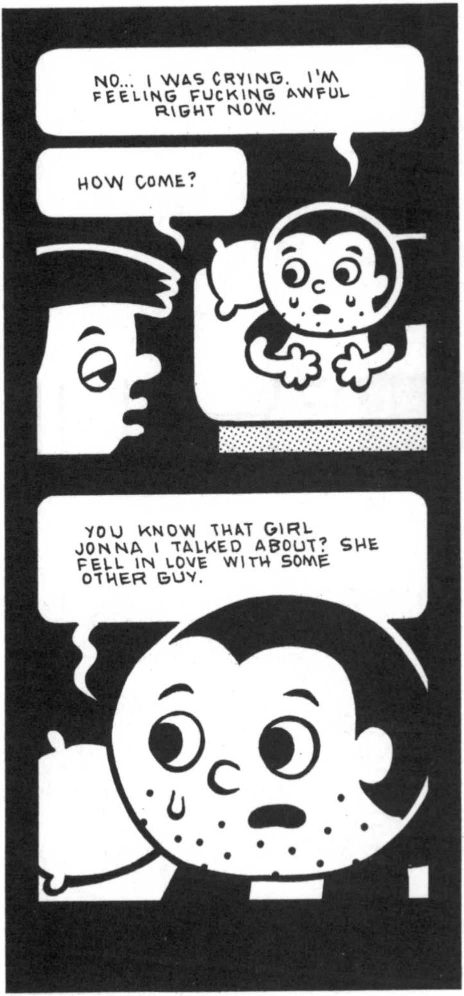
NO... I WAS CRYING. I'M FEELING FUCKING AWFUL RIGHT NOW.
HOW COME?
YOU KNOW THAT GIRL JONNA I TALKED ABOUT? SHE FELL IN LOVE WITH SOME OTHER GUY.

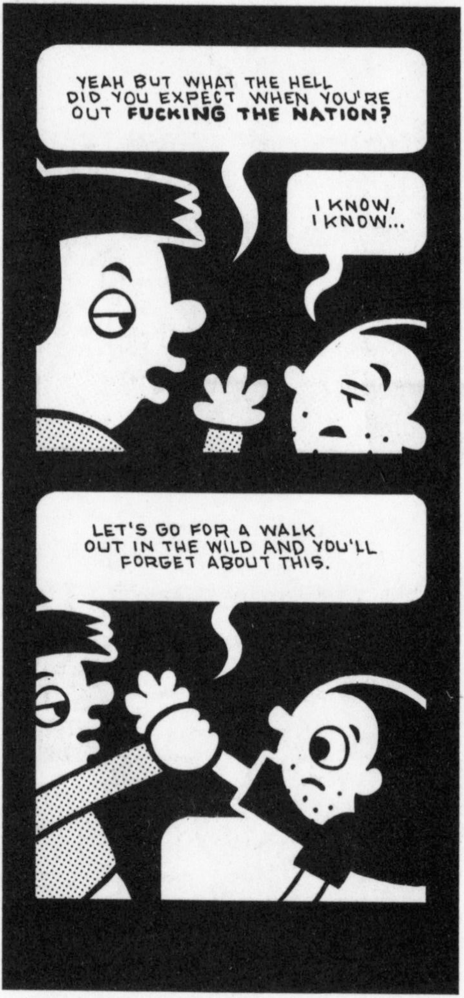
YEAH BUT WHAT THE HELL DID YOU EXPECT WHEN YOU'RE OUT **FUCKING THE NATION?**
I KNOW, I KNOW...
LET'S GO FOR A WALK OUT IN THE WILD AND YOU'LL FORGET ABOUT THIS.

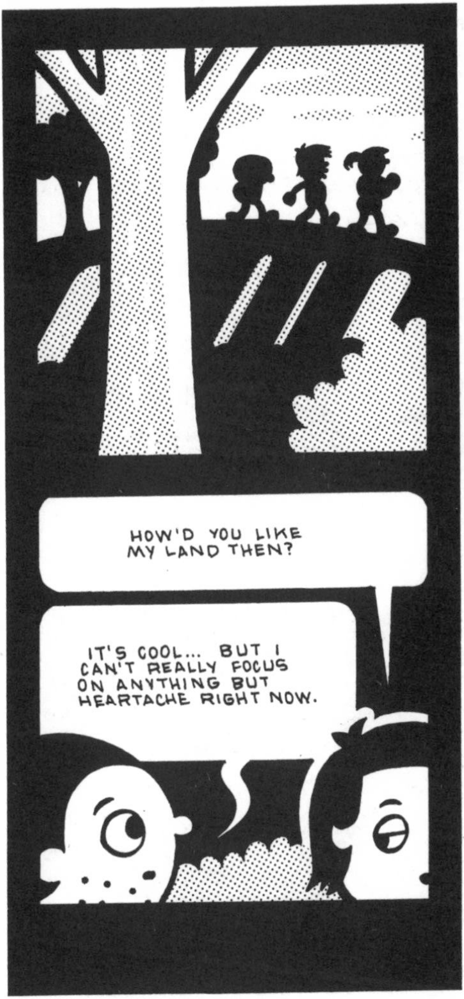
HOW'D YOU LIKE MY LAND THEN?
IT'S COOL... BUT I CAN'T REALLY FOCUS ON ANYTHING BUT HEARTACHE RIGHT NOW.

YEAH... YOU SHOULD'VE MADE A SACRIFICE TO FREYA AS WELL... THE GODDESS OF LOVE. YOU FORGOT ABOUT HER.
DAMNIT. YOU'RE RIGHT.
IF YOU'D THROWN YOUR NEW IPOD IN THE FIRE... EVERYTHING WOULD'VE BEEN ALRIGHT.

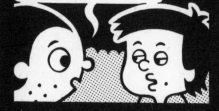

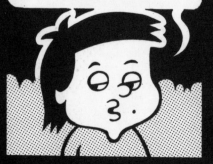

NAH... BUT THERE'S SOMETHING IN THAT. I SACRIFICED LOVE FOR ART INSTEAD.
YEAH, AND NOW YOU FEEL LIKE SHIT. TODAY WE LEARNED LOVE IS MORE IMPORTANT THAN COMICS AND SLEEPING AROUND.

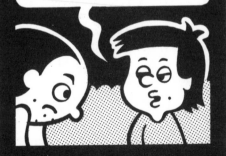

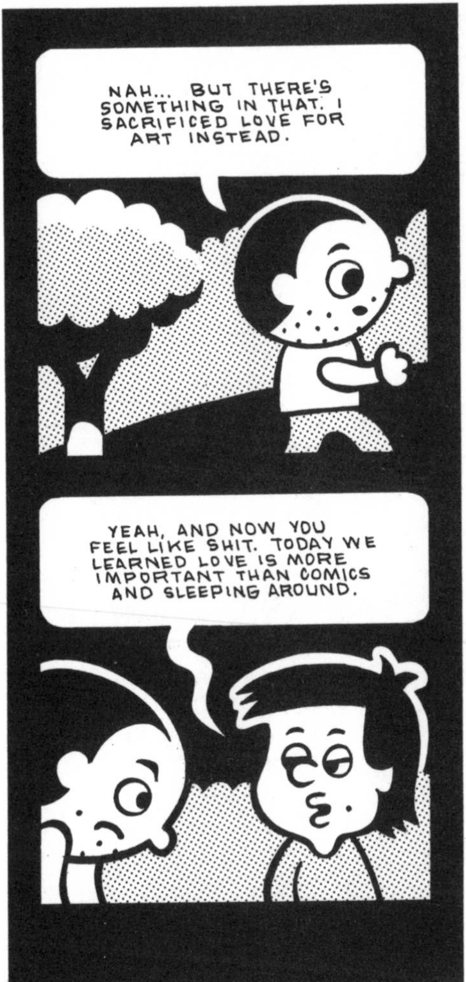

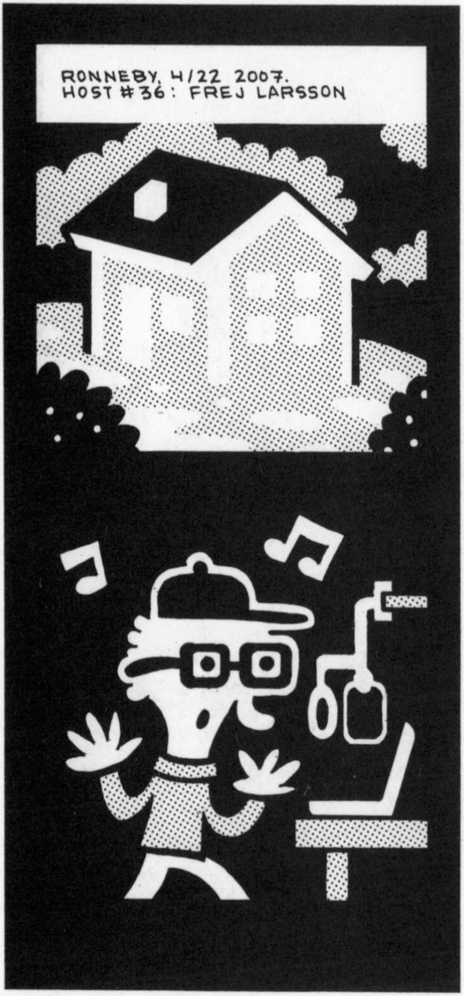
RONNEBY, 4/22 2007.
HOST #36: FREJ LARSSON

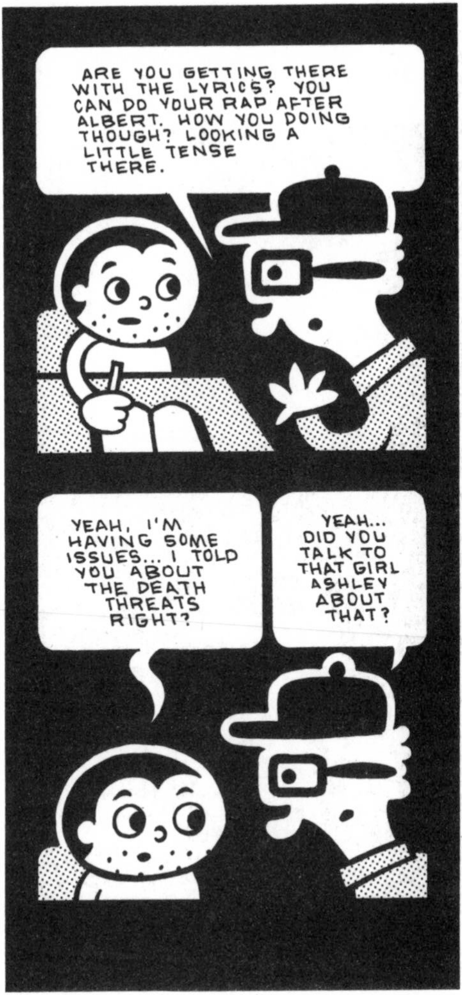

ARE YOU GETTING THERE WITH THE LYRICS? YOU CAN DO YOUR RAP AFTER ALBERT. HOW YOU DOING THOUGH? LOOKING A LITTLE TENSE THERE.
YEAH, I'M HAVING SOME ISSUES... I TOLD YOU ABOUT THE DEATH THREATS RIGHT?
YEAH... DID YOU TALK TO THAT GIRL ASHLEY ABOUT THAT?

MMM... WE TEXTED EACH OTHER YESTERDAY. SHE SAID HER BROTHER PROBABLY WON'T DO ANYTHING. IT'S NOT AN HONOUR CULTURE...
I'M STILL WORRIED THOUGH. WHEN HE CALLED HE TRIED TO LULL ME INTO A FALSE SENSE OF SECURITY.
HE EVEN PRETENDED NOT TO BE ANGRY... SO I'D GO OVER THERE. IF I HAD THEY'D HAVE BEATEN ME UP FOR SURE.
HE MIGHT BE DOING THE SAME THING NOW. OF COURSE HE'D TELL HIS SISTER EVERYTHING IS COOL.

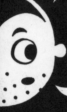

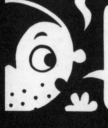

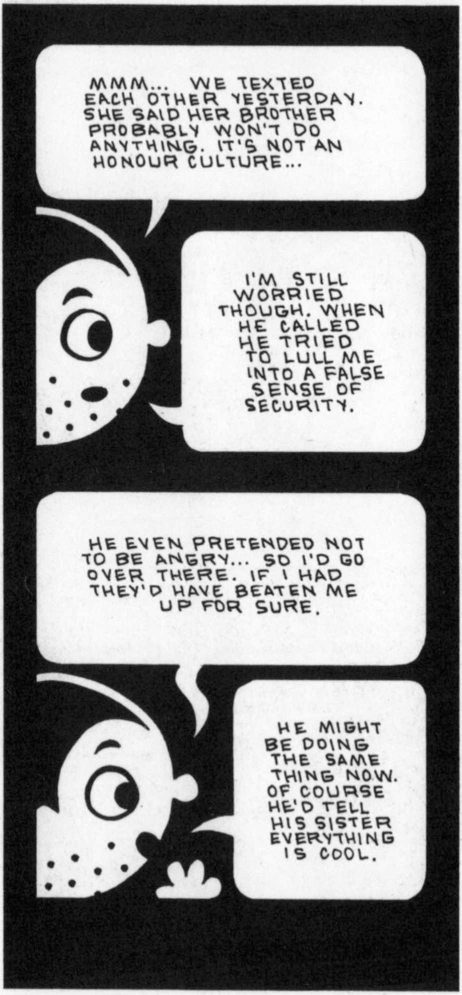

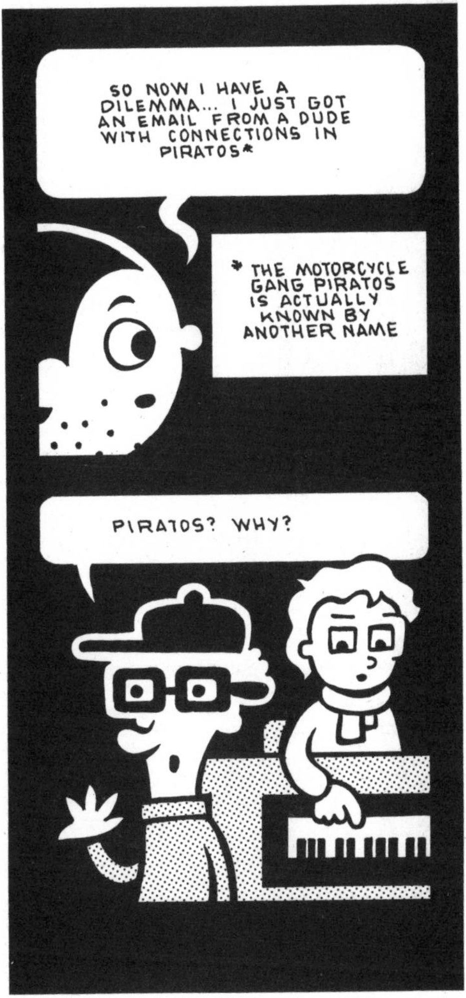
SO NOW I HAVE A DILEMMA... I JUST GOT AN EMAIL FROM A DUDE WITH CONNECTIONS IN PIRATOS*
* THE MOTORCYCLE GANG PIRATOS IS ACTUALLY KNOWN BY ANOTHER NAME
PIRATOS? WHY?

HMM... IT STARTED AT THE HULTSFRED FESTIVAL A COUPLE OF YEARS AGO. WE'D JUST DONE A GIG ON THE DEMO STAGE AND WE WERE HANGING OUT BACKSTAGE.

THIS DUDE COMES UP, REALLY TOUGH LOOKING. I THINK HE WAS SOME ARTIST'S BODY-GUARD OR SOMETHING.

DUDE! YOU'RE A RAPPER, RIGHT? LAS PALMAS?

UH... YEAH.

ON ONE OF YOUR TRACKS YOU SAY "THE PIRATOS BOSS SELLS PHONE SEX."

NAAAH... I KNOW WHAT LINE YOU MEAN... BUT THAT'S US FEATURING SPAKUR. HE'S KIDDING, SAYING **HE'S** IN PIRATOS AND SELLING PHONE SEX.

HE SHOWED ME PHOTOS ON HIS CELL PHONE OF SOME EMBLEMS AND PEOPLE WEARING PIRATOS VESTS.

YOU SHOULDN'T SAY THINGS LIKE THAT.

I NEARLY SHAT MYSELF **COMPLETELY.**

BUT... LIKE... IT'S...

NEVERMIND THAT NOW! WE DIG LAS PALMAS! WE WERE LISTENING TO YOU GUYS IN THE CAR ALL THE WAY HERE. HA HA!
I GOT A BEER AND A SMALL PIECE OF HASHISH.
YOU GUYS SHOULD DO A GIG AT ONE OF OUR PARTIES... WHAT'S YOUR PHONE NUMBER?

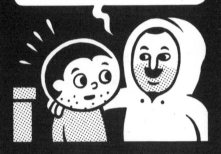

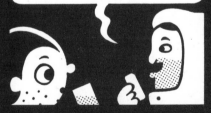

SO SINCE THEN, HE AND HIS FRIENDS CALL ME SOMETIMES... BUT I'VE BEEN VERY HESITANT TO GET INVOLVED.

NOW I'M SORT OF TOYING WITH THE IDEA. HE EMAILED ME YESTERDAY AND ASKED IF WE WANTED TO DO A GIG AT A MARITAL ARTS GALA IN GOTHENBURG.

MAYBE I COULD ARRANGE TO THREATEN THE GUYS WHO THREATENED ME.

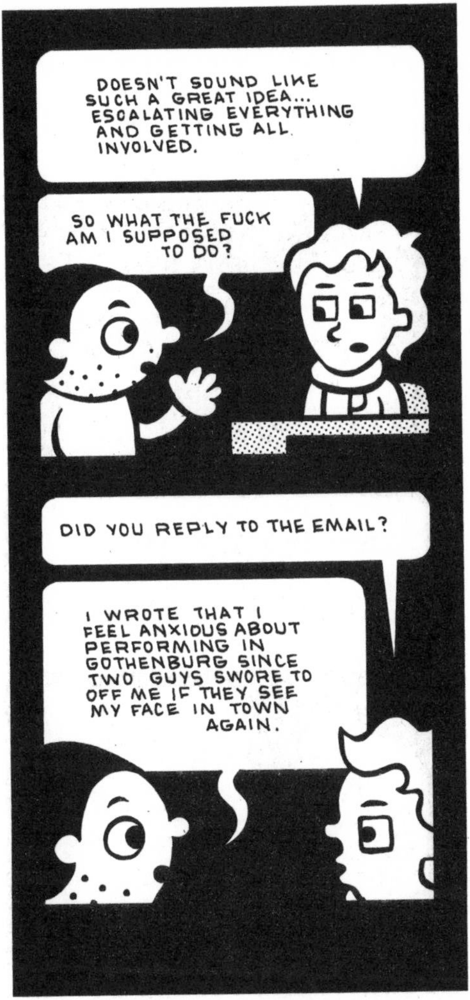
DOESN'T SOUND LIKE SUCH A GREAT IDEA... ESCALATING EVERYTHING AND GETTING ALL INVOLVED.
SO WHAT THE FUCK AM I SUPPOSED TO DO?
DID YOU REPLY TO THE EMAIL?
I WROTE THAT I FEEL ANXIOUS ABOUT PERFORMING IN GOTHENBURG SINCE TWO GUYS SWORE TO OFF ME IF THEY SEE MY FACE IN TOWN AGAIN.

GODDAMN... THAT SOUNDS MESSED UP... BUT YEAH... I GET IT. TOUGH.
YEAH... BUT THE HARDEST THING RIGHT NOW IS THE WHOLE DEAL WITH JONNA.
WITH THE NEW DUDE?
YEAH.

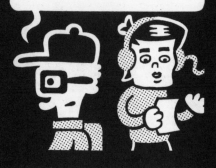

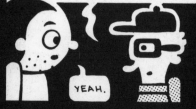

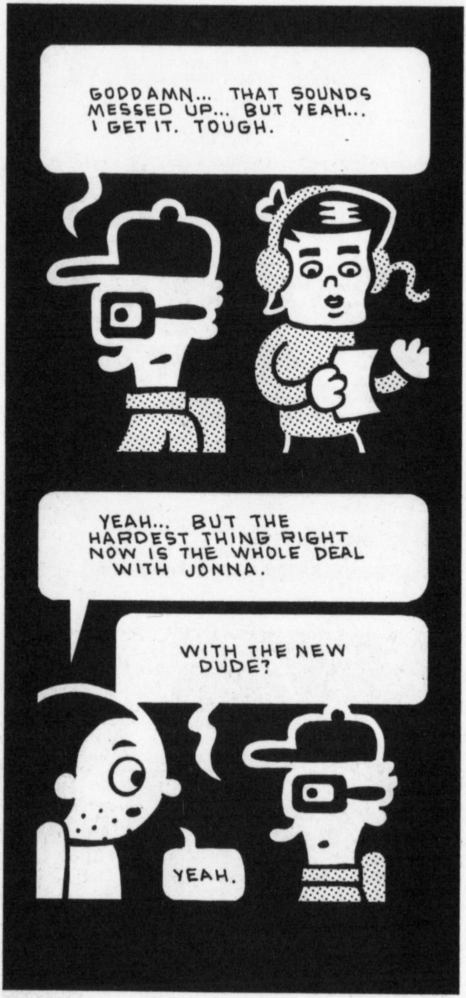

SIMON... ARE YOU SURE SHE'S NOT JUST SAYING THAT TO FUCK WITH YOUR HEAD?
I REALLY DON'T THINK SHE WOULD.
OK HONESTLY... I MET QUITE A FEW OF THE GUYS SHE'S BEEN DATING... THEY'RE... UH...

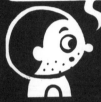

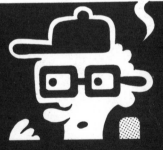

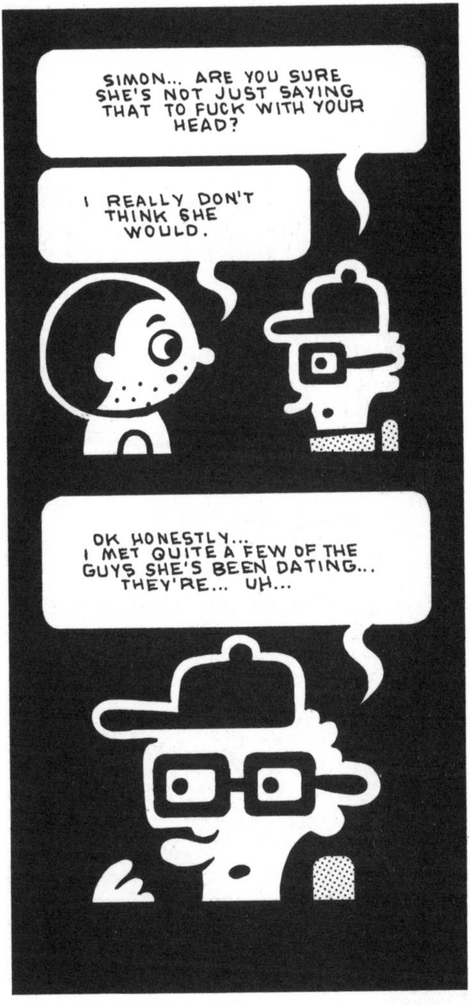

LET ME PUT IT THIS WAY... I CAN ALMOST GUARANTEE SHE'LL RECEIVE YOU WITH OPEN ARMS WHEN YOU COME HOME.
THANKS, FREJ. YEAH... I'M SURE YOU'RE RIGHT. SHE FOUND SOME HOOD RAT IN NORRKÖPING. THAT'S ALL.

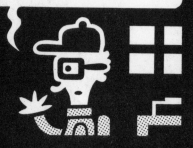

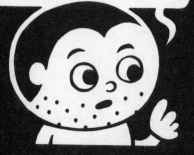

I'M FUCKING SIMON GÄRDENFORS.
ONCE YOU'VE TRIED THE MACK THERE'S NO TURNING BACK!
bibi-bibi-biPF
IT NEVER SHUTS UP. THERE'S BARELY ANY RECEPTION OUT HERE IN THE BOONDOCKS EITHER.

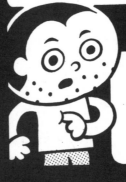

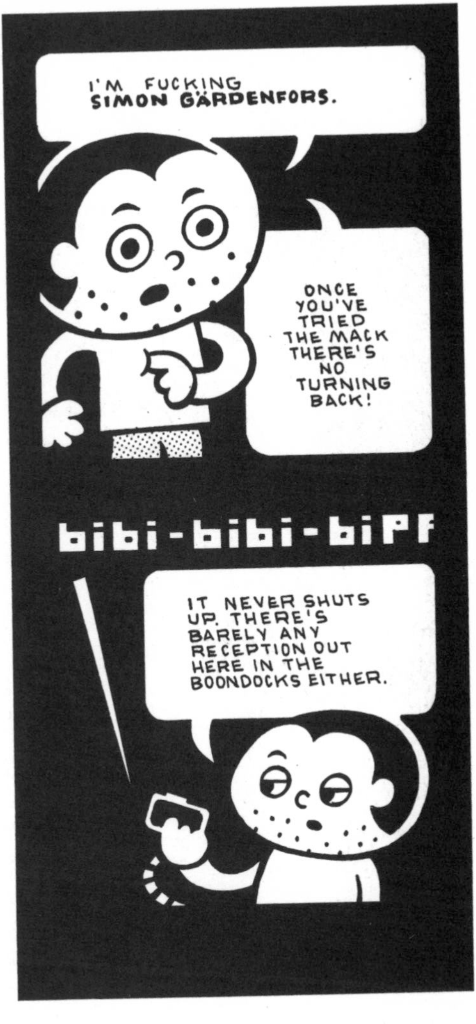

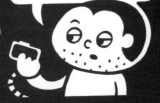

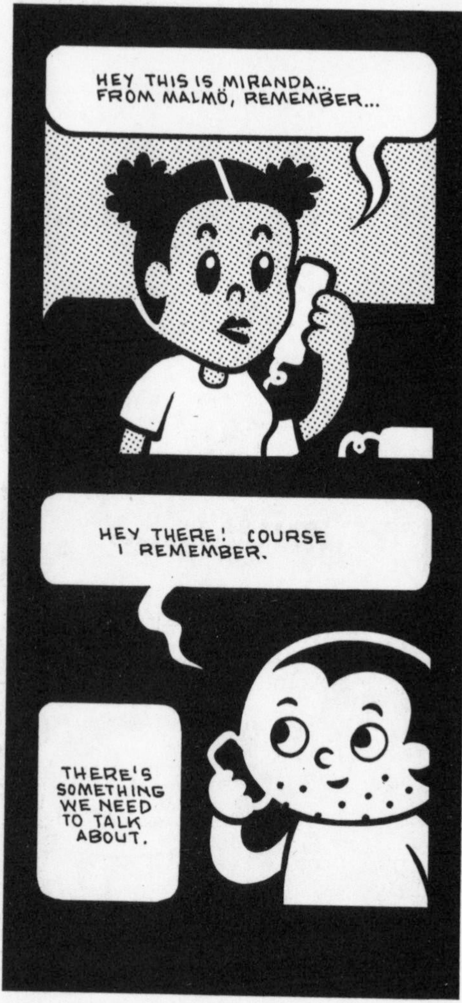
HEY THIS IS MIRANDA... FROM MALMÖ, REMEMBER...
HEY THERE! COURSE I REMEMBER.
THERE'S SOMETHING WE NEED TO TALK ABOUT.

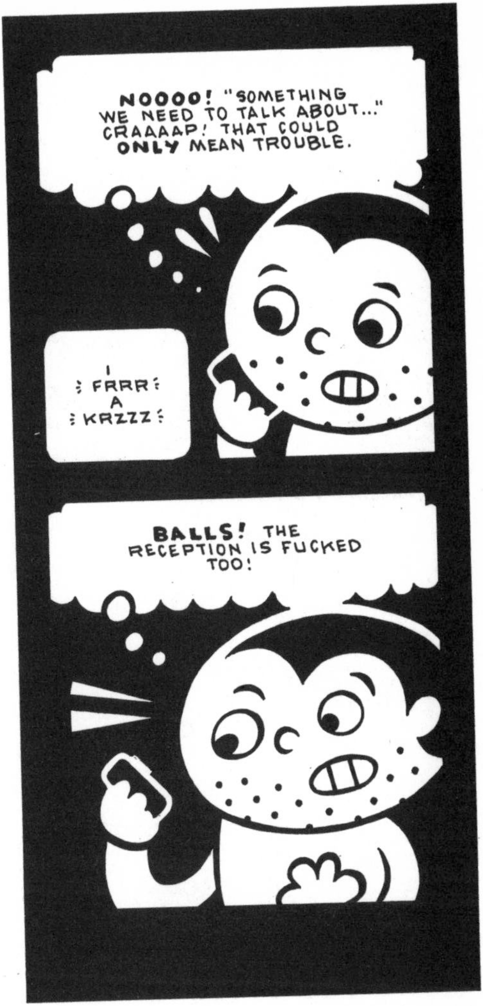
NOOOO! "SOMETHING WE NEED TO TALK ABOUT..." CRAAAAP! THAT COULD ONLY MEAN TROUBLE.
I FRRR A KRZZZ
BALLS! THE RECEPTION IS FUCKED TOO!

SHE'S PREGNANT. I CAN FEEL IT. AAARGH! WHAT THE HELL WAS I THINKING?
SMACK!
I'M SO DAMN STUPID. I DON'T WANT A BABY. NOT EVEN ONE THAT'S SPARKLING AND GOLDEN IN COLOUR. FUCK-ING-HELL!

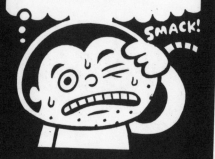

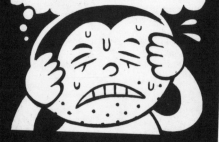

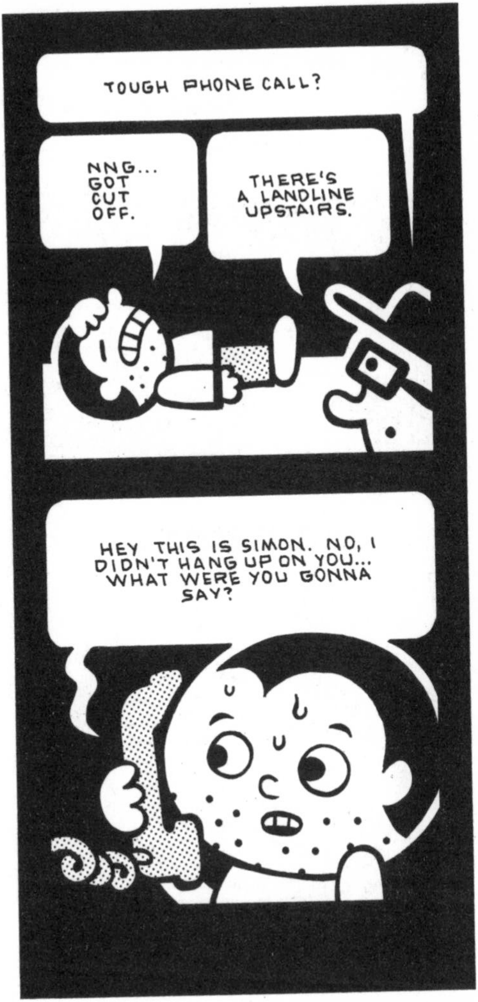
TOUGH PHONE CALL?
NNG... GOT CUT OFF.
THERE'S A LANDLINE UPSTAIRS.
HEY THIS IS SIMON. NO, I DIDN'T HANG UP ON YOU... WHAT WERE YOU GONNA SAY?

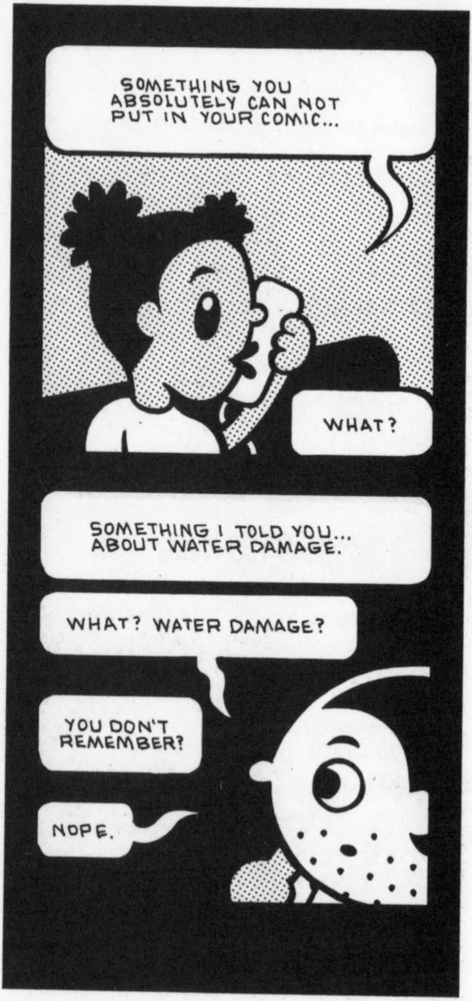
SOMETHING YOU ABSOLUTELY CAN NOT PUT IN YOUR COMIC...
WHAT?
SOMETHING I TOLD YOU... ABOUT WATER DAMAGE.
WHAT? WATER DAMAGE?
YOU DON'T REMEMBER?
NOPE.

WELL YOU WERE COMPLETELY DRUNK. NO WONDER YOU FORGOT I GUESS.
I HAVE NO IDEA WHAT YOU'RE ON ABOUT
GOOD, THEN I DON'T HAVE TO WORRY ABOUT YOU INCLUDING THIS IN YOUR BOOK.
AAAH! I'M SO HAPPY. I THOUGHT YOU WERE KNOCKED UP.
NOPE... NO NEED TO WORRY.
PHEW. GOT AWAY THIS TIME!

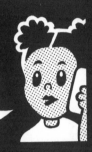

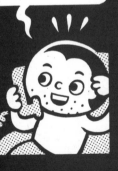

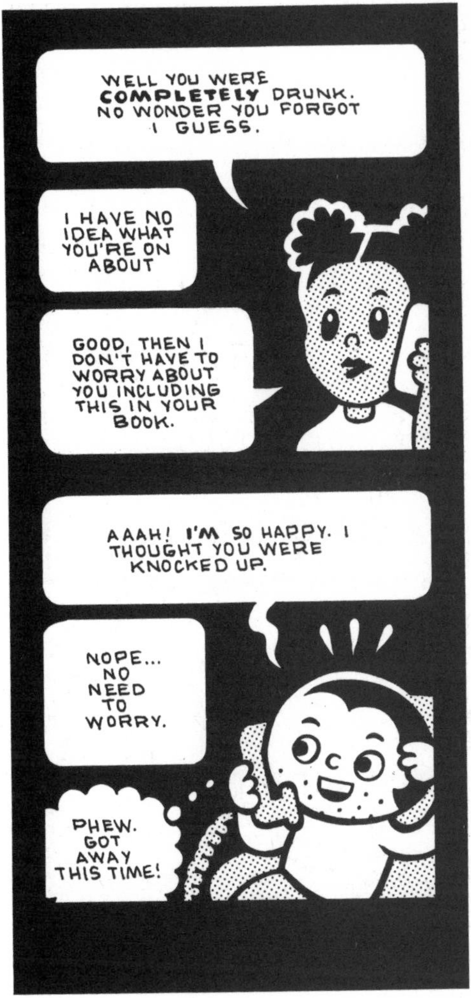

SO WHAT WAS THE WATER DAMAGE THING?
LET'S NOT GET INTO THAT. YOU HAVE A GOOD DAY NOW.
CLICK!

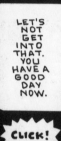

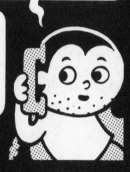

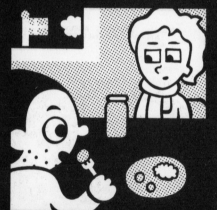

YOU THINK YOUR COMIC WILL BE GOOD THEN? YOU SEEM TO'VE COLLECTED QUITE A BIT OF MATERIAL.
YEAH... THERE'S ALREADY AN ABUNDANCE OF ANECDOTES. I JUST HAVE TO PICK OUT THE BEST ONES.

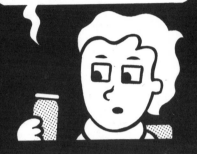

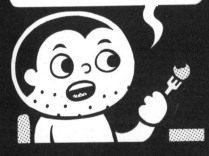

BUT DAMN... I'M AGONIZING ABOUT THIS RELEASE.
WHY'S THAT?
UH, YOU KNOW... GETTING DIRTY WITH SCHOOLGIRLS AND STUFF. LIKE... HOW WILL I EVER LOOK MY MOTHER IN THE EYE?

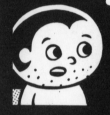

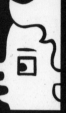

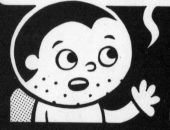

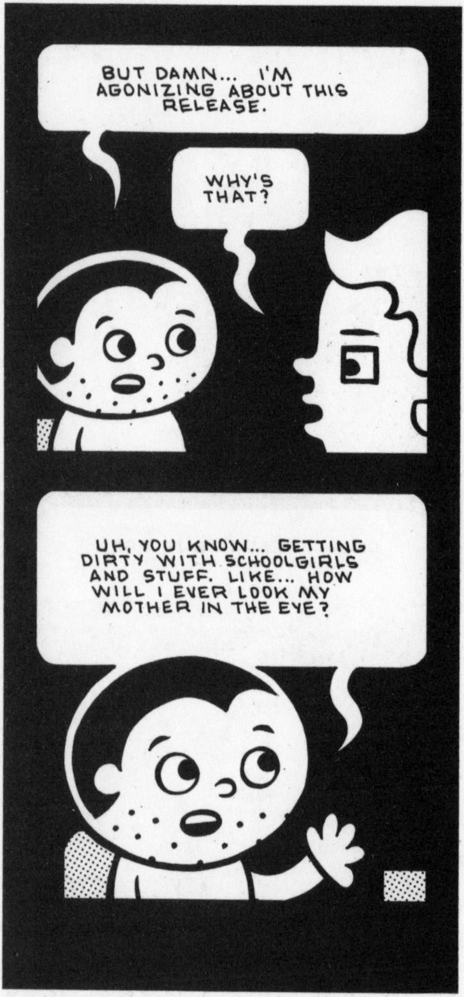

WHAT YOU'RE DOING IS TOTALLY LEGAL, SIMON.

YOU KNOW THE RULES.

LEGAL, YEAH... BUT NOT SOCIALLY ACCEPTABLE.

SEX WITH ANIMALS IS LEGAL... BUT NOT MANY PEOPLE WOULD CONSIDER THAT OK.

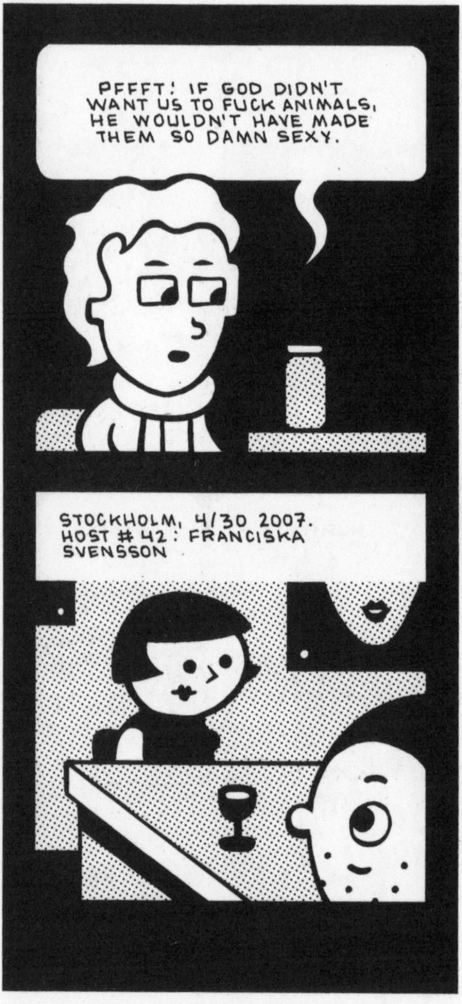
PFFFT! IF GOD DIDN'T WANT US TO FUCK ANIMALS, HE WOULDN'T HAVE MADE THEM SO DAMN SEXY.
STOCKHOLM, 4/30 2007. HOST # 42: FRANCISKA SVENSSON

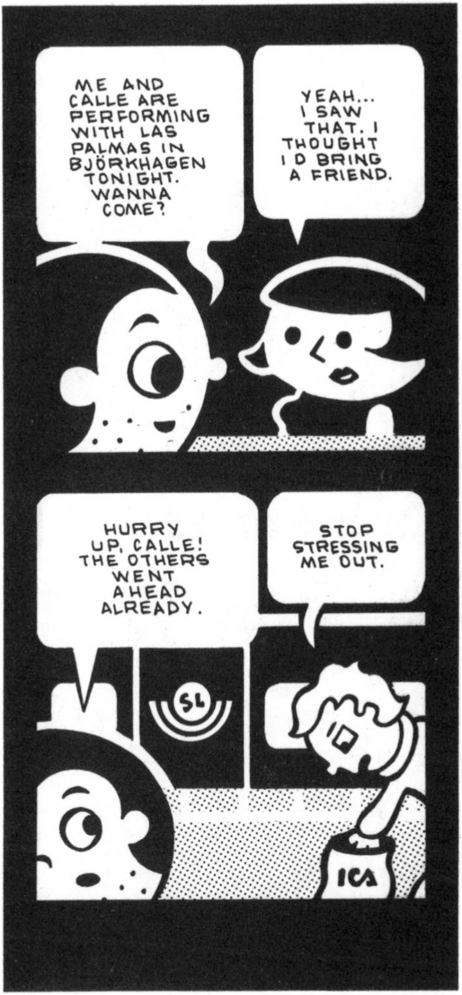
ME AND CALLE ARE PERFORMING WITH LAS PALMAS IN BJÖRKHAGEN TONIGHT. WANNA COME?
YEAH... I SAW THAT. I THOUGHT I'D BRING A FRIEND.
HURRY UP, CALLE! THE OTHERS WENT AHEAD ALREADY.
STOP STRESSING ME OUT.
SL
ICA

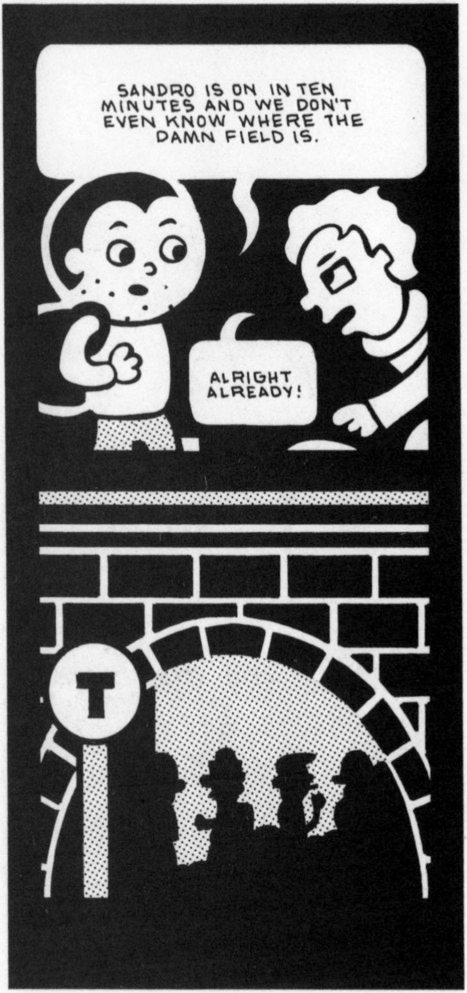
SANDRO IS ON IN TEN MINUTES AND WE DON'T EVEN KNOW WHERE THE DAMN FIELD IS.
ALRIGHT ALREADY!

EXCUSE ME KIDS... WE'RE LOOKING FOR A FIELD NEARBY WHERE A BUNCH OF BANDS ARE SUPPOSED TO PLAY.
IT'S THAT WAY.
NAH, LIKE WE'RE SUPPOSED TO FOLLOW THE TRACKS THAT WAY... BUT AFTER THAT I DUNNO.

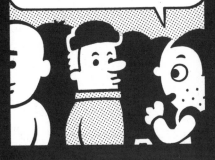

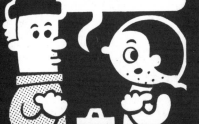

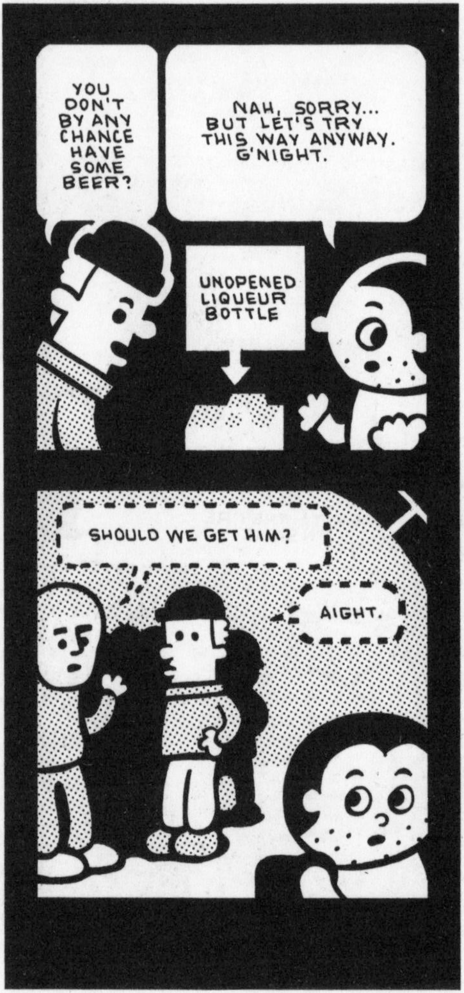
YOU DON'T BY ANY CHANCE HAVE SOME BEER?
NAH, SORRY... BUT LET'S TRY THIS WAY ANYWAY. G'NIGHT.
UNOPENED LIQUEUR BOTTLE
SHOULD WE GET HIM?
AIGHT.

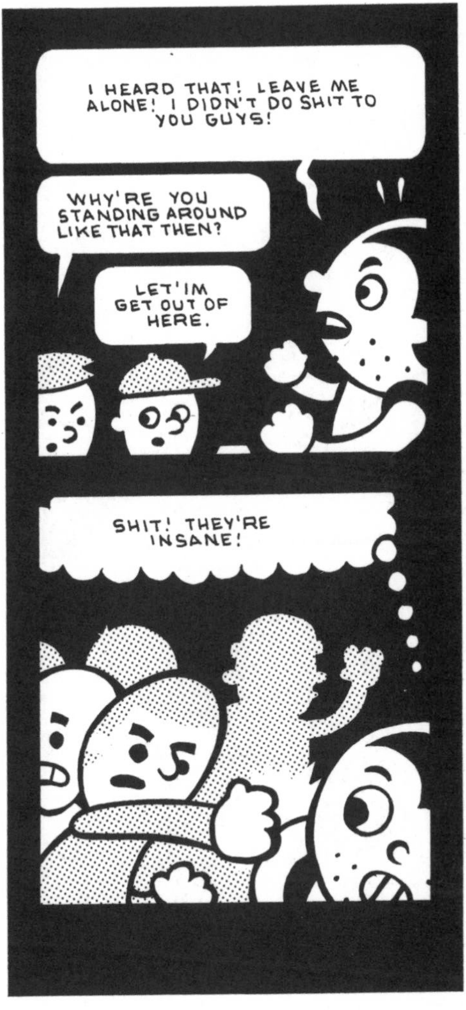
I HEARD THAT! LEAVE ME ALONE! I DIDN'T DO SHIT TO YOU GUYS!
WHY'RE YOU STANDING AROUND LIKE THAT THEN?
LET'IM GET OUT OF HERE.
SHIT! THEY'RE INSANE!

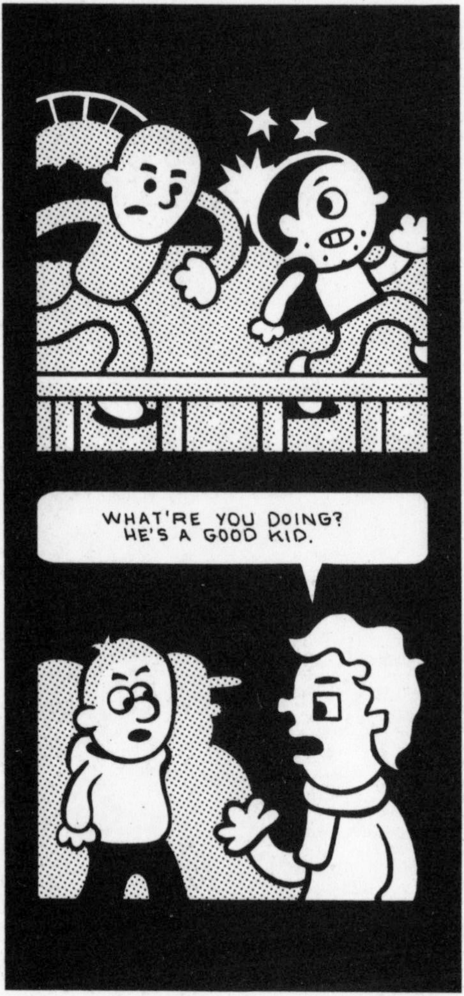
WHAT'RE YOU DOING? HE'S A GOOD KID.

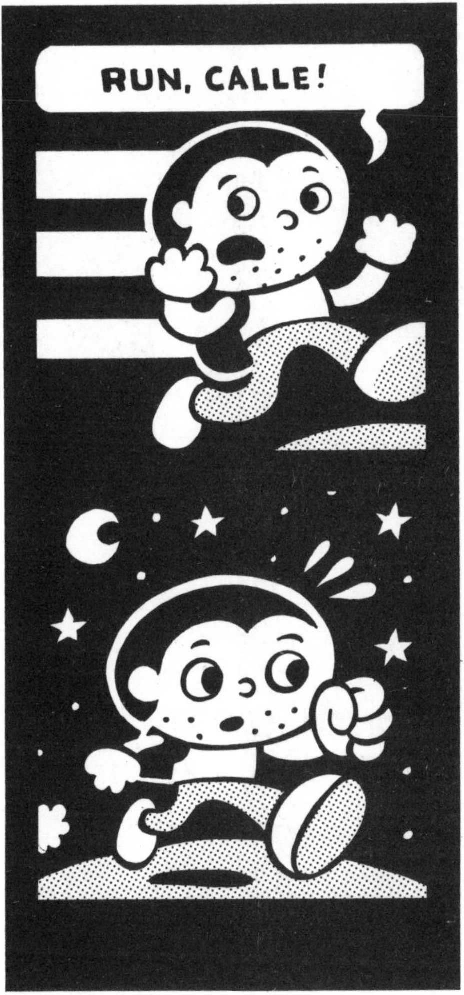
RUN, CALLE!

I THINK I GOT AWAY... BUT WHERE IS CALLE? I GOTTA GO BACK AND CHECK...
PANT! PANT!
WHAT THE FUCK! THEY'RE KICKING HIM IN THE HEAD!

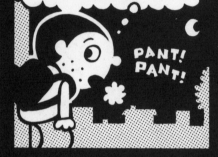

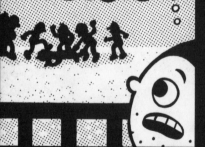

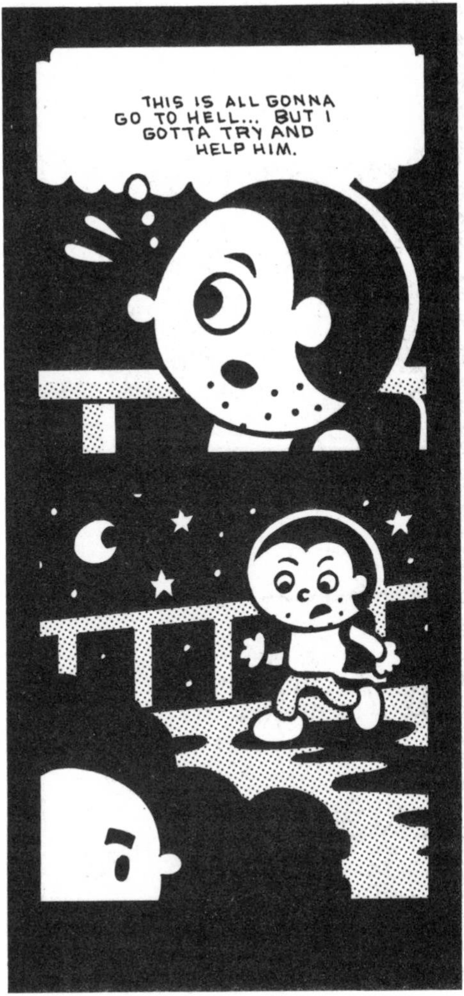
THIS IS ALL GONNA GO TO HELL... BUT I GOTTA TRY AND HELP HIM.

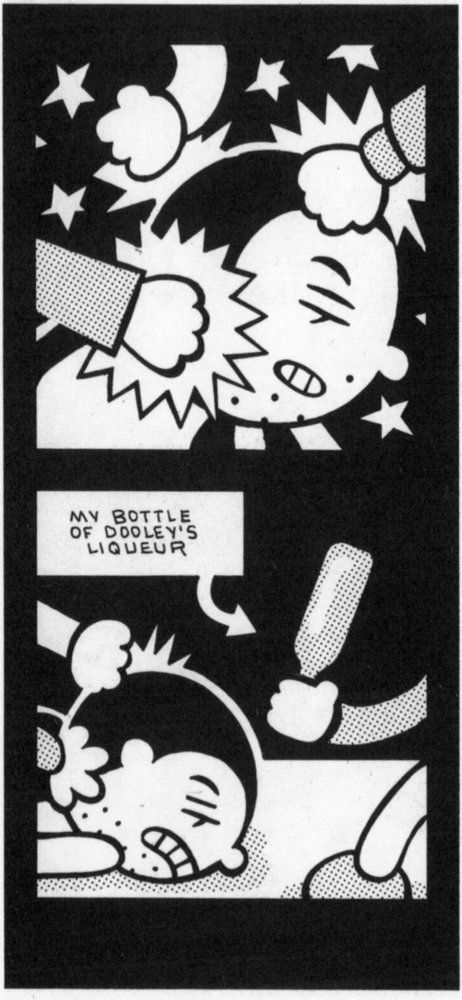
MY BOTTLE OF DOOLEY'S LIQUEUR

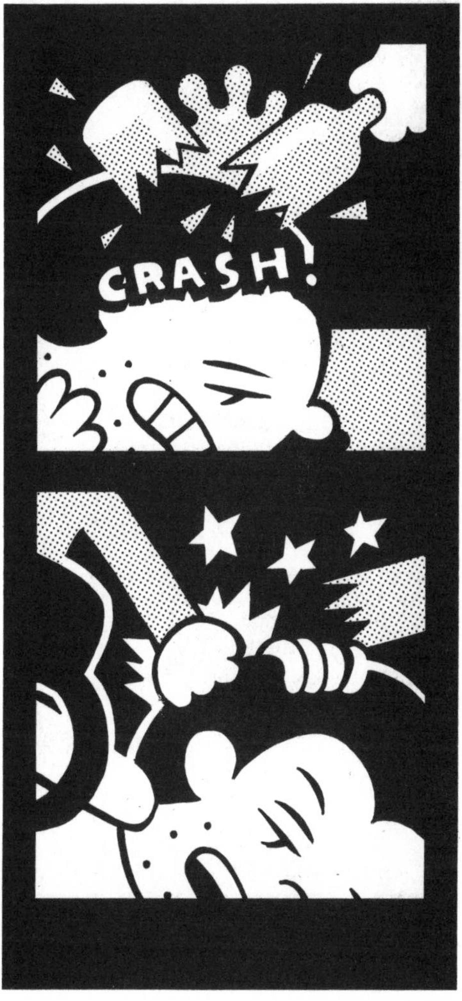
CRASH!

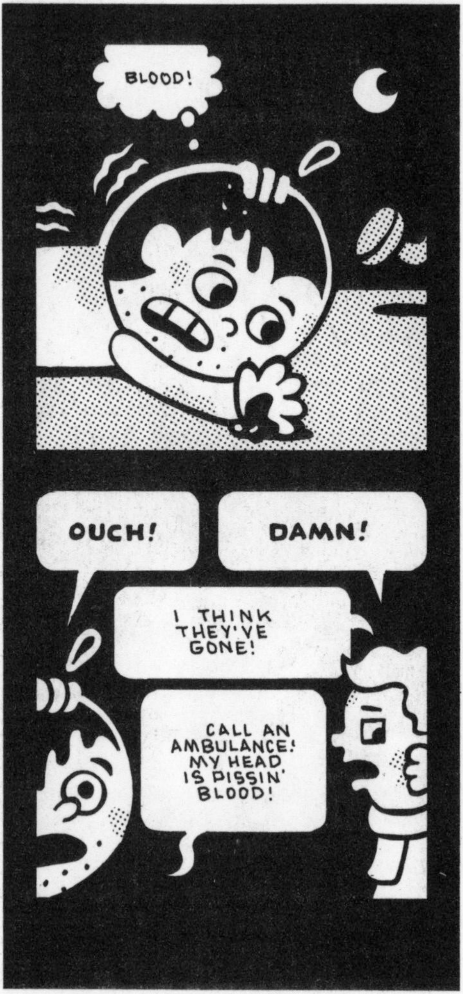
BLOOD!
OUCH!
DAMN!
I THINK THEY'VE GONE!
CALL AN AMBULANCE! MY HEAD IS PISSIN' BLOOD!

AND THEY STOLE ALL MY SHIT!
ASSHOLES!

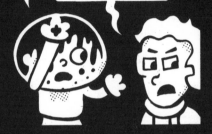

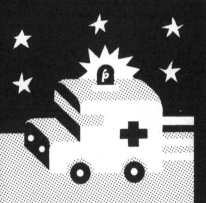

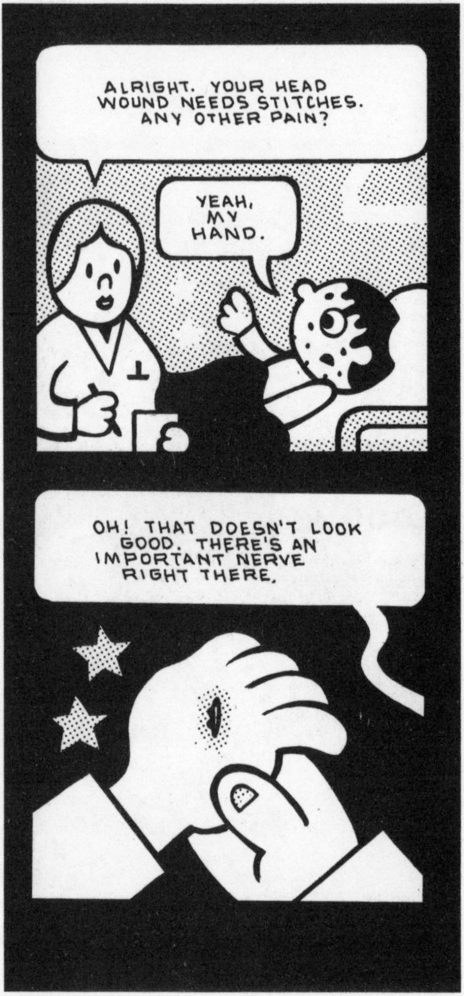

ALRIGHT. YOUR HEAD WOUND NEEDS STITCHES. ANY OTHER PAIN?
YEAH, MY HAND.
OH! THAT DOESN'T LOOK GOOD. THERE'S AN IMPORTANT NERVE RIGHT THERE.

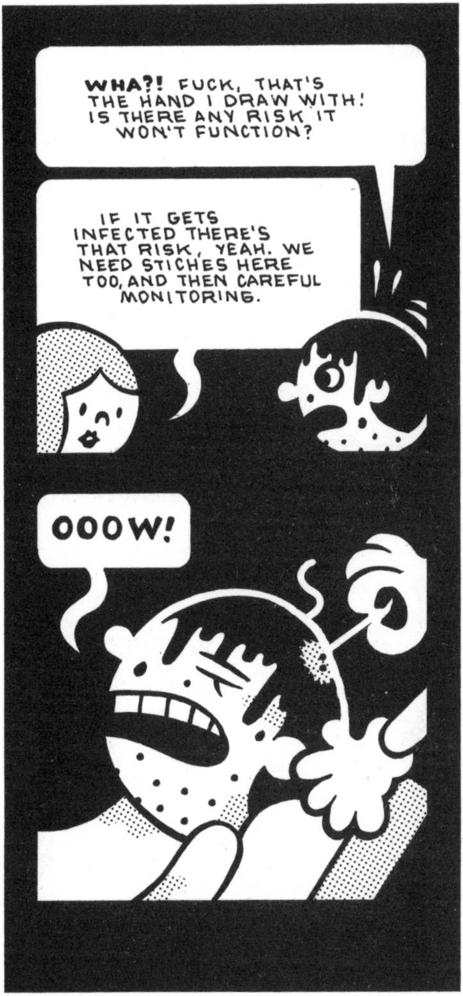
WHA?! FUCK, THAT'S THE HAND I DRAW WITH! IS THERE ANY RISK IT WON'T FUNCTION?
IF IT GETS INFECTED THERE'S THAT RISK, YEAH. WE NEED STICHES HERE TOO, AND THEN CAREFUL MONITORING.
OOOW!

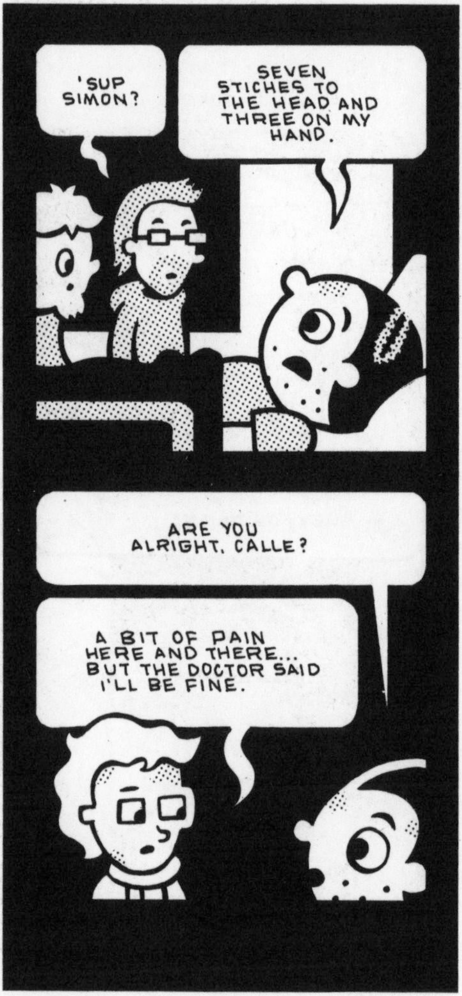
'SUP SIMON?
SEVEN STICHES TO THE HEAD AND THREE ON MY HAND.
ARE YOU ALRIGHT, CALLE?
A BIT OF PAIN HERE AND THERE... BUT THE DOCTOR SAID I'LL BE FINE.

STOCKHOLM, 5/1 2007.
HOST # 43: SARA
NORMAN HECKSCHER
KNOCK
KNOCK
HEY, OH DAMN!

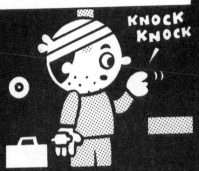

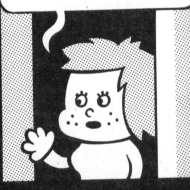

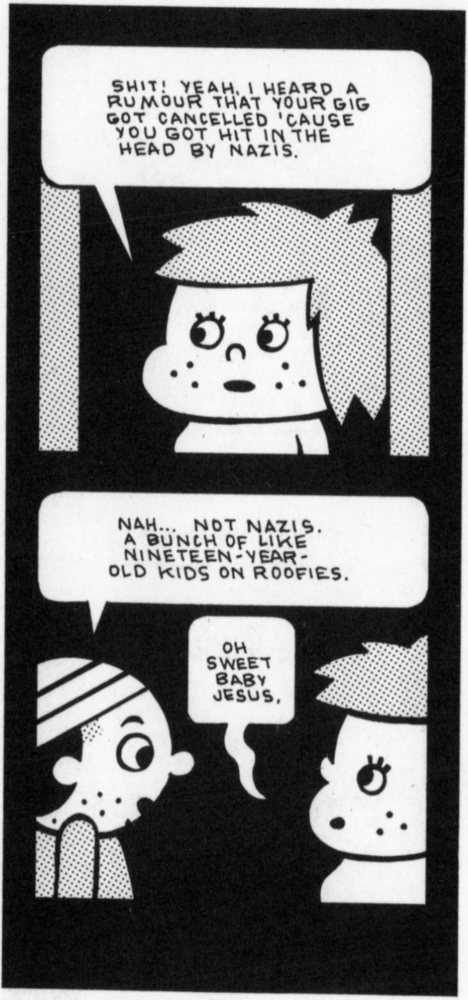
SHIT! YEAH, I HEARD A RUMOUR THAT YOUR GIG GOT CANCELLED 'CAUSE YOU GOT HIT IN THE HEAD BY NAZIS.
NAH... NOT NAZIS. A BUNCH OF LIKE NINETEEN-YEAR-OLD KIDS ON ROOFIES.
OH SWEET BABY JESUS.

BLAH BLAH AND SO MY DAD SHOWS DRUNK OFF HIS ASS IN THE MIDDLE OF THE DAY AND I THREW HIM OUT BLAH BLAH SO TODAY I GOT THIS EMAIL WHERE HE SAID I WAS LIKE A REGULAR MALCONTENT SWEDISH PERSON AND I FOUND THAT INCREDIBLY UNFAIR AND BLAH BLAH
SHE SEEMS LIKE A LOT OF FUN, BUT I CAN'T CONCENTRATE ON WHAT SHE'S SAYING.
I'M SORRY, BUT I HAVE TO GO TO BED SOON, I HAVEN'T BEEN ABLE TO SLEEP MUCH.
SURE! TAKE THE COUCH.

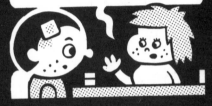

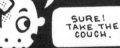

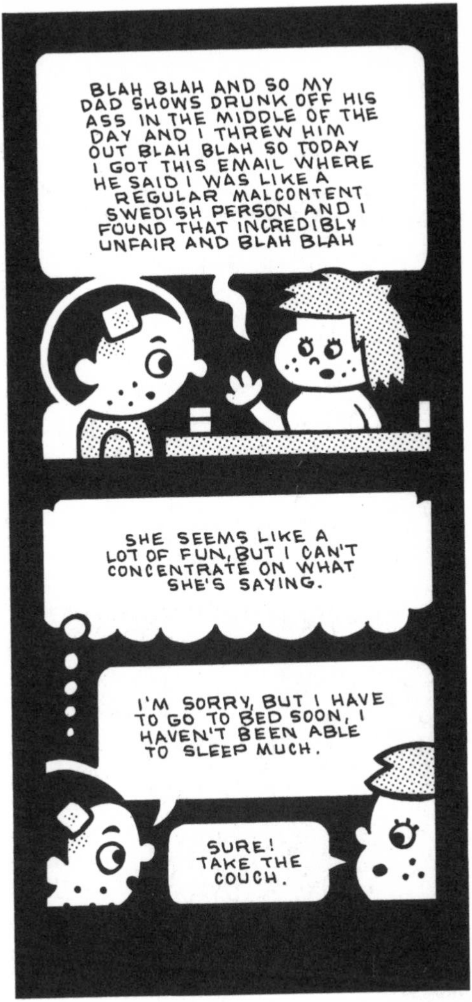

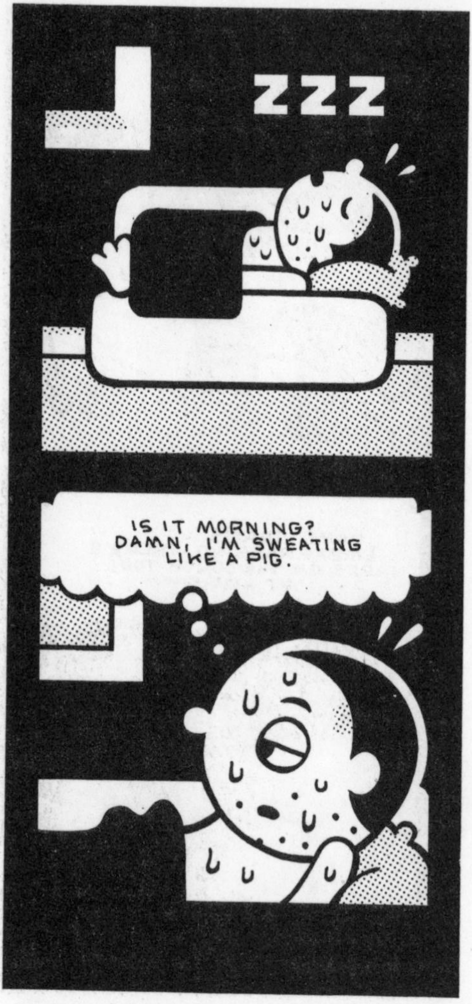
ZZZ
IS IT MORNING? DAMN, I'M SWEATING LIKE A PIG.

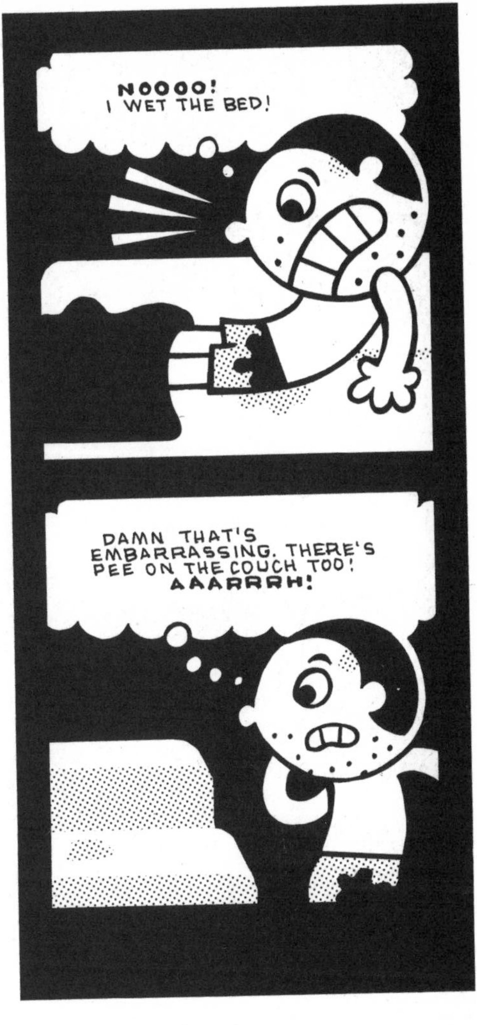
NOOOO!
I WET THE BED!
DAMN THAT'S EMBARRASSING. THERE'S PEE ON THE COUCH TOO! AAARRRH!

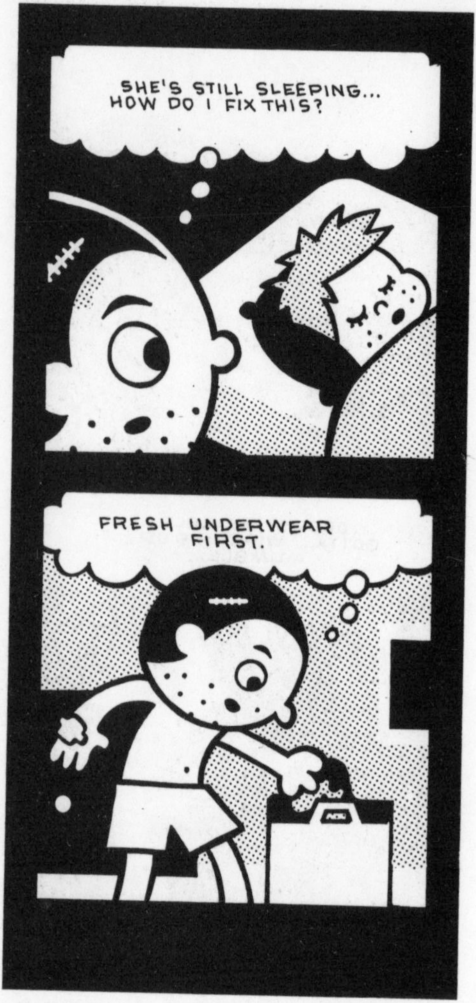
SHE'S STILL SLEEPING... HOW DO I FIX THIS?
FRESH UNDERWEAR FIRST.

THEN A GLASS OF WATER THAT I'LL PRETEND TO'VE KNOCKED OVER.
OOOPS! MUMBLE... GOTTA... WIPE THIS UP... MUMBLE...
PLINK

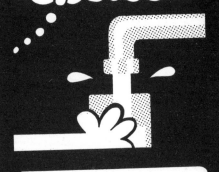

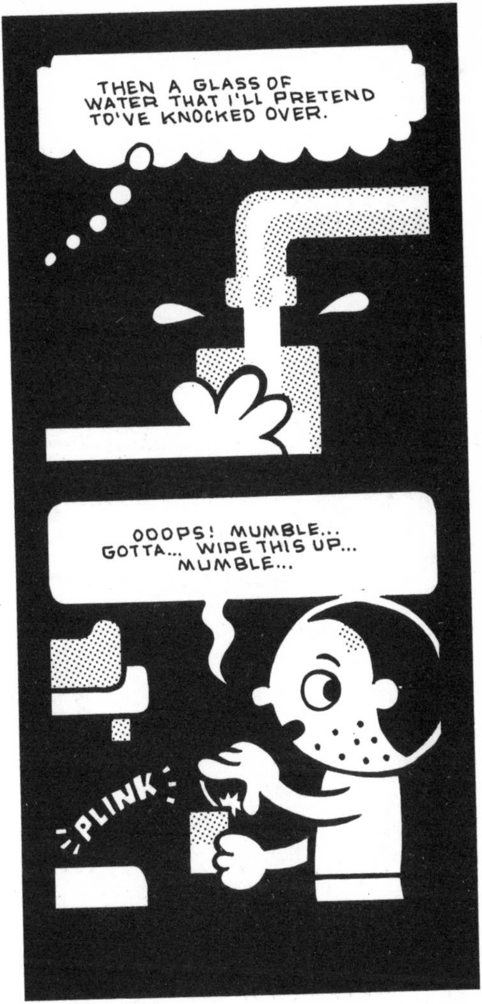

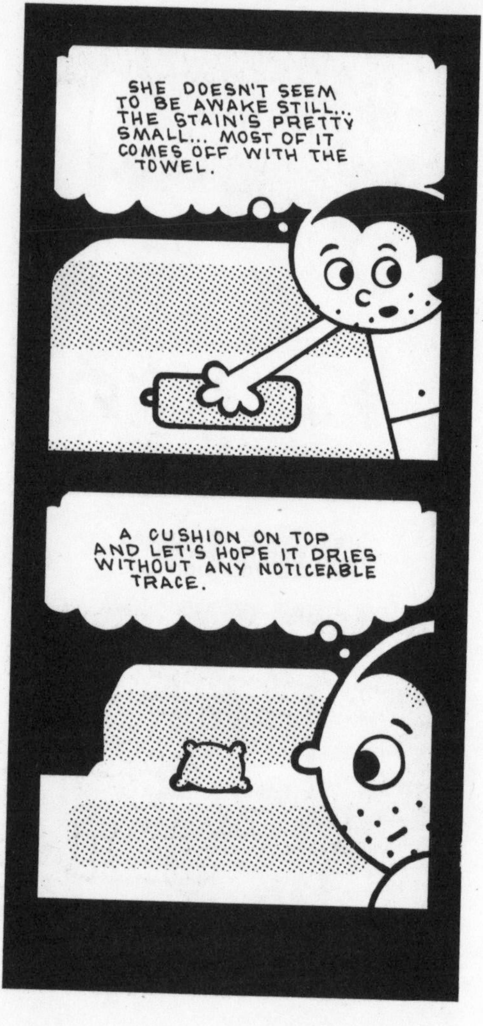
SHE DOESN'T SEEM TO BE AWAKE STILL... THE STAIN'S PRETTY SMALL... MOST OF IT COMES OFF WITH THE TOWEL.
A CUSHION ON TOP AND LET'S HOPE IT DRIES WITHOUT ANY NOTICEABLE TRACE.

bibi-bibi
biPPi-bi
HEY, THIS IS LINDA,
YOUR SUBTENANT...
HOW'RE YOU DOING?

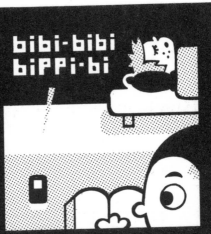

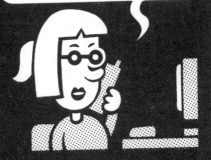

UH... NOT SO GOOD. I JUST HAD TEN STITCHES AT THE HOSPITAL. I GOT MUGGED AND BEAT UP LAST NIGHT.
OH MY GOD THAT SOUNDS AWFUL!
IT MIGHT BE THE WRONG TIME TO BRING THIS UP THEN BUT... THE REASON I'M CALLING IS THAT YOU HAVE FLEAS IN YOUR APARTEMENT. I HAVE BITES ALL OVER.

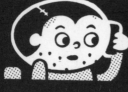

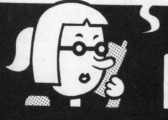

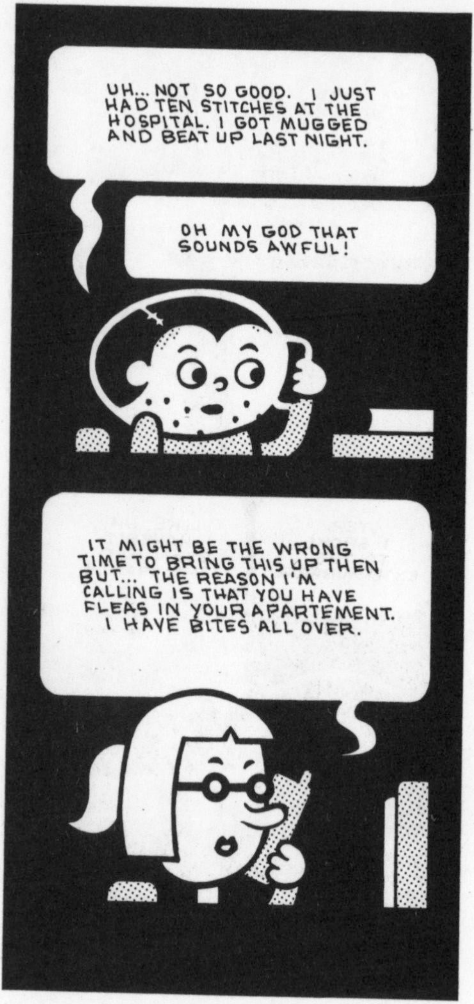

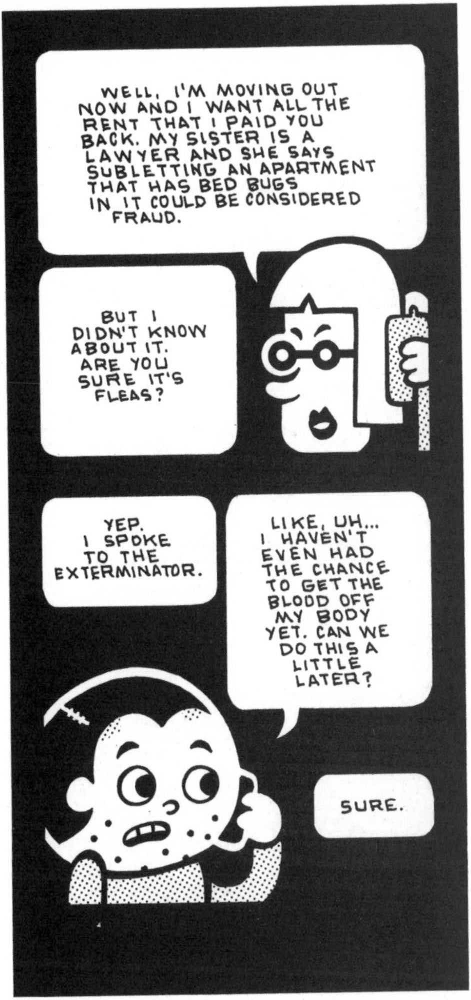
WELL, I'M MOVING OUT NOW AND I WANT ALL THE RENT THAT I PAID YOU BACK. MY SISTER IS A LAWYER AND SHE SAYS SUBLETTING AN APARTMENT THAT HAS BED BUGS IN IT COULD BE CONSIDERED FRAUD.
BUT I DIDN'T KNOW ABOUT IT. ARE YOU SURE IT'S FLEAS?
YEP. I SPOKE TO THE EXTERMINATOR.
LIKE, UH... I HAVEN'T EVEN HAD THE CHANCE TO GET THE BLOOD OFF MY BODY YET. CAN WE DO THIS A LITTLE LATER?
SURE.

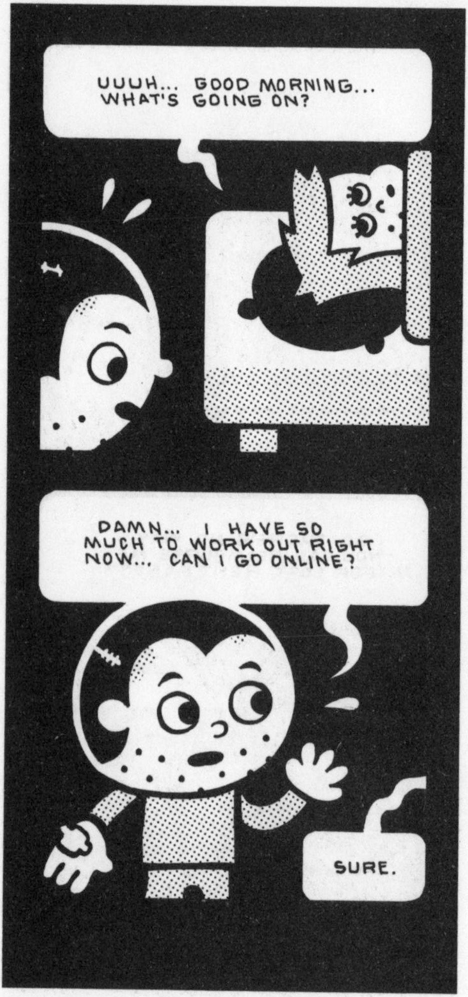
UUUH... GOOD MORNING... WHAT'S GOING ON?
DAMN... I HAVE SO MUCH TO WORK OUT RIGHT NOW..., CAN I GO ONLINE?
SURE.

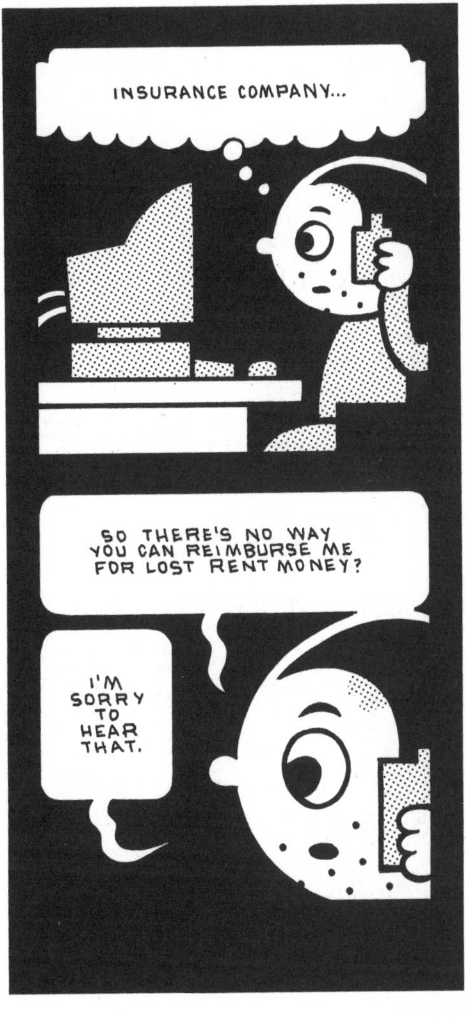
INSURANCE COMPANY...
SO THERE'S NO WAY YOU CAN REIMBURSE ME FOR LOST RENT MONEY?
I'M SORRY TO HEAR THAT.

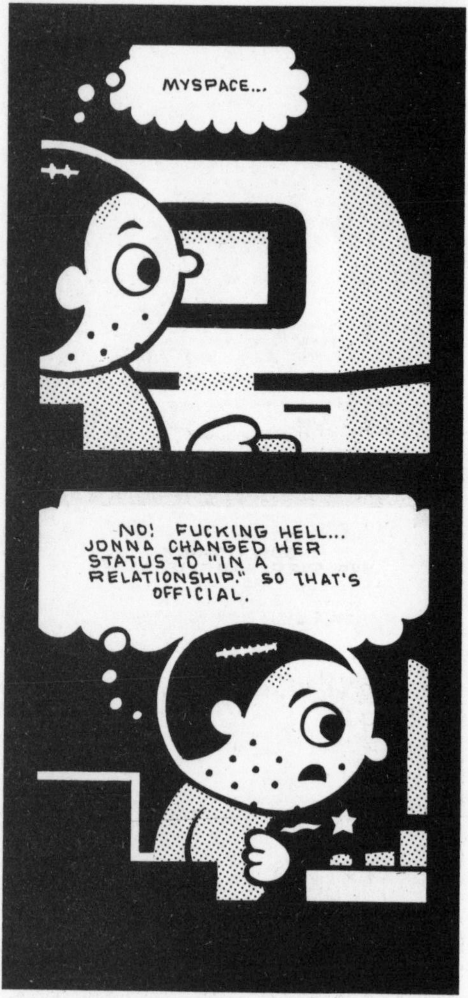
MYSPACE...
NO! FUCKING HELL... JONNA CHANGED HER STATUS TO "IN A RELATIONSHIP." SO THAT'S OFFICIAL.

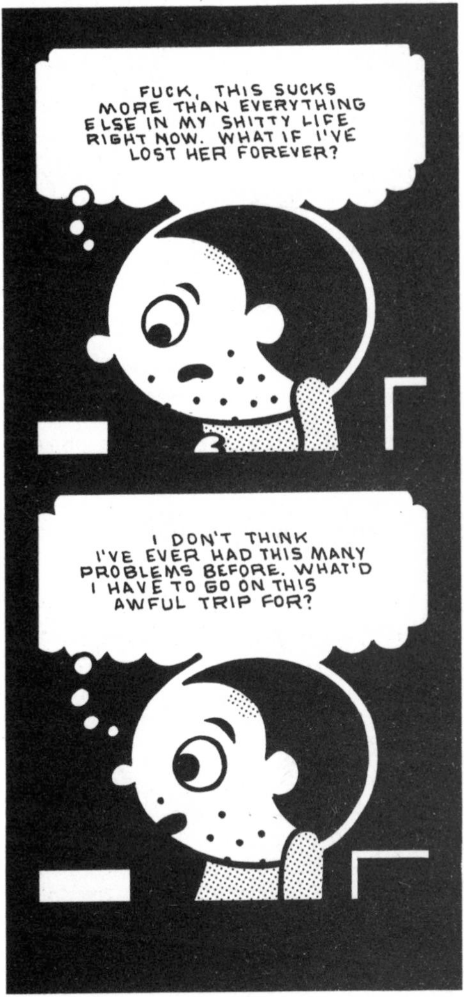
FUCK, THIS SUCKS MORE THAN EVERYTHING ELSE IN MY SHITTY LIFE RIGHT NOW. WHAT IF I'VE LOST HER FOREVER?
I DON'T THINK I'VE EVER HAD THIS MANY PROBLEMS BEFORE. WHAT'D I HAVE TO GO ON THIS AWFUL TRIP FOR?

GOTTA MAKE A LIST OF EVERYTHING. MIGHT GIVE A BIT OF STRUCTURE TO MY MISERY.

PROBLEM # 1: MY THINGS HAVE BEEN STOLEN. THE WORST PART: MY DIARY IS GONE. THE COMIC WILL REALLY SUFFER WITHOUT ALL THE DETAILS I WROTE DOWN AND SKETCHED.

the 120 days of Simon

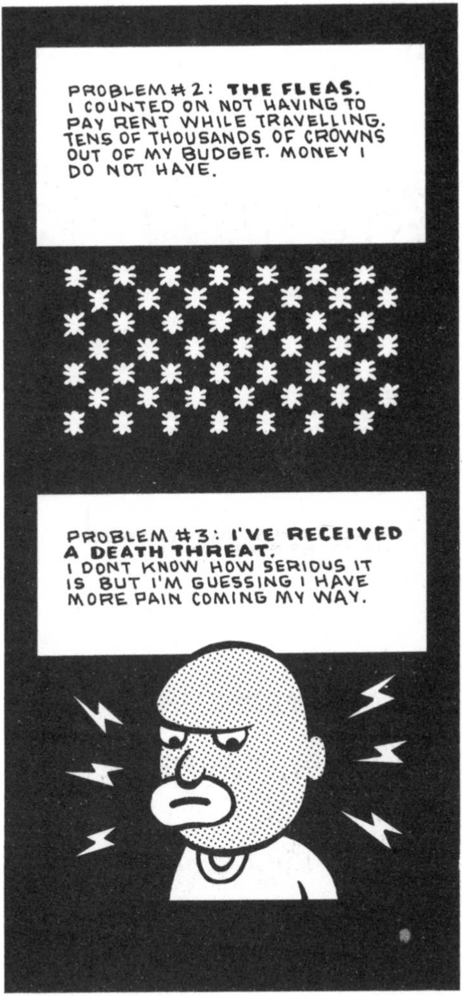

PROBLEM #2: **THE FLEAS.**
I COUNTED ON NOT HAVING TO
PAY RENT WHILE TRAVELLING.
TENS OF THOUSANDS OF CROWNS
OUT OF MY BUDGET. MONEY I
DO NOT HAVE.

PROBLEM #3: **I'VE RECEIVED
A DEATH THREAT.**
I DON'T KNOW HOW SERIOUS IT
IS BUT I'M GUESSING I HAVE
MORE PAIN COMING MY WAY.

PROBLEM #4: **THE WOUND ON MY HAND.**
IF IT DOESN'T HEAL PROPERLY I'LL LOSE MY ABILITY TO DRAW, WHICH MEANS LOSING A BIG PART OF MY LIFE.

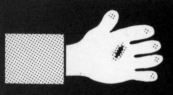

PROBLEM #5: *JONNA.*
I BLEW IT, AND IT WAS THE MOST PROMISING RELATIONSHIP IV'E EVER HAD.

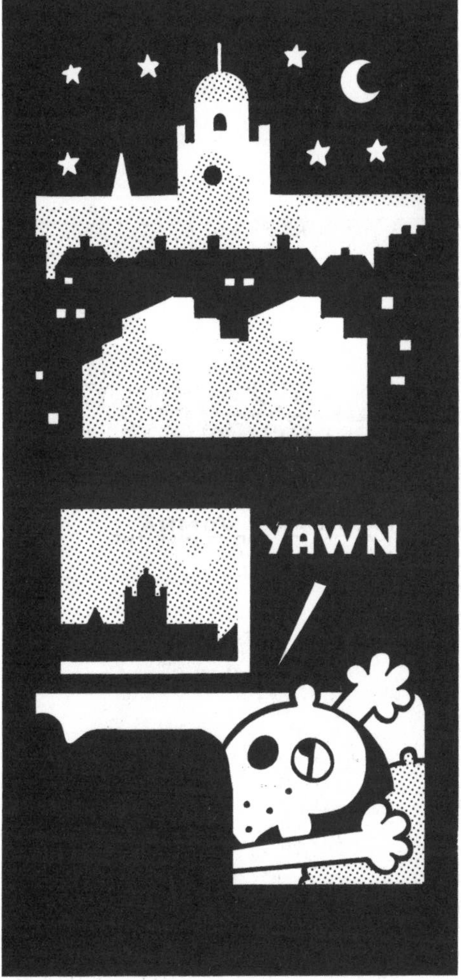
YAWN

HEY... ARE YOU SIMON?

I FOUND A BAG THIS MORNING WHEN I WAS OUT WALKING MY DOG. IT WAS THROWN ON A LAWN. YOUR PHONE NUMBER WAS IN A DIARY THAT LAY NEXT TO IT.

ALMOST EVERYTHING ELSE WAS STOLEN.
melina

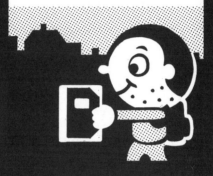

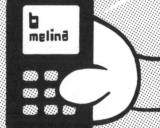

HELLO THERE...
HOW'S YOUR HEAD?
WELL... NO PAIN ACTUALLY. YOU KNOW... I BORROWED FREJ AND MAJA'S APARTMENT TO GET A COUPLE OF DAYS REST. WANNA KEEP ME COMPANY?
COOL. SEE YOU TONIGHT.

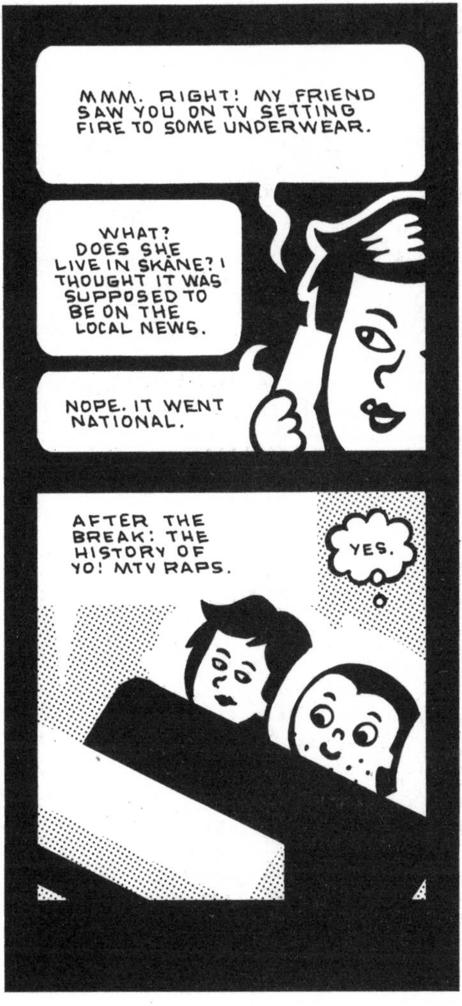
MMM. RIGHT! MY FRIEND SAW YOU ON TV SETTING FIRE TO SOME UNDERWEAR.
WHAT? DOES SHE LIVE IN SKÅNE? I THOUGHT IT WAS SUPPOSED TO BE ON THE LOCAL NEWS.
NOPE. IT WENT NATIONAL.
AFTER THE BREAK: THE HISTORY OF YO! MTV RAPS.
YES.

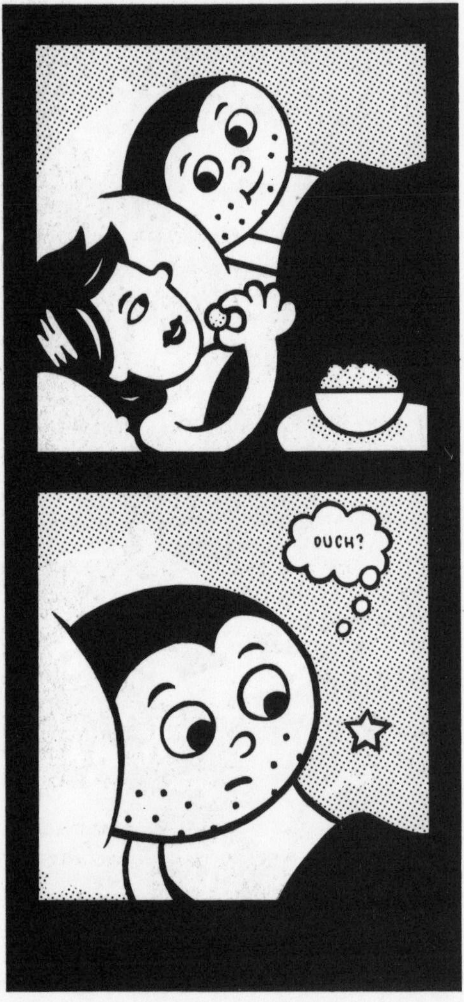
OUCH?

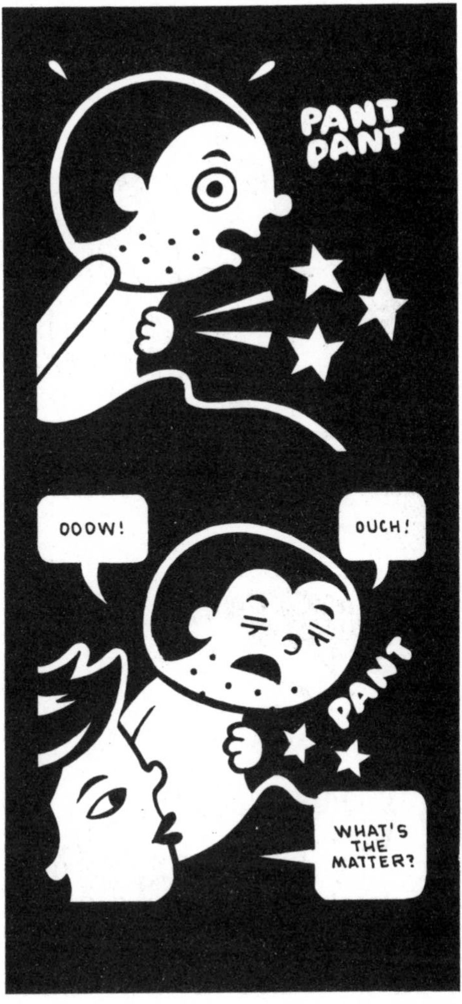

PANT PANT
OOOW!
OUCH!
PANT
WHAT'S THE MATTER?

I'M GETTING... OW... CHEST PAINS. I CAN BARELY BREATHE IN.
THERE'S LIKE PRESSURE AND TENSION OR SOMETHING.
AAAAY! WHAT THE HELL COULD THIS BE?

TYPICAL PANIC ATTACK. I RECOGNIZE IT VERY WELL.
PROBABLY SUBCONSCIOUS STRESS AFTER YOU WERE BEAT UP.
LIE DOWN AND TRY TO BREATHE.
PANIC ATTACK?

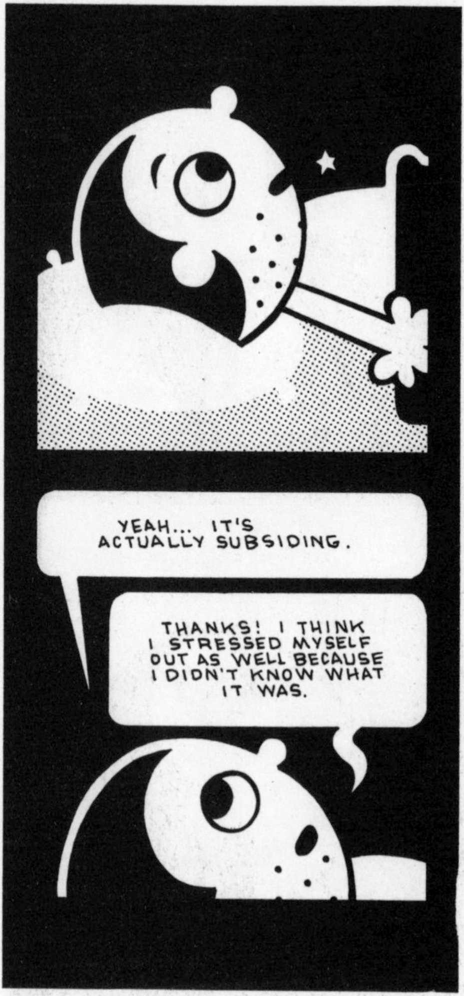
YEAH... IT'S ACTUALLY SUBSIDING.
THANKS! I THINK I STRESSED MYSELF OUT AS WELL BECAUSE I DIDN'T KNOW WHAT IT WAS.

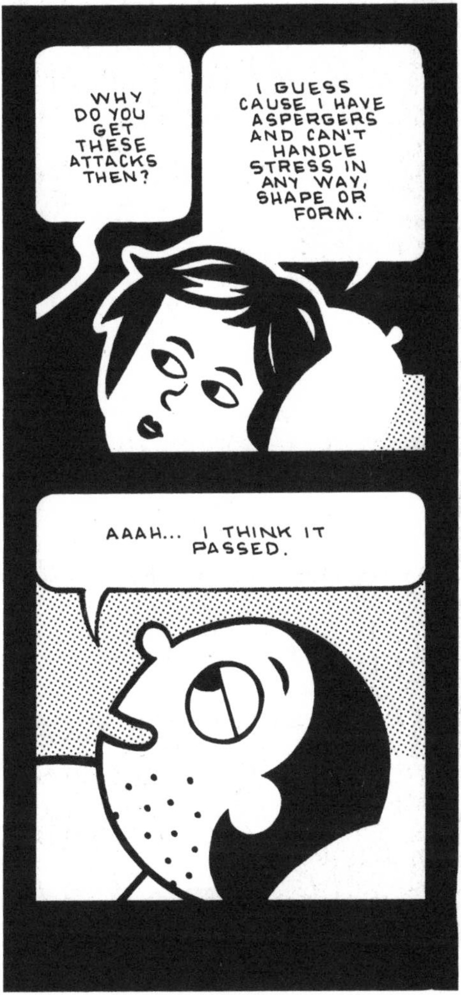
WHY DO YOU GET THESE ATTACKS THEN?
I GUESS CAUSE I HAVE ASPERGERS AND CAN'T HANDLE STRESS IN ANY WAY, SHAPE OR FORM.
AAAH... I THINK IT PASSED.

THIS FEELS GOOD. I FEEL RELIEVED... AS IF I'D HAD A GOOD CRY.
I THINK I'M A LITTLE TOO GOOD AT SUPPRESSING UNCOMFORTABLE FEELINGS.
MAYBE I SHOULD CRY OR SOMETHING.

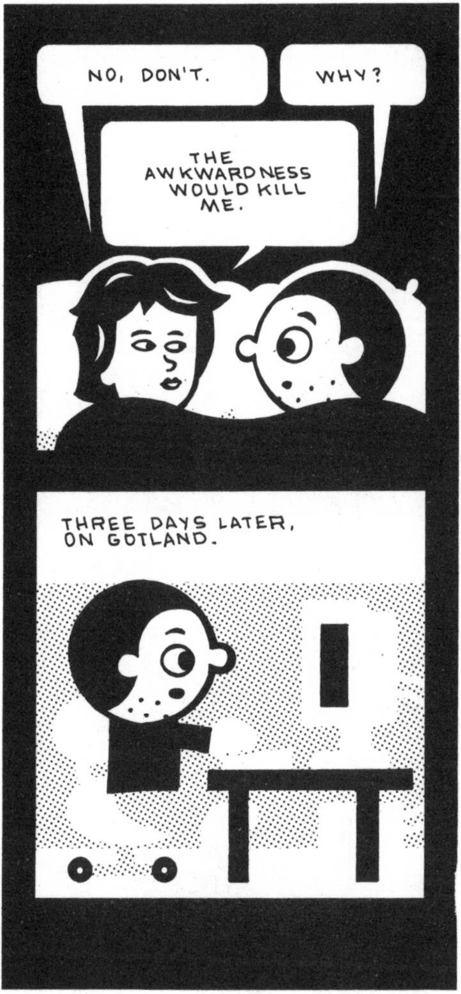
NO, DON'T.
WHY?
THE AWKWARDNESS WOULD KILL ME.
THREE DAYS LATER, ON GOTLAND.

FROM: PIRATE DAHLKVIST
SUBJECT: GIG
HEY, NO NEED TO WORRY WHEN IN GOTHENBURG. IF YOU HAVE THEIR NUMBER I'LL SORT IT OUT. I'LL ASK PIRATOS' GOTHENBURG CHAPTER TO TAKE CARE OF IT SMOOTHLY.
HMM...

HEY, THIS IS ASHLEY.
THIS IS SIMON.
WHAT'S UP WITH YOU?
UH... YOU KNOW WHAT... THIS THING WITH YOUR BROTHER... STILL NOT COMFORTABLE WITH IT.
IS HE IN?
THANKS.

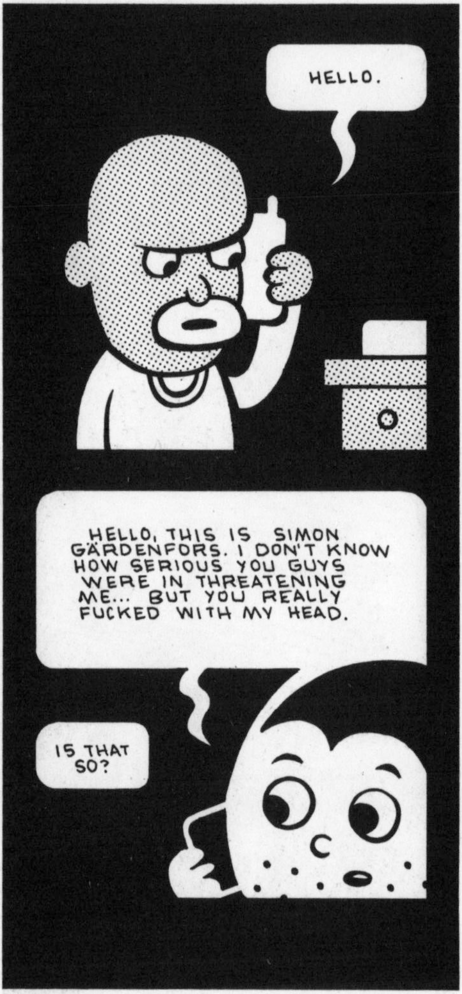
HELLO.
HELLO, THIS IS SIMON GÄRDENFORS. I DON'T KNOW HOW SERIOUS YOU GUYS WERE IN THREATENING ME... BUT YOU REALLY FUCKED WITH MY HEAD.
IS THAT SO?

SO IT'S LIKE THIS... WE WERE ASKED TO DO A GIG IN GOTHENBURG THAT THIS GUY WITH PIRATOS CONNECTIONS IS HELPING ORGANIZE... AND I TOLD HIM ABOUT THE THREAT.

HE ASKED FOR YOUR PHONE NUMBER AND SAID PIRATOS IN GOTHENBURG COULD SORT THIS... I JUST WANTED TO LET YOU KNOW THAT I WON'T GIVE IT TO HIM.

RIGHT.

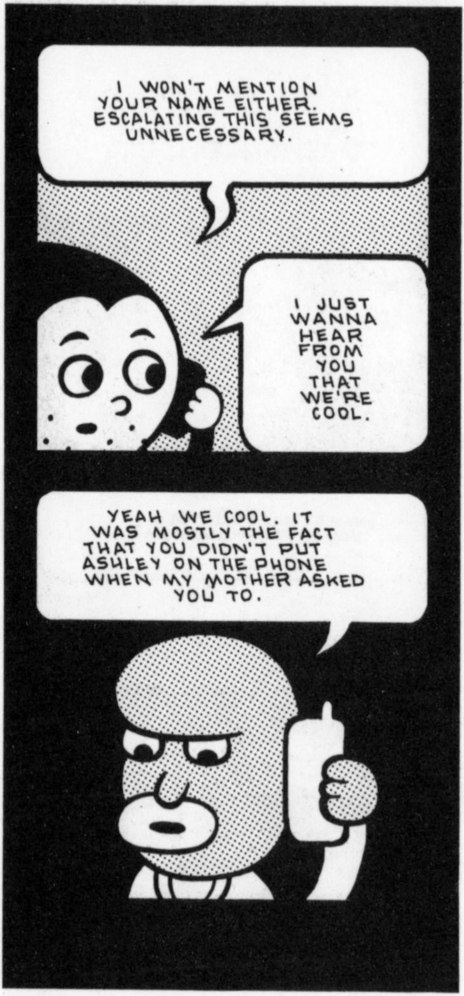
I WON'T MENTION YOUR NAME EITHER. ESCALATING THIS SEEMS UNNECESSARY.
I JUST WANNA HEAR FROM YOU THAT WE'RE COOL.
YEAH WE COOL. IT WAS MOSTLY THE FACT THAT YOU DIDN'T PUT ASHLEY ON THE PHONE WHEN MY MOTHER ASKED YOU TO.

MY MOM WAS AWAKE ALL NIGHT CRYING. GET IT? I LOVE HER SO MUCH... YOU UPSET MY MOTHER I FLIP OUT.
HMM.
WHAT'LL YOU TELL YOUR FRIENDS THEN?
IT'S COOL. THEY DON'T EVEN KNOW WHAT YOU LOOK LIKE.

ALRIGHT... SO NO THREATS ANYMORE THEN?
NOPE.
THEN LET'S FORGET ABOUT ALL THIS.
LJUNG, 5/13 2007. HOST # 49: PONTUS LUNDKVIST

YOU STILL NERVOUS ABOUT RETURNING TO GOTHENBURG THEN?
NOT AT ALL. IT'S ALL COOL.

WHO'RE YOU STAYING WITH THIS TIME?
IT'S WITH HARE KRISHNA. DIDN'T I TELL YOU?
THAT'S RIGHT... BUT HOW'D THEY FIND YOU?

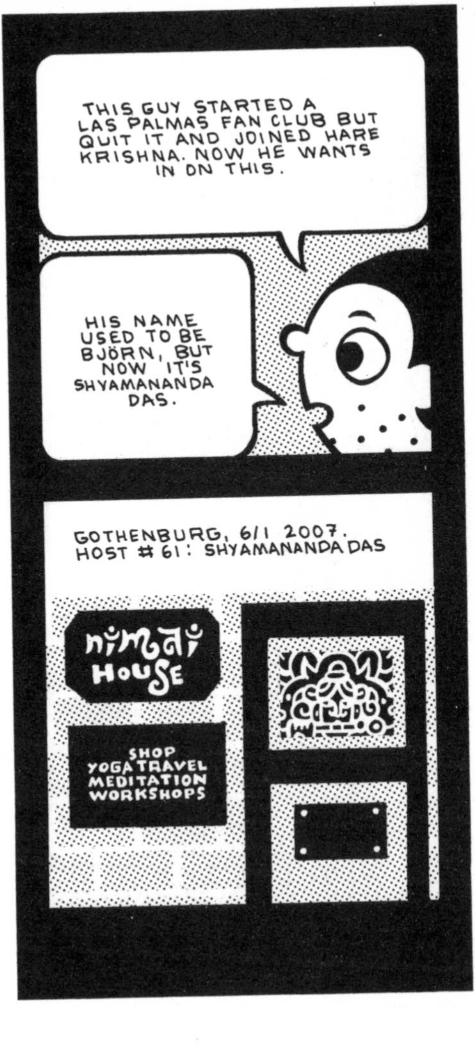
THIS GUY STARTED A LAS PALMAS FAN CLUB BUT QUIT IT AND JOINED HARE KRISHNA. NOW HE WANTS IN ON THIS.
HIS NAME USED TO BE BJÖRN, BUT NOW IT'S SHYAMANANDA DAS.
GOTHENBURG, 6/1 2007.
HOST # 61: SHYAMANANDA DAS
NIMAI HOUSE
SHOP
YOGA TRAVEL
MEDITATION
WORKSHOPS

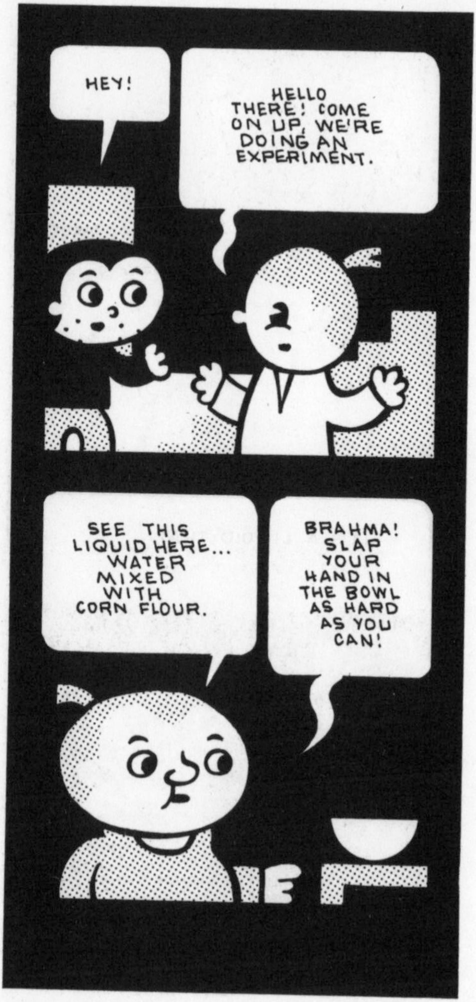
HEY!
HELLO THERE! COME ON UP, WE'RE DOING AN EXPERIMENT.
SEE THIS LIQUID HERE... WATER MIXED WITH CORN FLOUR.
BRAHMA! SLAP YOUR HAND IN THE BOWL AS HARD AS YOU CAN!

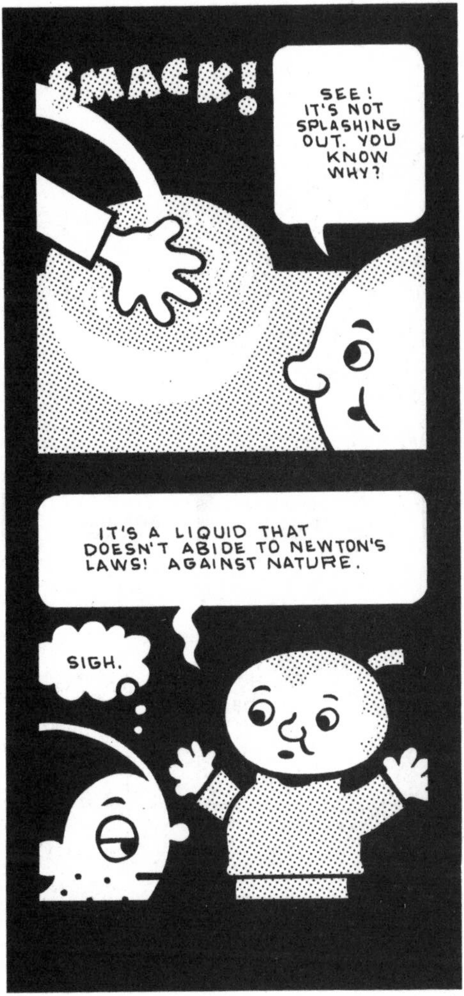
SMACK!
SEE! IT'S NOT SPLASHING OUT. YOU KNOW WHY?
IT'S A LIQUID THAT DOESN'T ABIDE TO NEWTON'S LAWS! AGAINST NATURE.
SIGH.

SIMON, YOU WANNA JOIN US WHEN WE SING AND PLAY NEAR THE NORDSTAN MALL LATER?
SURE.
HARE KRISHNA HARE KRISHNA KRISHNA KRIS

WHAT'RE YOU ON?
JUNKIE
09:30 PM
YOU ALWAYS GO TO BED THIS EARLY?
6 PEOPLE ON 300 SQUARE FT.

NOPE, SOMETIMES WHEN WE'RE NOT TIRED WE LIE AWAKE AND TALK.
IT'S USUALLY WHEN WE'VE BEEN HAVING A PARTY, EATING TOO MUCH SUGAR.
04:00 AM
HARE KRISHNA, HARE KRISHNA, KRISHNA KRISHNA, HARE HARE HARE RAMA, HARE RAMA RAMA RAMA, HARE HARE...
DOES THIS 1728 TIMES EVERY MORNING

GLUTEN-PROTEIN CHUNKS WITH MANNA AND HING*
* A SPICE ALSO KNOWN AS ASAFOETIDA OR DEVIL'S DUNG. REPLACES ONION AND GARLIC WHICH ARE SAID TO BE APHRODISIACS.
CAN I TAKE SOME BROCHURES WITH ME?
YEAH. AS MANY AS YOU LIKE.
SEX THAT HURTS OTHERS
SUICIDE

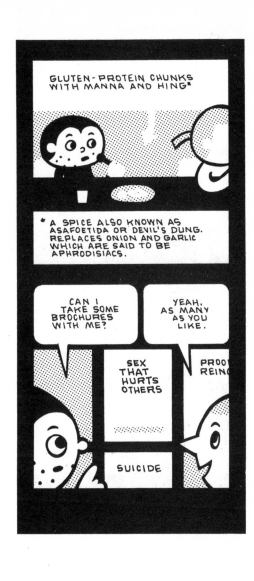

HE WHO ABANDONS HIS WIFE WILL BE AN ABANDONED WIFE IN THE FUTURE. SHE WHO ABORTS A FOETUS WILL COME INTO A MOTHERS WOMB AND BE ABORTED.
SEX THAT
ALSO, IF YOU'RE NOT RESPONSIBLE IN YOUR RELATIONSHIPS YOU WILL FEEL THAT YOUR LIFE IS SHADOWED BY A BIG, DARK CLOUD.
NO SHIT SHERLOCK.

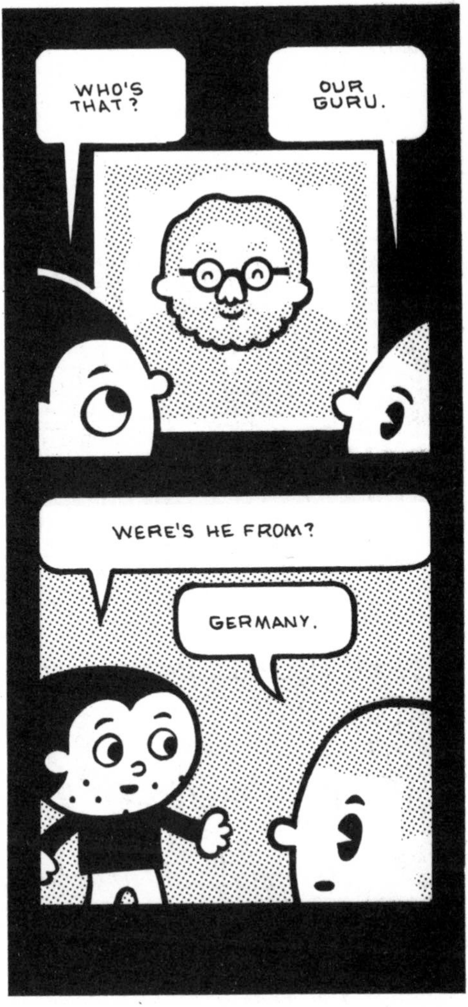
WHO'S THAT?
OUR GURU.
WERE'S HE FROM?
GERMANY.

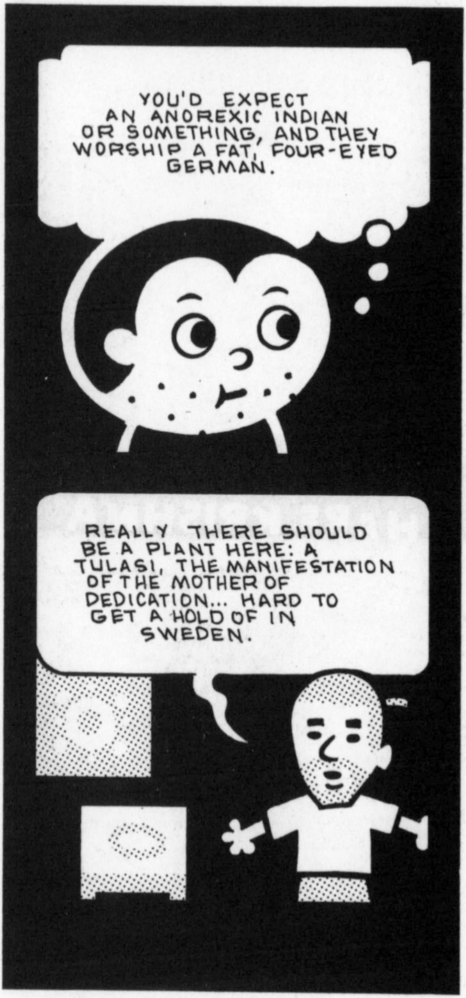
YOU'D EXPECT AN ANOREXIC INDIAN OR SOMETHING, AND THEY WORSHIP A FAT, FOUR-EYED GERMAN.
REALLY THERE SHOULD BE A PLANT HERE: A TULASI, THE MANIFESTATION OF THE MOTHER OF DEDICATION... HARD TO GET A HOLD OF IN SWEDEN.

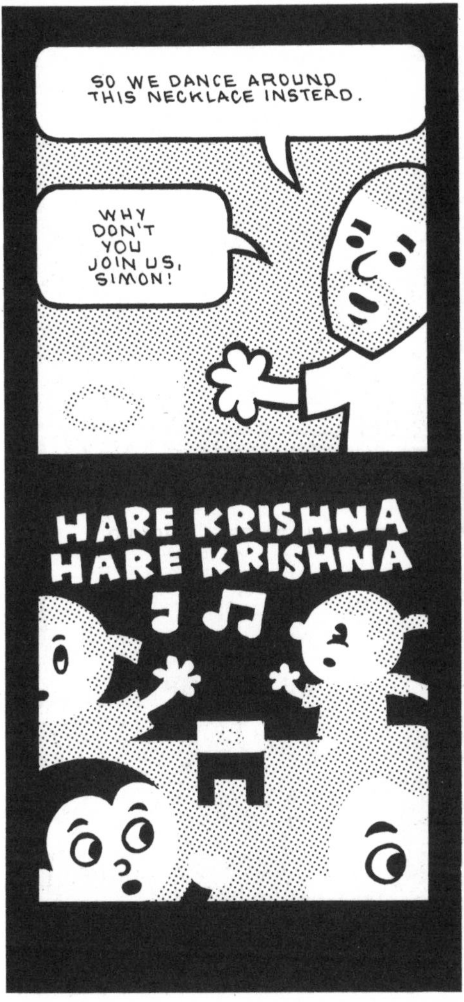

SO WE DANCE AROUND THIS NECKLACE INSTEAD.
WHY DON'T YOU JOIN US, SIMON!
HARE KRISHNA
HARE KRISHNA

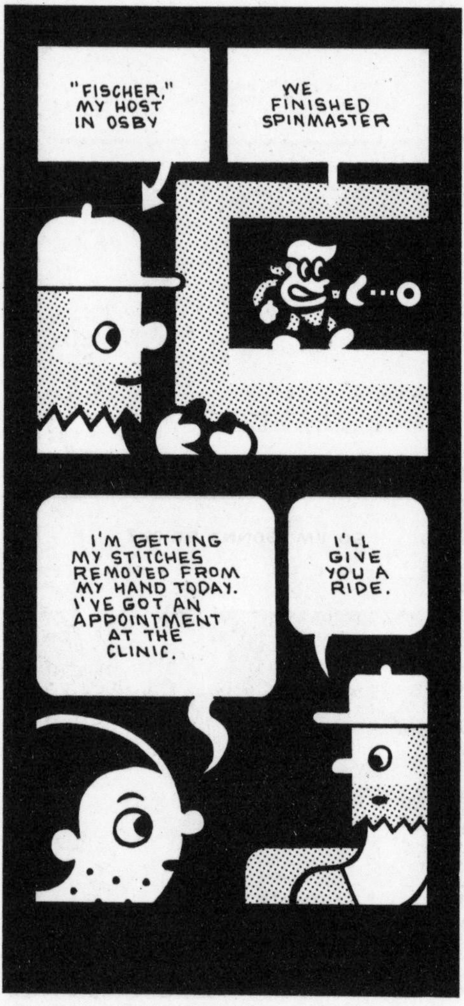
"FISCHER," MY HOST IN OSBY
WE FINISHED SPINMASTER
I'M GETTING MY STITCHES REMOVED FROM MY HAND TODAY. I'VE GOT AN APPOINTMENT AT THE CLINIC.
I'LL GIVE YOU A RIDE.

THERE WE GO! THIS HEALED UP NICELY.

SO I'M GONNA BE OK? I'LL BE ABLE TO DRAW AND EVERYTHING?

SURE!

PHEW!

TROLLHÄTTAN, 6/3 2007.
HOST #62: INGER STARDUST

STARDUST... THAT'S
AN UNUSUAL NAME.

I MADE IT UP FOR
MYSELF A COUPLE OF
YEARS
AGO.

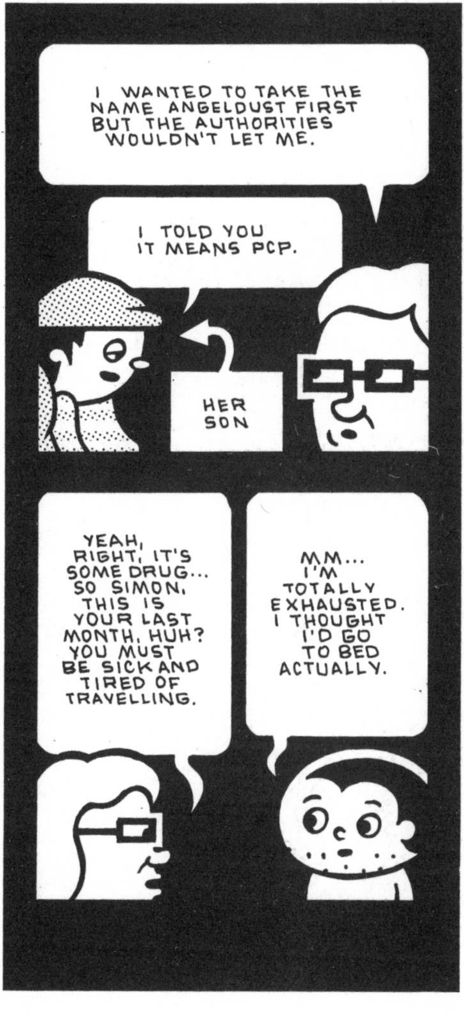
I WANTED TO TAKE THE NAME ANGELDUST FIRST BUT THE AUTHORITIES WOULDN'T LET ME.
I TOLD YOU IT MEANS PCP.
HER SON
YEAH, RIGHT, IT'S SOME DRUG... SO SIMON, THIS IS YOUR LAST MONTH, HUH? YOU MUST BE SICK AND TIRED OF TRAVELLING.
MM... I'M TOTALLY EXHAUSTED. I THOUGHT I'D GO TO BED ACTUALLY.

WE MADE A BED FOR YOU IN THERE... HA HA... I WAS JOKING WITH ADAM EARLIER THAT I'D SAY "TEAR YOUR CLOTHES OFF AND I'LL COME IN!" HA HA.
SIGH

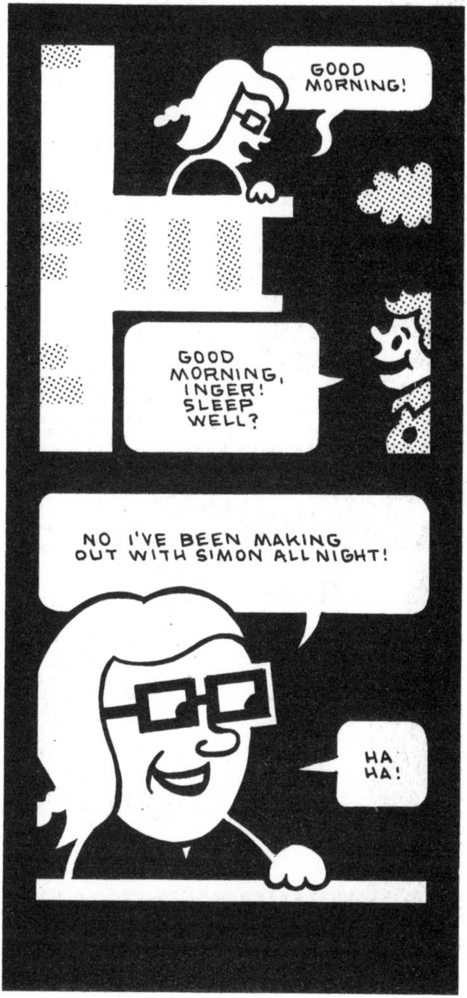
GOOD MORNING!
GOOD MORNING, INGER! SLEEP WELL?
NO I'VE BEEN MAKING OUT WITH SIMON ALL NIGHT!
HA HA!

I'M JUST KIDDING AROUND, YOU KNOW THAT RIGHT?
SURE, HEH HEH.

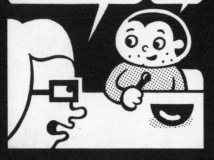

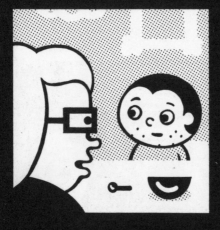

YOU GOT DANGEROUS EYES, SIMON. THE GIRLS BETTER WATCH OUT.
THANKS.
UH... COULD I USE THE LAUNDRY ROOM?
RIGHT... YOU WANTED TO DO SOME LAUNDRY.

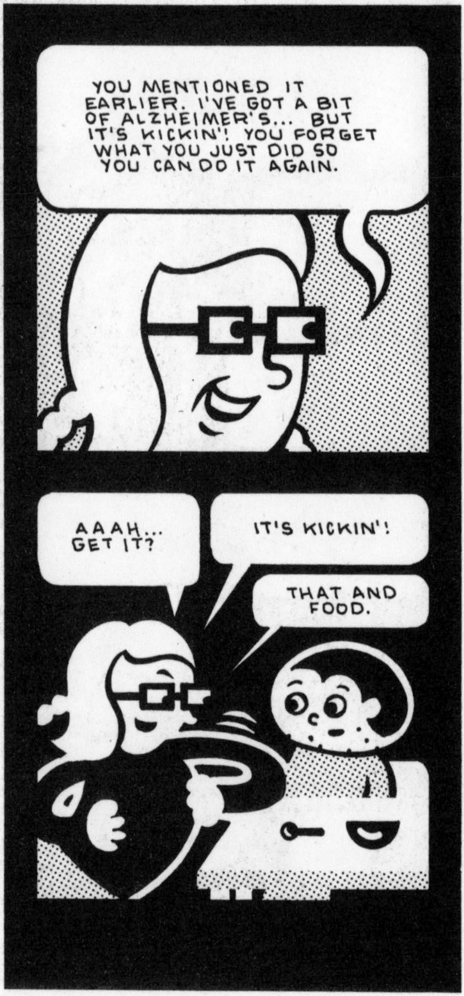
YOU MENTIONED IT EARLIER. I'VE GOT A BIT OF ALZHEIMER'S... BUT IT'S KICKIN'! YOU FORGET WHAT YOU JUST DID SO YOU CAN DO IT AGAIN.
AAAH... GET IT?
IT'S KICKIN'!
THAT AND FOOD.

THE LAUNDRY ROOM IS ALWAYS FREE AT THIS HOUR.
ADAM! SIMON AND I ARE GOING DOWN TO THE BASEMENT...
...WE'LL SEE WHAT HAPPENS!
JUST KIDDING... I WON'T MOLEST YOU!

WE SHOULD CHECK OUT MY MOTORCYCLE WHILE WE'RE DOWN HERE. IT'S IN THE GARAGE.

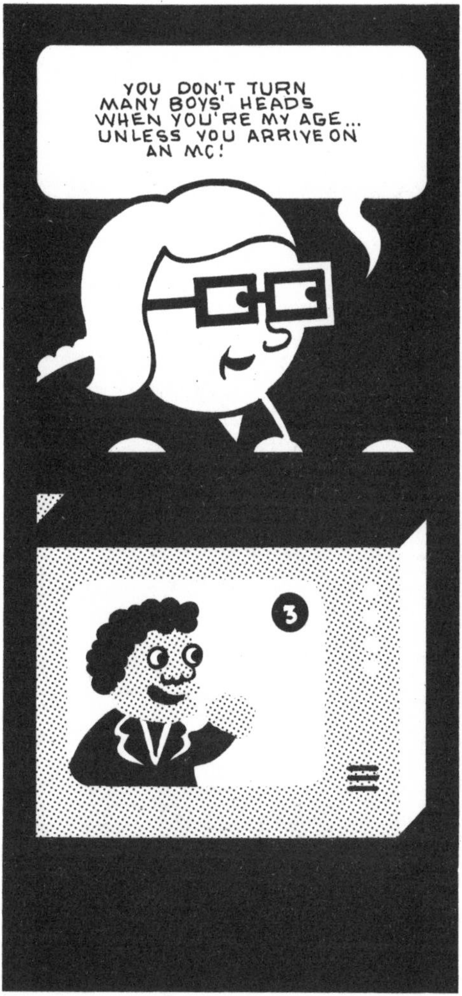
YOU DON'T TURN MANY BOYS' HEADS WHEN YOU'RE MY AGE... UNLESS YOU ARRIVE ON AN MC!
3

OOH! NEGROES! I LOVE THAT.
MOM, YOU'RE EMBARRASSING.
BUT I DO. THEY'RE SUCH GOOD ACTORS!

HAHAHA! INGER STARDUST... WHAT A COOL CAT.
MALTE VOIGT, MY HOST IN HÖÖR
BLUE SHADOW ON NINTENDO 8-BIT.
USE THE WRESTLING MISSILES!

ANOTHER ROUND?
YEAH, IN A BIT... IT'S TOTALLY ADDICTIVE, BUT I GOTTA CHECK MY EMAIL AND STUFF FIRST.
HMMM... MAIL FROM THE ARTIST'S GRANT BOARD.

I APPLIED FOR A GRANT BEFORE I WENT ON THE TRIP BUT I GAVE UP ON THAT AGES AGO.
GULP WHA?
GHHH!

THE BOARD HAS GRANTED
YOUR APPLICATION FOR
HIGH COST ARTISTIC
WORK/ PROJECT.
SUM: 266,000 SWEDISH
CROWNS (40,000 USD)

YEAAAAH!

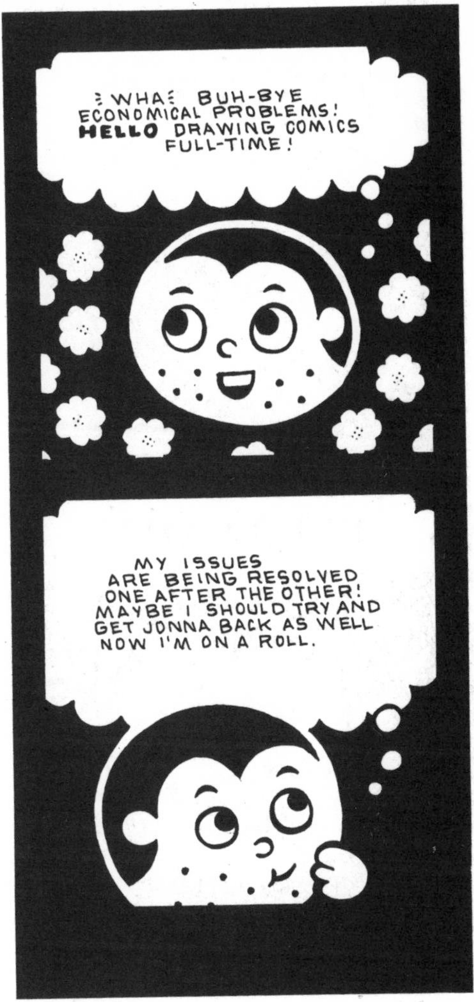
WHA BUH-BYE ECONOMICAL PROBLEMS! **HELLO** DRAWING COMICS FULL-TIME!
MY ISSUES ARE BEING RESOLVED ONE AFTER THE OTHER! MAYBE I SHOULD TRY AND GET JONNA BACK AS WELL NOW I'M ON A ROLL.

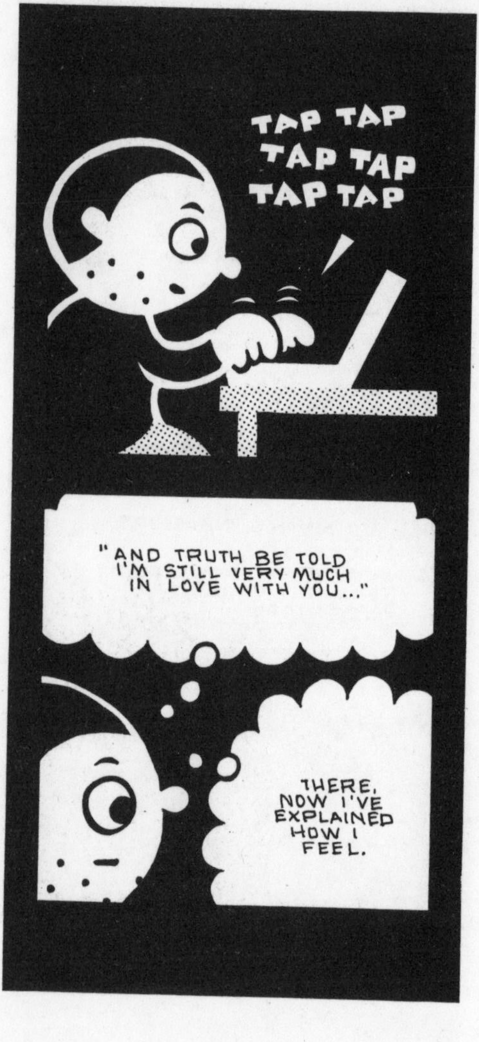
TAP TAP
TAP TAP
TAP TAP
"AND TRUTH BE TOLD I'M STILL VERY MUCH IN LOVE WITH YOU..."
THERE, NOW I'VE EXPLAINED HOW I FEEL.

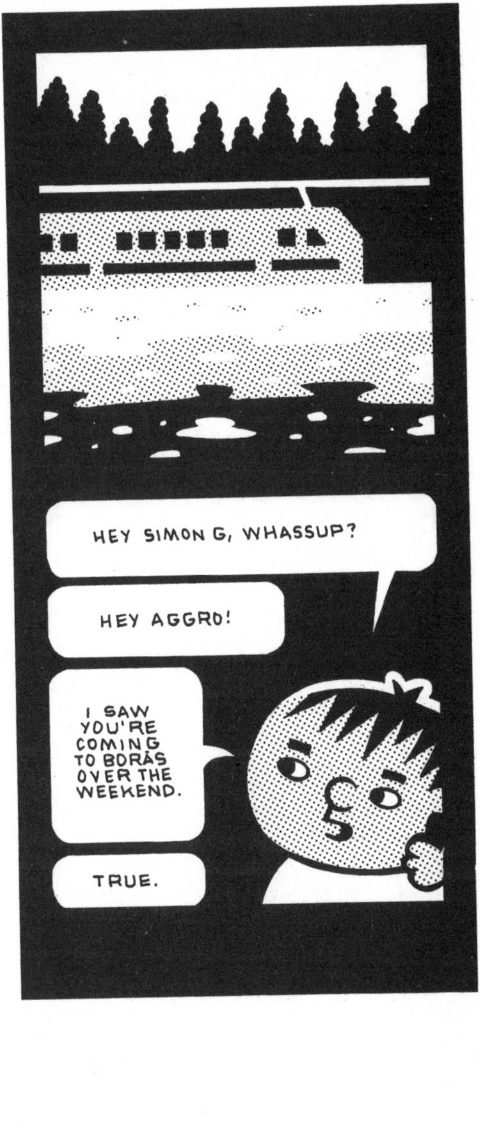
HEY SIMON G, WHASSUP?
HEY AGGRO!
I SAW YOU'RE COMING TO BORÅS OVER THE WEEKEND.
TRUE.

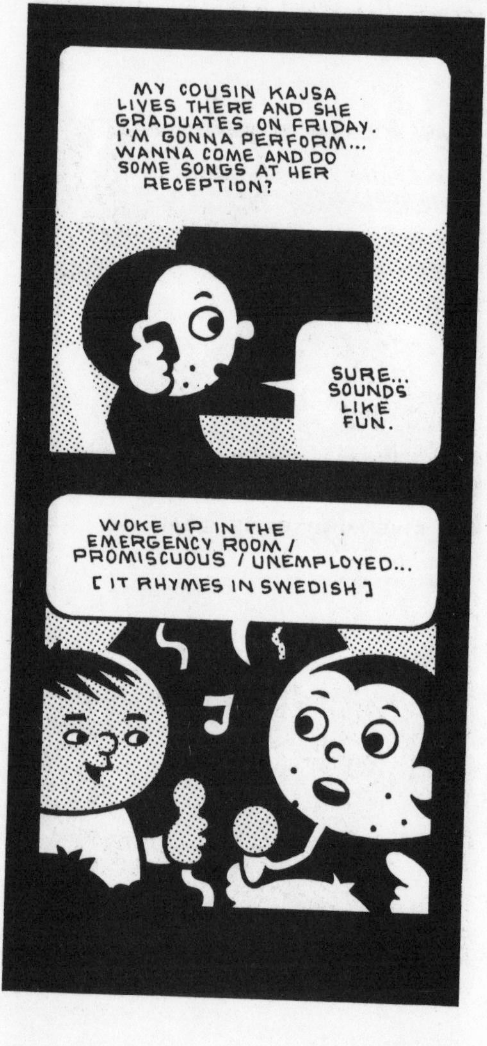
MY COUSIN KAJSA LIVES THERE AND SHE GRADUATES ON FRIDAY. I'M GONNA PERFORM... WANNA COME AND DO SOME SONGS AT HER RECEPTION?
SURE... SOUNDS LIKE FUN.
WOKE UP IN THE EMERGENCY ROOM / PROMISCUOUS / UNEMPLOYED...
[IT RHYMES IN SWEDISH]

YOU GUYS KICKED ASS.
THANKS. I'M SIMON.
LINNÉA.
FIVE MINUTES OF SMALL TALK LATER.

HEH HEH RIGHT ON THE MONEY... OR NOT... OR WHATEVER.
SOME SORT OF WORKSHOP/ HOBBY ROOM
NO OBJECTIONS HERE. DAMN SHE'S HOT.

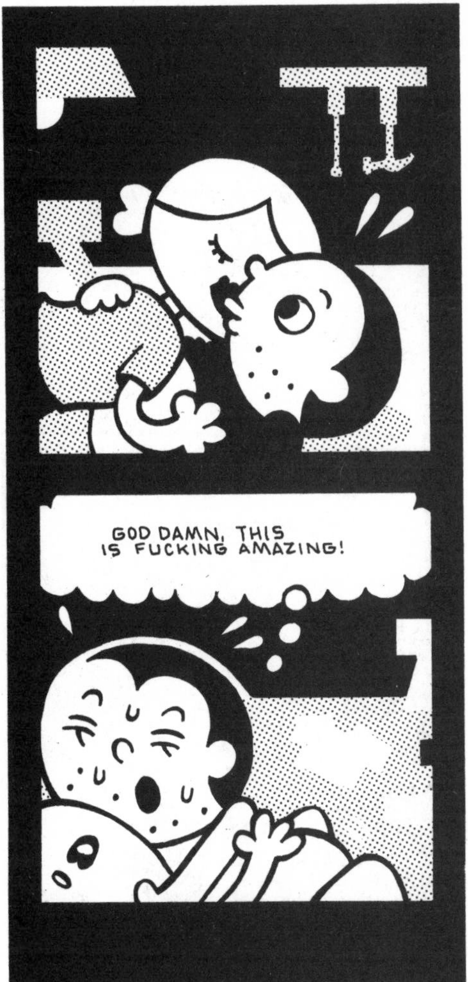
GOD DAMN, THIS IS FUCKING AMAZING!

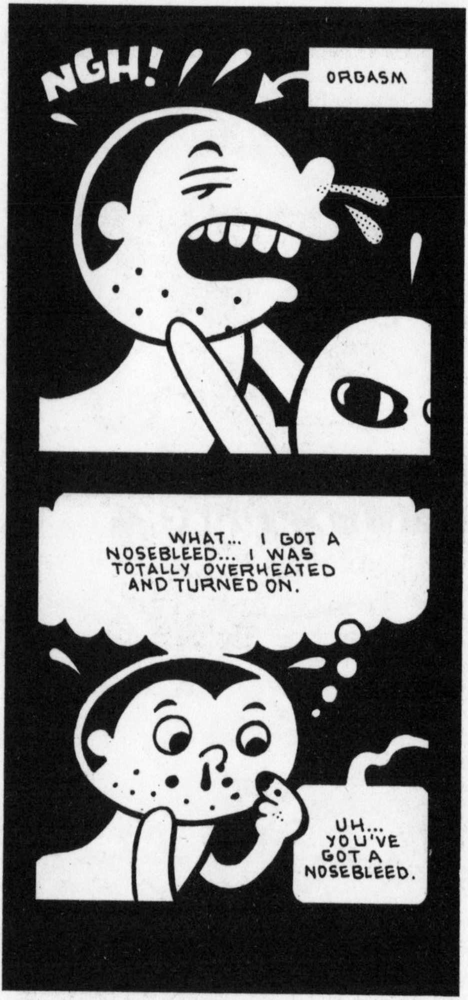
NGH!
ORGASM
WHAT... I GOT A NOSEBLEED... I WAS TOTALLY OVERHEATED AND TURNED ON.
UH... YOU'VE GOT A NOSEBLEED.

QUICKLY! WHAT IS THIS? SOME LIMP PIECE OF CHAMOIS LEATHER? IT'LL DO TO STEM THE FLOW.
KNOCK KNOCK
LINNÉA!

DUNK! DUNK!
COME OUT OF THERE!
SHIT. IT'S MY SISTER. I GOTTA GO TALK TO HER.
WHAT THE HELL ARE YOU DOING?! I SAW YOU GUYS SNEAKING IN THERE.
JUST TALKING!
RIGHT... AND HOW DO YOU THINK YOUR BOYFRIEND FEELS ABOUT THAT? AND WHAT'S THE RED STUFF ON YOUR NECK?

AAAY! I GOTTA WIPE OFF THOSE GENITAL FLUIDS AS WELL.
IMPORTANT NOTE TO SELF: GET RID OF THIS RAG AT A SAFE LOCATION.
CUM, PUSSY JUICE & BLOOD.

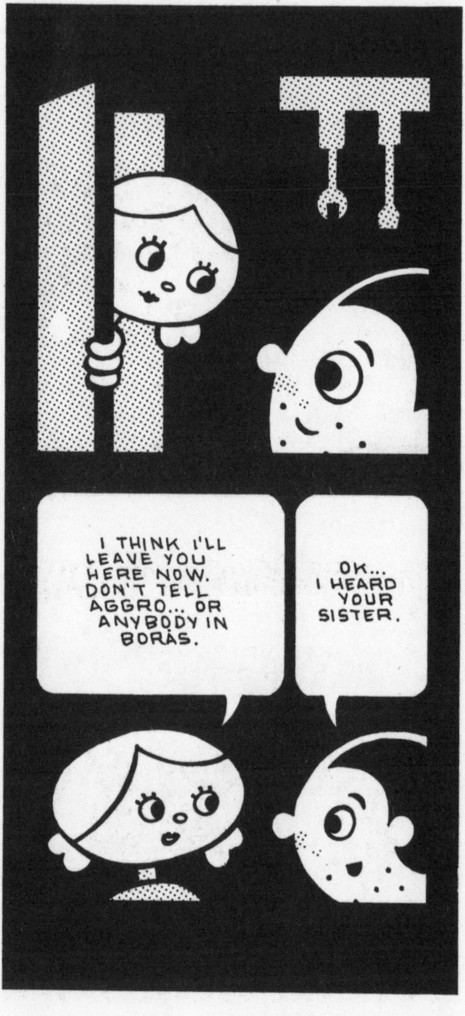
I THINK I'LL LEAVE YOU HERE NOW. DON'T TELL AGGRO... OR ANYBODY IN BORÅS.
OK... I HEARD YOUR SISTER.

BUT THAT WAS FUCKING SWEET.
YEAH. AWESOME.
NEXT DAY...
THREE HOURS LEFT UNTIL BOLLNÄS AND I FEEL ON TOP OF THE WORLD.
SJ

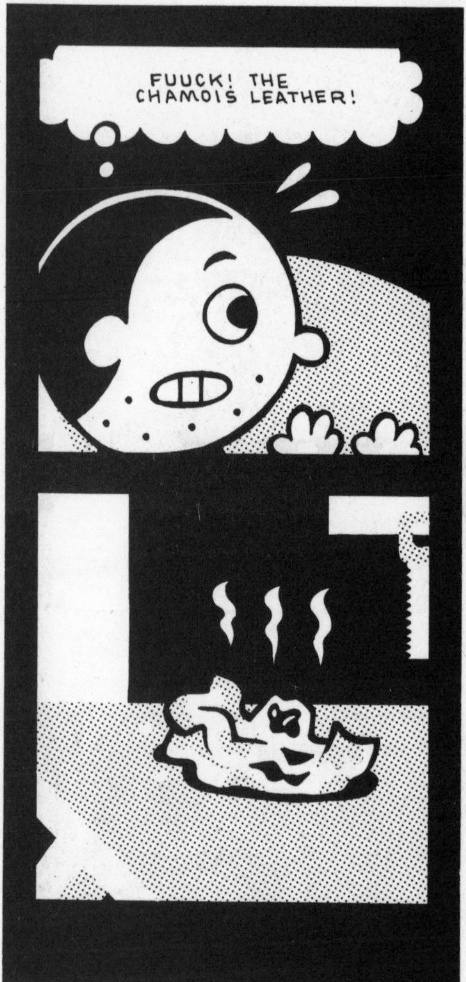
FUUCK! THE CHAMOIS LEATHER!

VÄSTERÅS, 6/11 2007.
HOST#69: MÅRTEN ARVIDSSON

bibi-bibi biPPi

OH. I'LL GO OUTSIDE AND TALK.

HEY... IT'S JONNA...
THANKS FOR THE EMAIL...
IT WAS LOVELY.

MMM...
BEEN A
WHILE
SINCE I
SENT
IT.

I KNOW... BUT I'M A LITTLE DRUNK SO I PLUCKED UP THE COURAGE TO TALK ABOUT THIS.

GOOD.

IT WAS BRAVE OF YOU TO WRITE YOU'RE IN LOVE WITH ME... YOU KNEW I COULDN'T WRITE ANYTHING BACK RIGHT THEN.

I WAS JUST TRYING TO BE HONEST.

DO YOU REALLY MEAN IT OR ARE YOU JUST TRYING TO CHARM ME NOW?
I MEAN IT, I SWEAR... I WOULDN'T LIE TO YOU ABOUT SOMETHING LIKE THAT.
I WANTED TO TELL YOU THIS FOR A WHILE BUT HAVEN'T BEEN ABLE TO. THIS RELATIONSHIP I TALKED ABOUT... PROBABLY GONNA COME TO NOTHING.

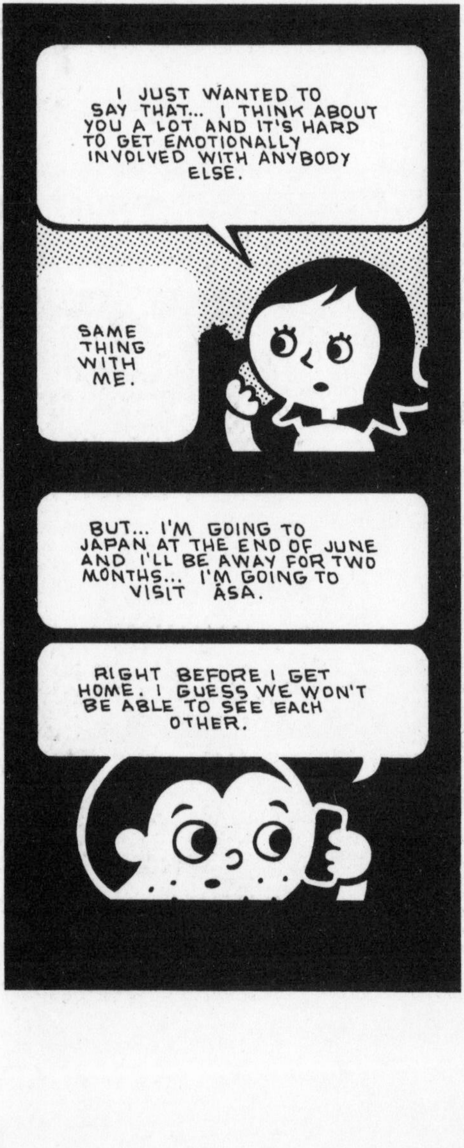
I JUST WANTED TO SAY THAT... I THINK ABOUT YOU A LOT AND IT'S HARD TO GET EMOTIONALLY INVOLVED WITH ANYBODY ELSE.
SAME THING WITH ME.
BUT... I'M GOING TO JAPAN AT THE END OF JUNE AND I'LL BE AWAY FOR TWO MONTHS... I'M GOING TO VISIT ÅSA.
RIGHT BEFORE I GET HOME. I GUESS WE WON'T BE ABLE TO SEE EACH OTHER.

MM... BUT THAT COULD BE A GOOD THING. I MISS YOU, BUT I NEED SOME TIME TO THINK IT OVER.

JUMPING FROM ONE THING TO ANOTHER GETS SUPERFICIAL VERY EASILY.

I DUNNO ABOUT THAT... I DON'T THINK THERE'S ANY RISK THINGS WOULD GET SUPERFICIAL BETWEEN US.

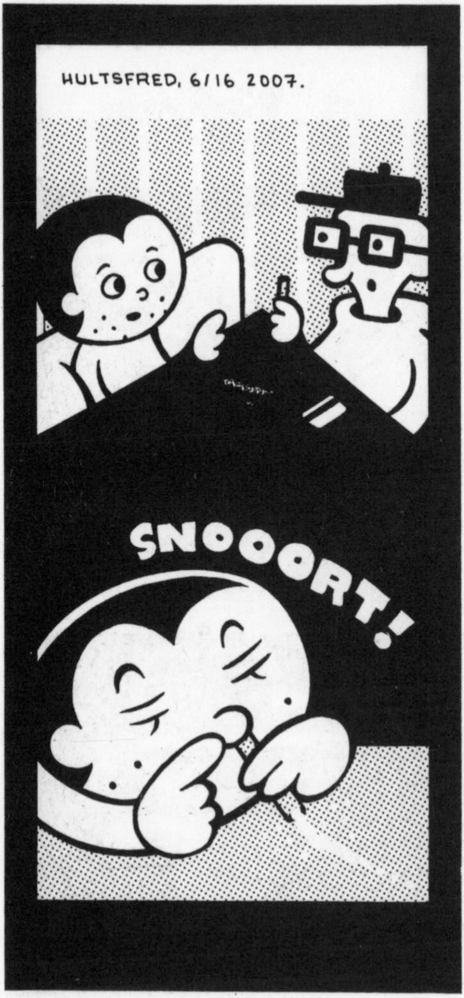
HULTSFRED, 6/16 2007.
SNOOORT!

OOOUCH! MY NOSE IS REALLY STINGING! ARE YOU SURE THIS IS METH?
YEAH... BUT I BOUGHT IT IN MALMÖ. THAT MEANS IT'S PROBABLY MIXED WITH LAUNDRY DETERGENT.

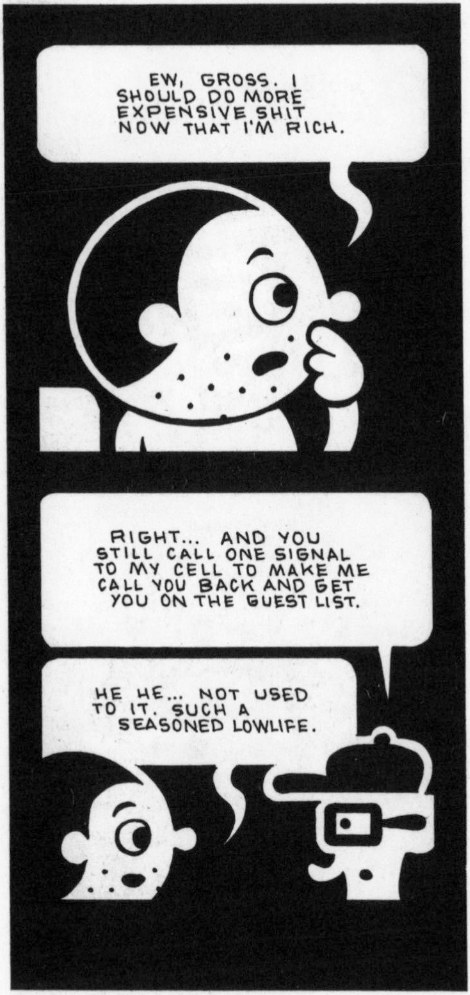
EW, GROSS. I SHOULD DO MORE EXPENSIVE SHIT NOW THAT I'M RICH.
RIGHT... AND YOU STILL CALL ONE SIGNAL TO MY CELL TO MAKE ME CALL YOU BACK AND GET YOU ON THE GUEST LIST.
HE HE... NOT USED TO IT. SUCH A SEASONED LOWLIFE.

WELL WELL... CONGRATULATIONS ARE IN ORDER, SIMON. QUARTER-MILLIONAIRE... HOW DO YOU FEEL?
EVERYTHING FEELS SO DAMN GOOD RIGHT NOW. I HAD A TON OF PROBLEMS JUST RECENTLY... AND ALL OF A SUDDEN ALL OF THEM ARE GONE WITH THE WIND.

I FEEL LIKE THINGS MIGHT WORK OUT WITH JONNA AS WELL. WE MIGHT END UP TOGETHER AFTER ALL.
SO I WAS RIGHT.
HOW MANY OF YOUR 120 DAYS DO YOU HAVE LEFT?
LESS THAN TWO WEEKS.

SO YOU'VE BASICALLY LANDED THE THING. DID YOU STICK TO THE RULES?
YUP, TWO NIGHTS MAXIMUM IN THE SAME PLACE, AND I HAVEN'T SET A FOOT IN MY OWN APARTMENT.
SIMON GÄRDENFORS **CAN'T** LOSE!

KIRUNA, 6/25 2007. HOST #79:
MIKAEL ANDERSSON

FINAL STOP ON MY
JOURNEY BEFORE THE LAST
COUPLE OF DAYS IN
STOCKHOLM. MY HOST FAMILY
TOOK ME ON A TOUR OF THE
STATE MINING PLANT AND ON
A FIELD TRIP TO JUKKASJÄRVI.

WE VISITED THE CHURCH WITH BROR HJORT'S JESUS PORTRAIT AND THE PRIEST LARS LEVI LAESTADIUS.

LAESTADIANISM IS A CHRISTIAN MOVEMENT THAT STRICTLY BANISHES LIQUOR, GAMBLING AND OTHER SINFUL THINGS.

OUT OF THIS REVIVAL MOVEMENT THE KARELA-SECT WAS FORMED, COMPLETELY RECONSIDERING EVERYTHING AND REVELLING IN DANCE, DRINKING, AND FREE SEXUAL EXPLOITS.

AMONG OTHER THINGS, THEY WOULD STROKE EACH OTHER'S ANUSES WITH PASTRY BRUSHES IN RELIGIOUS RITUAL.

STOCKHOLM, 6/29 2007.
HOST #81: DAVID LILJEMARK
(SOMEWHAT) CHEQUERED SCARF
WHA?
SO YOUR TRIP IS OVER... I'M WAVING YOU OVER THE FINISH LINE, LIKE IN A CAR RACE.
SHAKE!

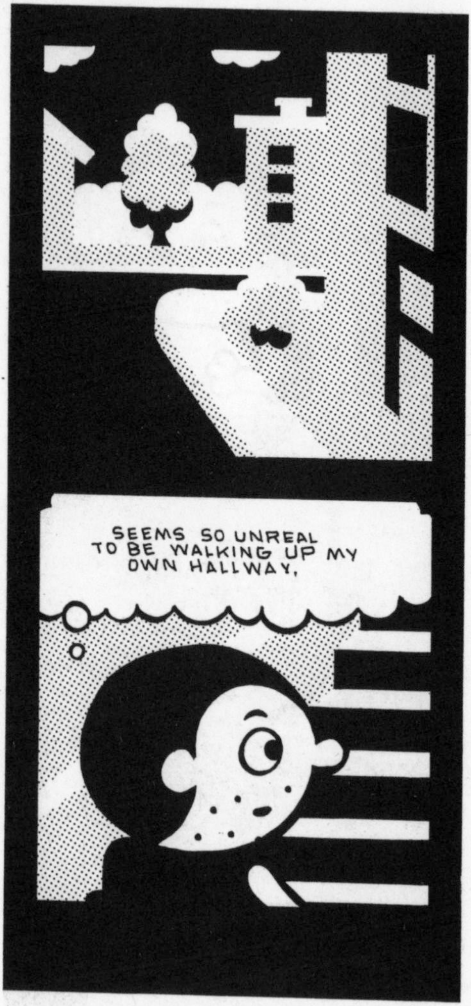
SEEMS SO UNREAL TO BE WALKING UP MY OWN HALLWAY.

AAAH!
SO THE EXTERMINATOR'S ALREADY BEEN? TOO BAD MY BED IS OVERTURNED AND SPRAYED... I WOULD'VE LOVED TO CHILL IN IT RIGHT NOW.

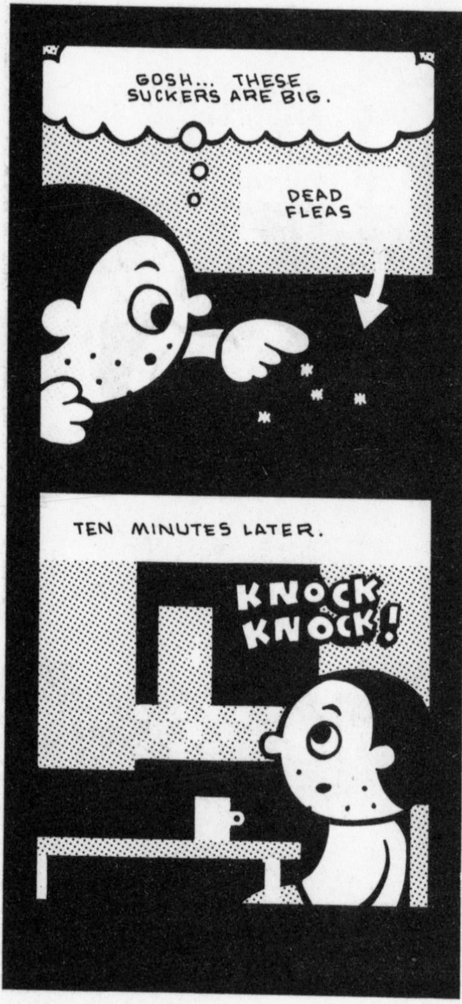
GOSH... THESE SUCKERS ARE BIG.
DEAD FLEAS
TEN MINUTES LATER.
KNOCK KNOCK!

HELLO THERE! WE'RE GOING TO KEEP SPRAYING. YOU SHOULD GET OUT OF HERE FOR AT LEAST ANOTHER FOUR HOURS.
ALRIGHT... BACK ON THE STREETS. FLEAS... I GUESS THAT'S MY PUNISHMENT FOR LIVING LIKE A PARASITE ON SOCIETY.

7/1 2007.
AAAH... FIRST MORNING IN MY OWN BED... IN FOUR MONTHS.
WHAT THE FUCK?

I FOUND A FLEA THAT WAS STILL ALIVE.
I LET IT CRAWL UP ON MY HAND.

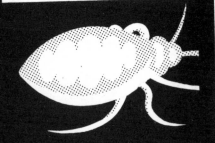

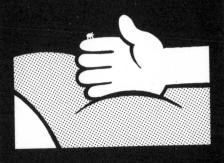

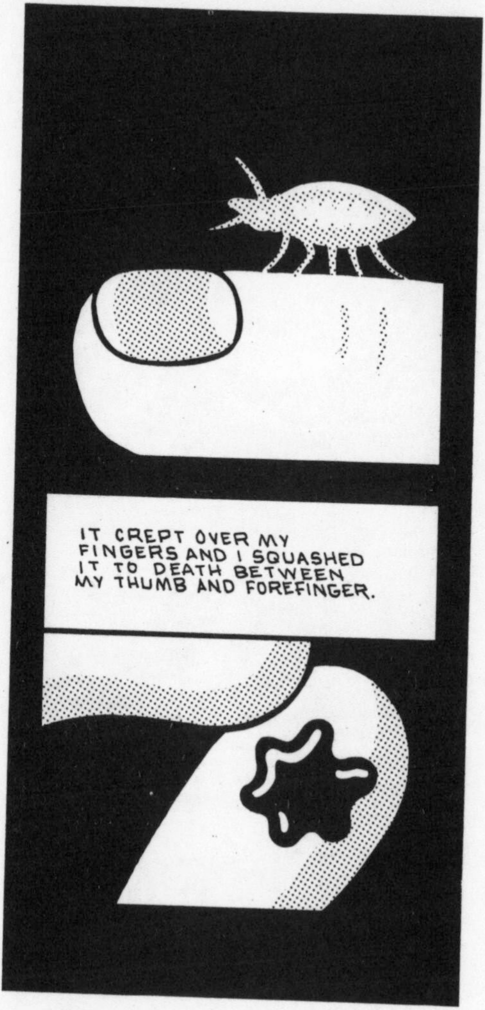
IT CREPT OVER MY FINGERS AND I SQUASHED IT TO DEATH BETWEEN MY THUMB AND FOREFINGER.

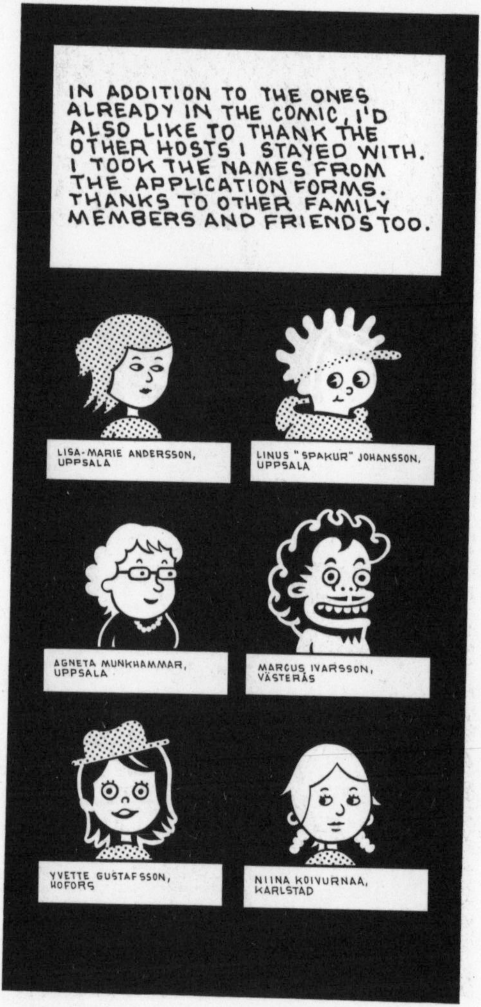
IN ADDITION TO THE ONES ALREADY IN THE COMIC, I'D ALSO LIKE TO THANK THE OTHER HOSTS I STAYED WITH. I TOOK THE NAMES FROM THE APPLICATION FORMS. THANKS TO OTHER FAMILY MEMBERS AND FRIENDS TOO.
LISA-MARIE ANDERSSON, UPPSALA
LINUS "SPAKUR" JOHANSSON, UPPSALA
AGNETA MUNKHAMMAR, UPPSALA
MARCUS IVARSSON, VÄSTERÅS
YVETTE GUSTAFSSON, HOFORS
NIINA KOIVURNAA, KARLSTAD

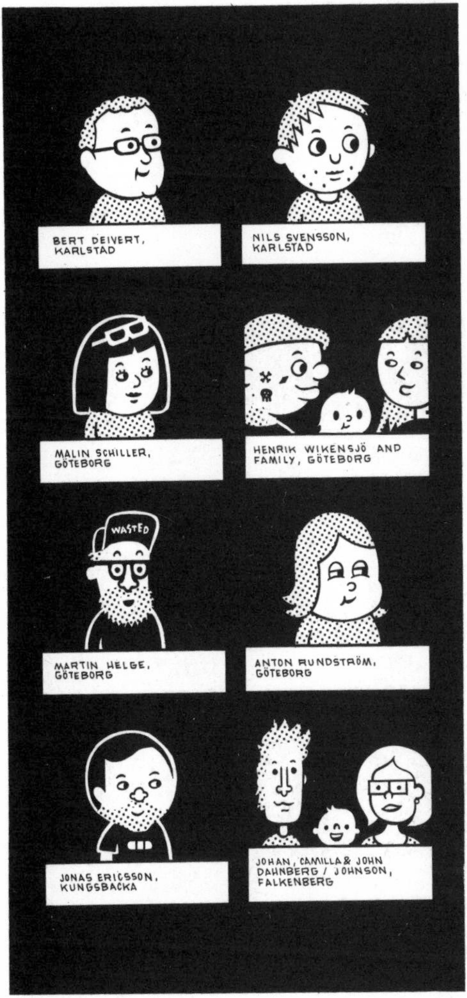

BERT DEIVERT, KARLSTAD
NILS SVENSSON, KARLSTAD
MALIN SCHILLER, GÖTEBORG
HENRIK WIKENSJÖ AND FAMILY, GÖTEBORG
WASTED
MARTIN HELGE, GÖTEBORG
ANTON RUNDSTRÖM, GÖTEBORG
JONAS ERICSSON, KUNGSBACKA
JOHAN, CAMILLA & JOHN DAHNBERG / JOHNSON, FALKENBERG

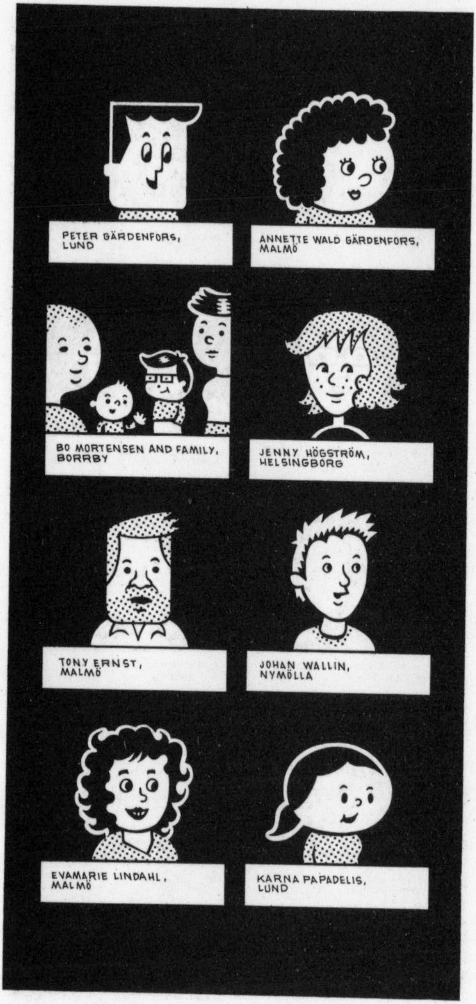
PETER GÄRDENFORS, LUND
ANNETTE WALD GÄRDENFORS, MALMÖ
BO MORTENSEN AND FAMILY, BORRBY
JENNY HÖGSTRÖM, HELSINGBORG
TONY ERNST, MALMÖ
JOHAN WALLIN, NYMÖLLA
EVAMARIE LINDAHL, MALMÖ
KARNA PAPADELIS, LUND

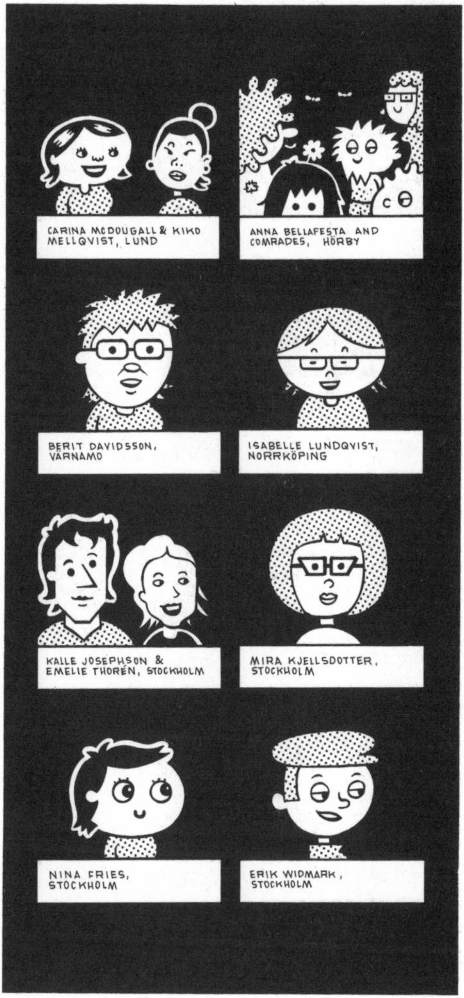

CARINA MCDOUGALL & KIKO MELLQVIST, LUND
ANNA BELLAFESTA AND COMRADES, HÖRBY
BERIT DAVIDSSON, VÄRNAMO
ISABELLE LUNDQVIST, NORRKÖPING
KALLE JOSEPHSON & EMELIE THORÉN, STOCKHOLM
MIRA KJELLSDOTTER, STOCKHOLM
NINA FRIES, STOCKHOLM
ERIK WIDMARK, STOCKHOLM

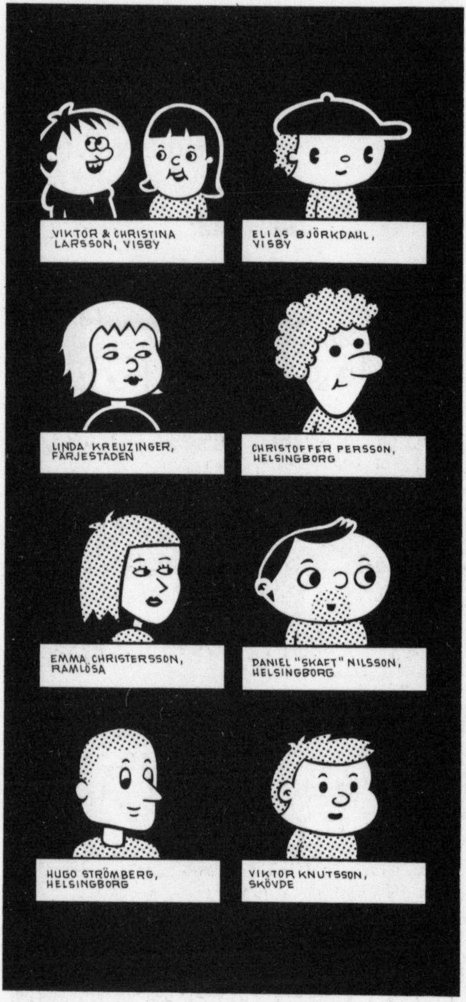

VIKTOR & CHRISTINA LARSSON, VISBY
ELIAS BJÖRKDAHL, VISBY
LINDA KREUZINGER, FÄRJESTADEN
CHRISTOFFER PERSSON, HELSINGBORG
EMMA CHRISTERSSON, RAMLÖSA
DANIEL "SKAFT" NILSSON, HELSINGBORG
HUGO STRÖMBERG, HELSINGBORG
VIKTOR KNUTSSON, SKÖVDE

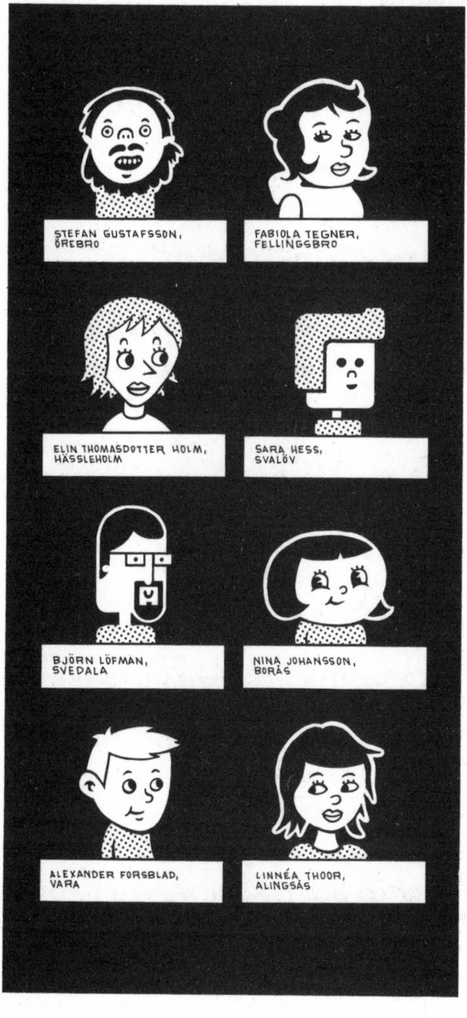
STEFAN GUSTAFSSON,
ÖREBRO
FABIOLA TEGNER,
FELLINGSBRO
ELIN THOMASDOTTER HOLM,
HÄSSLEHOLM
SARA HESS,
SVALÖV
BJÖRN LÖFMAN,
SVEDALA
NINA JOHANSSON,
BORÅS
ALEXANDER FORSBLAD,
VARA
LINNÉA THOOR,
ALINGSÅS

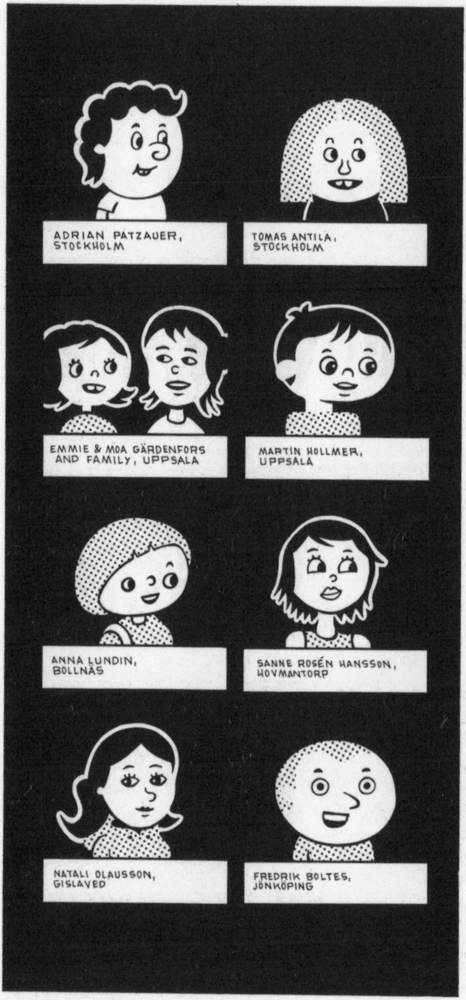
ADRIAN PATZAUER,
STOCKHOLM
TOMAS ANTILA,
STOCKHOLM
EMMIE & MOA GÄRDENFORS
AND FAMILY, UPPSALA
MARTIN HOLLMER,
UPPSALA
ANNA LUNDIN,
BOLLNÄS
SANNE ROSÉN HANSSON,
HOVMANTORP
NATALI OLAUSSON,
GISLAVED
FREDRIK BOLTES,
JÖNKÖPING

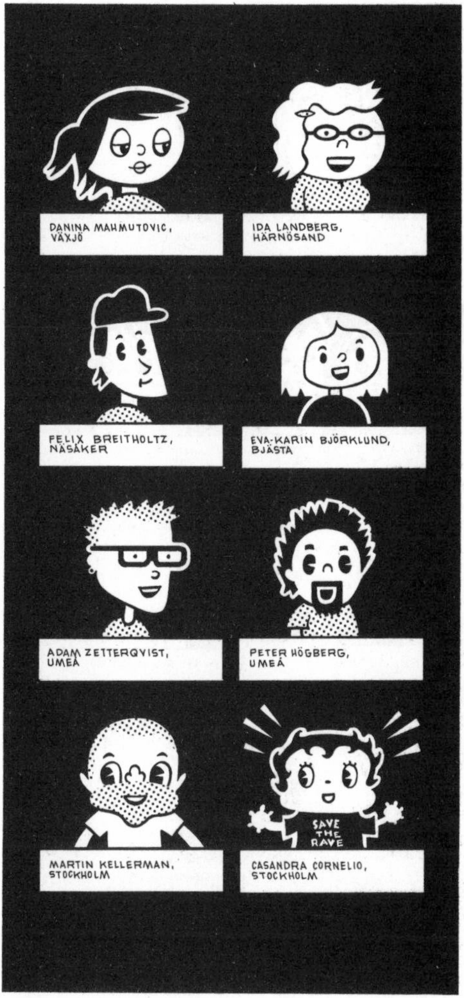
DANINA MAHMUTOVIC, VÄXJÖ
IDA LANDBERG, HÄRNÖSAND
FELIX BREITHOLTZ, NÄSÅKER
EVA-KARIN BJÖRKLUND, BJÄSTA
ADAM ZETTERQVIST, UMEÅ
PETER HÖGBERG, UMEÅ
MARTIN KELLERMAN, STOCKHOLM
SAVE THE RAVE
CASANDRA CORNELIO, STOCKHOLM

SIMON GÄRDENFORS ACKNOWLEDGES THE FINANCIAL CONTRIBUTION OF
THE SWEDISH ARTS GRANTS COMMITTEE (KONSTNÄRSNÄMNDEN) AND
THE FOUNDATION FOR THE CULTURE OF THE FUTURE (FRAMTIDENS KULTUR)